TROILUS AND CRISEYDE

(Abridged)

GEOFFREY CHAUCER

EDITED BY D. S. BREWER
Lecturer in English, University of Cambridge
Fellow of Emmanuel College

AND L. ELISABETH BREWER
Lecturer in English,
Homerton College of Education,
Cambridge

ROUTLEDGE & KEGAN PAUL

LONDON, HENLEY AND BOSTON

First published 1969
by Routledge & Kegan Paul Ltd
39 Store Street
London. WC1E 7DD,
Broadway House, Newtown Road
Henley-on-Thames
Oxon. RG9 1EN and
9 Park Street
Boston, Mass. 02108, USA
Reprinted 1969, 1970 (thrice) and 1971
First published as a paperback 1977
Printed in Great Britain
by The Camelot Press Ltd
Southampton
© *Routledge & Kegan Paul 1969*
The text is taken from
Chaucer's Major Poetry, *edited*
by Albert C. Baugh, Copyright ©
1963 Meredith Corporation. Reprinted
by permission of Appleton-Century-Crofts

ISBN 0 7100 6488 8 (c)
ISBN 0 7100 8719 5 (p)
ISBN 0 7100 6642 2 (l)

TROILUS AND CRISEYDE

ROUTLEDGE ENGLISH TEXTS

GENERAL EDITOR: T. S. Dorsch, M.A. (Oxon)
Professor of English Literature, Durham University

Volumes in the series include:

ELIZABETHAN LYRICAL POETS, edited by Patricia Thomson

ELIZABETHAN VERSE ROMANCES, edited by M. M. Reese

POETS OF THE EARLY SEVENTEENTH CENTURY, edited by Bernard and Elizabeth Davis

JOHNSON: 'RASSELAS' AND ESSAYS, edited by Charles Peake

WORDSWORTH: 'THE PRELUDE', BOOKS I–IV, edited by P. M. Yarker

BYRON: 'DON JUAN', BOOKS I–IV, edited by T. S. Dorsch

CHAUCER: 'TROILUS AND CRISEYDE', edited by D. S. Brewer and L. E. Brewer

GIBBON: 'AUTOBIOGRAPHY', edited by M. M. Reese

MORRIS: 'NEWS FROM NOWHERE', edited by J. Redmond

FOR MICHAEL

CONTENTS

SERIES EDITOR'S PREFACE

THE ROUTLEDGE ENGLISH TEXTS are designed primarily for the use of sixth-form pupils and undergraduates. Each volume is edited by a scholar who is an authority on the period which it represents and who has also had experience of teaching and examining at the school-leaving or the undergraduate level. The aim is to provide, in the introductions and notes, both sufficient explanatory material to enable the texts to be read with full understanding, and critical commentary of a kind that will stimulate thought and discussion.

The series includes both single works of some length and collections of shorter works. Where a work is too long to fit within the limits of size necessarily laid down for a textbook series – such a work, for example, as *The Prelude*, or *Don Juan* – it will normally be represented by a single extended extract of several consecutive books or cantos rather than by an abridgement of the whole, since an abridgement runs the risk of losing the cumulative effects that are important in a work of some scope. In the anthologies a few authors of a particular period will be well represented, in the belief that a reasonably thorough study of a limited field is more profitable than a superficial study of a wide field, and that a more than passing acquaintance with an author is of value in itself.

T. S. DORSCH

NOTE ON THIS EDITION

THE aim of this edition is to make available to students who may have no previous knowledge of Chaucer a fair representation of his greatest poem in a self-contained volume.

The Selection of Passages is intended to reflect the nature of the poem and the course of the story; but, inevitably, in taking just over 5,000 lines out of the original text of about 8,000, much has been omitted. We have tried to choose those passages that are most central to the poem and also most immediately appealing, without sacrificing the poem's essential variety. Book IV has regrettably had to be sacrificed almost entirely. Elsewhere we have given long integral sections which represent the turns and variety of the narrative as no series of snippets could do. We hope we have given a fair and comprehensible selection which will be enjoyed, and will encourage the reader to go on to the whole poem, and indeed to other of Chaucer's works.

The Introduction supplies necessary basic information along with interpretation. The interpretation must be judged on its correspondence with the poem, and space has not permitted argument with those critics whose views differ. Comment has been limited largely, but by no means entirely, to the text of the selection made here; reference is occasionally made to parts of the poem not represented here, but this should offer no difficulty, and we believe the observations apply with equal force to the present selection as to the poem as a whole. The Introduction is divided into topics for the convenience of teacher and student, but the treatment is suggestive, not exhaustive.

The Commentary is especially aimed to help the understanding of the text. Words that may mislead the student have often been noted, as well as syntactically difficult passages. A few observations on the nature of the action and style have also been made, though obviously many more might have been made. There has been no attempt to indicate sources and parallels except in the most general way; these can for the most part be found in Robinson's edition (see Bibliographical Note), and the emphasis here is on Chaucer's own text.

The Text is that printed by A. C. Baugh (see Bibliographical Note), with a few corrections. Baugh's text is mainly based on the manuscript in Corpus Christi College, Cambridge, but slightly modernized in form. The spelling is original, but tolerably regular.

The Glossary is directed to the understanding of the present text, and partly based on that in Baugh's edition.

The Bibliographical Note suggests some of the more readily available books that the teacher and student may wish to seek, and which contain further, more elaborate information about the scholarship and criticism of Chaucer and his age.

INTRODUCTION

I

GENERAL

CHAUCER'S *Troilus and Criseyde*, finished about 1385, was the next great poem in English after *Beowulf* – a gap of some 600 years. In that gap the old heroic world was lost; from it a new chivalric world emerged. The old heroic poem had seen the hero in a social role, representing society, without private life. The new chivalric poem, the romance, sees the hero as a representative, but individual and not typical, man. He is a lover, whose love is private, irrelevant to society, or even condemned by it; different from marriage and war, which are public and social acts and responsibilities. The individualism of love is one of the great organizing emotions of medieval Christendom as mass anger and protest are of the humanistic mid-twentieth century. Through his love the hero discovers the nature of existence, and of his own true functions, testing his personal values against those of other people and of society at large.

With *Troilus and Criseyde* English culture, after three centuries of assimilation following the deprivations of the Norman Conquest, finds itself again, in its own language and with a new richness of resource, breadth of feeling, and intellectual power. The poem has roots deep in the varied strata of English and European culture, and is the fine flower of the courtly chivalric culture of Richard II's court.

The problems of what life *should* be like in relation to what it *is* like, of Fortune, destiny, free will, surround the events of the story; yet these events are common enough. Troilus, a brave and good young man, falls desperately in love with a beautiful young woman, Criseyde; he seduces her; they enjoy mutual love; the harsh world of adult expediencies in politics and society separates them; she forgets him in the interest of a newer, less worthy seducer, Diomede. Troilus is miserable and cannot forget her for a quarter of a day. Eventually he dies. Love and loss happen every day, which gives the story much of its interest. But it is a most unusual poem because of the wider significance with which this story, so ordinary and yet so important, is invested.

2

THE POET

It is natural to be interested in who tells this poem. In one sense the poem is told by that well-documented, middle-aged courtier, wit, diplomat and Customs-collector, Geoffrey Chaucer (c. 1340–1400). A brief summary of the life of this interesting man will be found below, p. xl. But we are primarily interested in his poem. A poem is a symbolic structure with many different facets which can be only briefly noticed in the various sections of this introduction; but the facet which most immediately presents itself to us when we read is the tone of personal narration adopted by the poet. The story is enclosed between prologue and epilogue, so that the poem is longer than the story. It is as if a novelist's preface, containing comments on the story, were included within his novel; and also as if the novel finished by saying, 'After all, it is only a story, though it makes us think so-and-so about life'. The poet also continually makes us conscious of his own act of story-telling in the very course of the poem, sometimes claiming to see into a character's mind, sometimes claiming to be reporting only what his source says, sometimes expressing ignorance. How valuable this device is may be suggested by the number of novelists who today adopt first-person narratives. It gives a sort of historical solidity to the work. But a first-person narrator is *inside* the story. Chaucer the poet is not. He is always the story-teller in our presence, as it were. Therefore his telling has not the aim of the complete illusion attempted by the ordinary modern novel. Or rather, the illusion lies not at the level of character and event, but at the level of narration. Accepting Chaucer-the-poet as story-teller, we accept the story as he tells it, and the range of style from formality to realism, without difficulty.

The fascination of the poet's comments lies partly in their frequent irony. Not everything he tells us is to be taken at its face value – for example, his remark at the beginning of the poem that he is ignorant about love is self-evidently untrue. He does not seem to be *always* ironical, but he is ironical so often that critics often disagree about what he means or implies – and you must make up your own mind.

Even when the poet's comments, or manner of presenting his material, are not ironical, they are often ambiguous, as when he proclaims his ignorance of Criseyde's age. By an obvious paradox this ignorance increases the realism. Such partial knowledge is very like what we have about other people in real life. But at other times the poet knows even what is going on in Criseyde's mind. Why does he proclaim his ignorance of her age? Is he hinting that she is rather older than Troilus (as is indeed likely)? She describes herself as young in Book II – but what does that mean? Chaucer so often introduces a note of doubt in his comments on Criseyde that we are bound to feel there is something slippery about her.

A similar authorial device is the poet's wish to excuse Criseyde (V, 1093–9). Is it to be taken at face value? Or is it an ironical device to draw attention to her fault by seeming to gloss it over?

This occasional pose of ignorance or simplicity adopted by the poet has led some critics to speak as if the whole poem should be thought of as told by a fictional person, who is the Narrator, and is as it were a character as much 'within' the poem as any of the named characters. Although such a notion may allow interesting critical comments, it seems mistaken. There must always be a level of reality in the poem, some things meant literally. It is better to think of the poet as sometimes adopting a pose of simplicity, as any clever story-teller has to. The effect of the pose lies in the double image it creates, of a clever man pretending for a moment to be a simple man (as at the beginning of the whole poem) which thus creates two levels of meaning in the poem, simple meaning and deeper meaning, a doubleness which works almost like a metaphor and gives a poetic richness to the poem. One must not completely separate the poet from the pose, the complex meaning from the simple meaning. Their relationship is their chief strength. Therefore we do not usually speak of the Narrator of the poem, though some good critics have done so, but of the poet. The 'poet' may well have been different in some ways from the actual man 'Geoffrey Chaucer'. You cannot explain the poet or poetry by reference to the man's life, though they must have been related. The man is dead and gone, while the poet lives in the poem.

3

THE STORY AND ITS SOURCES

The poet tells a story, though the poem is longer, and more than, the story. By the story here we mean the account of events, what Chaucer called the 'matere'. This 'matter' may be thought of as of two kinds: first the particular story of Troilus; second, the general story of Troy. Both came to Chaucer as a kind of history, not merely fiction. He knew there had been a good deal of invention in telling them, and he used some in his own re-telling; but the whole point of accepting a traditional story is that one accepts the main outline – otherwise it would be a different story. Chaucer and his audience knew from the start that the story of Troilus was a story of truth and betrayal, and that the great city of Troy had been eventually destroyed after a ten-year siege by the Greeks in revenge for Helen's adultery with Paris, brother of Troilus.

The story of Troilus

Chaucer found the particular story of Troilus in Boccaccio's poem *Il Filostrato*, written in Italian about 1330. Boccaccio has three main characters, Troilo, Criseida, Pandaro. He says he has written the poem partly with autobiographical intent, to show, through the sufferings of Troilo, how the poet has suffered in real life from his own lady's rejection of him. Troilo is a lively, passionate young man, son of King Priam of Troy; Pandaro is his friend and Criseida's cousin, equally lively. Criseida is a young widow, who readily agrees to sleep with Troilo when approached by Pandaro. The action is rapid. Criseida is sad when she must part from Troilo, but soon consoles herself with Diomede. It is not surprising that this somewhat sexy poem finishes on a decidedly jaundiced, anti-feminist note. But it is a good poem, interesting, passionate, relatively quick-moving, and a fascinating companion to Chaucer's poem, with which it has many times been compared. Many of the philosophical and general elements in Chaucer's poem are foreshadowed in Boccaccio's, but much more super-ficially and briefly. The story bulks larger with him. Students should if possible read Boccaccio's poem, of which an English translation has been made (see Bibliographical Note). Boccaccio's poem is less detached, less rich in characterization, less courtly, less idealistic, less philosophical, less humorous than Chaucer's, but is more personal, intense, and perhaps more immediately appealing to the young than Chaucer's poem.

It has recently been discovered that Chaucer also used a French translation of *Il Filostrato* by Jean of Beauvau, Seneschal of Anjou, to help with details of translation, but this does not alter the fact of Chaucer's dependence on Boc-caccio.

Boccaccio did not invent all the story of Troilo. The essen-tial idea was the work of a twelfth-century poet writing in French, Benoît de Ste.-Maure, who wrote the enormous *Roman de Troie*. He told of the grief of the young but great warrior Troilus when separated from his beloved Briseida. What Boccaccio did was to invent the story of the wooing (which Chaucer in his turn greatly expanded) and change the name of the heroine from Briseida to Criseida.

Benoît's work was known to Chaucer, and he occasionally borrowed from it. Benoît was also the source of a Latin account, the *Historia Destructionis Troiae* by Guido de Columnis, written in 1287 – a moralistic and anti-feminist prose history (an Elizabethan translation of which was the principal source of Shakespeare's *Troilus and Cressida*). Chaucer occasionally consulted Guido.

The story of Troy

The personal story of Troilus the lover thus grew from Benoît through Boccaccio to Chaucer. Though Boccaccio isolates the story in personal terms, for all other writers the story of Troilus was merely an incident in the tale of Troy. In Chaucer's poem, too, a sense of the social and political pressures of the besieged city, and of its inevitable doom, is an essential part of the poem. Social and political forces divide the lovers, and the doom of Troy is itself an example of the transitory nature of all human joy and achievement. The story of Troy had also a special interest for medieval Englishmen because it was believed that Aeneas, who had escaped from Troy when it was burnt by the Greeks, later to found Rome, had had a grandson, Brut, who established the kingdom of Britain and founded a line of kings which included Lear, Cymbeline, and Arthur.

Benoît founded his long account of the Trojan War on two short Latin works, the *De Excidio Troiae Historia* of Dares, written about A.D. 600, and the *Ephemeridos Belli Troiani* of Dictys Cretensis, written about the fourth century. These are the basic authorities for the Trojan War known to medieval writers, the *Dares and Dyte* referred to by Chaucer, I, 146 and V, 1771. Chaucer probably did not read them, though he read a poetic version of Dares by the Englishman Joseph of Exeter called the 'Liber Frigic Daretis', and borrowed from it for the portraits at V, 799 ff.

The fall of Troy was described in Virgil's *Aeneid*, which tells of the later founding of Rome, and which was a medieval schoolbook. Finally, the principal source of knowledge was Homer, referred to by Chaucer, I, 145 and V, 1792. But hardly any medieval men knew Greek, and Chaucer certainly knew none. Homer was famous by hearsay, and was moreover thought to be a liar who favoured the Greeks. These writers mention Troilus as a great warrior, but only very briefly, and never as a lover.

The story of Troy was very well known throughout the Middle Ages, an image of worldly glory and tragedy, out of whose fall, however, had risen the grandeur of Rome, which fell in its turn, as all empires must.

Lollius

Chaucer never mentions Boccaccio as his source. Medieval writers tended to mention ultimate authorities rather than immediate sources, and in any case Chaucer was writing a poem, not a scholarly treatise. He does, however, mention 'myn auctour called Lollius', I, 394 (not in the present selection), and again V, 1653. He seems to have shared a general impression, arising out of a misunderstanding of one of the verse *Letters* of the Latin poet Horace, that Lollius was, like Homer, Dares, and Dictys, one of the principal and ultimate authorities for our knowledge of the Trojan War. Chaucer mentions him with the others in *The House of Fame*, 1466–70.

It is necessary to know about the tradition of the story of Troilus and Troy, and the general familiarity of Chaucer's audience with it. Their – and our – foreknowledge of the general outcome is part of the feeling of the poem. But Chaucer's own poem is the centre of interest in this edition.

4

THE CHARACTERS

Traditionally, when novelists write a novel they tend to think of a character and then imagine how he would act. We sometimes hear of 'the characters taking charge'. The story then is a function of the character. Perhaps something like this happened with Chaucer's Wife of Bath in *The Canterbury Tales*. But in *Troilus and Criseyde* the situation is different. The story, constituting the main actions of the characters, is given. In some sense, therefore, the characters are functions of the story, as is very much the case with Pandarus. But not entirely. Chaucer does not try to make his characters 'develop', but he gives Troilus and Criseyde quite clear sets of characteristics, and some degree of independence. The result, with these two, is that they are more than, or at least different from, the sum of their actions. What they *are*, and what they *do*, are slightly at odds (as may sometimes be observed of people in real life – 'Fancy *her* doing *that*!'). Hence some of the poignancy, especially of the charming Criseyde.

Again, in a novel we tend to identify ourselves with the chief characters. This poem, however, is told in such a way that, though we deeply sympathize with Troilus and Criseyde, we do not identify ourselves completely with them. We are always slightly detached, because the poet himself is.

Troilus

He is the central character, son of Priam, king of Troy. He falls in love, is faithful, is betrayed. Traditionally he was very young and an outstanding soldier. Chaucer makes him noble, sensitive, introspective, modest, not aggressive. He is morally much superior to, or at least much more innocent than, Boccaccio's Troilo. The result of Chaucer's changes is that Troilus could not possibly of his own accord have seduced Criseyde; he is much too modest, nice, and good. His character is described, V, 827 ff. He is not meant to be a 'usual' type of person. He is an extreme example, a young man in a thousand. But he is also a representative, or 'exemplary' character, the touchstone of the action; the person through whom the discoveries of the poem are made.

Pandarus

Pandarus is almost entirely a function of the action. He is not described as the other main characters are at V, 799 ff. Chaucer makes him Criseyde's uncle (perhaps to give him more authority over her), but though he is more experienced than Troilus, he is his constant companion and must be thought to be little older. We only see him as companion to Troilus and uncle to Criseyde and in the company of one or other or both, never in any action on his own account, as a soldier or otherwise, save in the briefest reference to his own unsuccessful love of an unknown lady. As go-between he represents the aggressive sexuality that Troilus lacks. He does Troilus's 'dirty work' for him. But also he represents the compliance of Criseyde. She is no wanton, and without Pandarus's pressure would never have loved Troilus. Since he promotes the action he also represents, in a sense, 'the way of the world', even Fortune, though he is in no way allegorical. His characteristics emerge with his actions and speech. He is fluent, quick-witted, jolly, well-educated in a literary way (for persuasion, proverbial wisdom, letter-writing), well-educated in science (for reading the stars to judge a good day for action, to foretell the weather, etc.). He is a liar and deceiver. He genuinely loves Troilus and, at first, Criseyde, though he hates her for betraying his friend. Vividly realistic as he is, he is what he does; he seems to have no core as a man, but he is very fascinating as a character.

Criseyde

Criseyde has the traditional beauty of the medieval heroine, though Chaucer only specifically mentions her golden hair, which her black widow's dress sets off so perfectly. Her figure was perfect, though Chaucer says she was of average height (whereas most heroines were tall) and that her eyebrows were joined together. This had been thought a mark of beauty by the Greeks, but by medieval as by modern minds was considered a flaw. The scientist and theologian Albertus Magnus says it is a sign of treachery. Besides suggesting her physical beauty, Chaucer gives her character, V, 806 ff. She is fully delightful and womanly. Her timidity is only one of the charming aspects of her womanhood, like her pity and her lovingness. It is not a 'fatal flaw'. Part of the tragedy is that such a delightful and virtuous lady should have been unfaithful. Chaucer always introduces a note of ambiguity or mystery when discussing her. We know her by glimpses, though they may be glimpses into the very working of her mind. We see her as a disdainful young lady, as a serene mistress of her household, as a girl merry and playful as a kitten with Pandarus, as prudent and worldly, always anxious about her reputation, as content with her situation both before she is beloved, and when loved. She does not initiate action: she is always worked on, and she always does what people want her to do – Pandarus, Troilus, the Trojan parliament, her father, and Diomede. She is a fascinatingly complex and real character, not allegorical, but she may be said to represent also the gifts of Fortune and Nature. She is also, therefore, 'exemplary', or representative.

Diomede

Little need be said of Diomede; he is bold, rich, handsome, active, selfish, lying; the sort of man whom many men dislike and almost all women are readily deceived by. He is 'large of tongue', according to some, as Chaucer tells us (V, 799 ff.) – big-mouthed?

5

THE STRUCTURE

Troilus and Criseyde follows Boccaccio's poem closely on the whole, but with a number of subtle alterations and some large additions. Chaucer expands the story of the wooing, in particular, and produces an almost perfectly symmetrical five-book structure, where the climax of joy and success comes in the middle book. This rise and fall represents the turn of Fortune's wheel. Troilus climbs on the wheel in the first book, reaches its height at the end of the third, and is eventually utterly cast down in the fifth.

This structure can hardly be accidental, but there is a puzzle. The poet translates from the handbook of rhetoric written about 1200 by Geoffrey of Vinsauf the lines about the need to consider the overall structure of any piece of work (I, 1065–71, not in present selection) before beginning, but in the prologue of the fourth book seems to anticipate finishing the poem in four books. Perhaps he once intended to, but changed his mind, and overlooked the remark in the various revisions he made.

The present selection necessarily omits much, and so does not do the structure full justice. But it concentrates on those elements where Chaucer himself expanded or added to Boccaccio's version, while keeping the main outline of rise and fall.

6

RHETORIC

Rhetoric can mean either 'the art of writing', or, more particularly, 'the art of adorning writing'. Medieval rhetoric descended from classical rhetoric, whose origin lay in instructions for persuasive speech in the law-courts, but which became broadened to include all the elements of a 'liberal education' and decent behaviour.

In the Middle Ages the classical ideals were weakened but not lost. There was a group of rhetoricians writing about the end of the twelfth century of whom Geoffrey of Vinsauf was the best-known. His *Poetria Nova* is quoted in *Troilus and Criseyde*, as already noted, and he is the Geoffrey referred to at the end of *The Nun's Priest's Tale* in *The Canterbury Tales*. Medieval writers also learned rhetoric with their (Latin) grammar, and by imitation of other writers.

Medieval rhetoric and writing usually maintained a strong element of persuasiveness and of communication, and were thus interested more in subject-matter and the audience than in the author's own personality. It was thought that the style should suit the subject (rather than, for example, express the poet's private personality). The aims of a writer were to create a work of harmony and beauty (rather than, for example, a close imitation of ordinary life). The writer wished to move his audience by the creation of meaning and pattern. The similarities and differences, we may say, between *Troilus and Criseyde* and a nineteenth-century novel are comparable to those between a fourteenth-century Gothic stained-glass window or manuscript illumination and a nineteenth-century realistic painting. Each tells a story, is colourful, and has realistic elements, but the Gothic work is really quite different and is not attempting a transcript of life. (It should be noticed, however, that modernist twentieth-century art, so much more fragmented and so much less realistic than nineteenth-century art, is in some respects nearer to Gothic art.)

To summarize: an adorned verbal structure; persuasive communication; a deliberately varied style; a pattern of beauty – these are among the chief aims of poetic rhetoric, such as that of *Troilus and Criseyde*. The texture of the style is very rich. Chaucer uses many stylistic devices, such as prologues, addresses to the audience, addresses to some personification (e.g. Fortune), comparisons, similes, metaphors, proverbs, contrasts, understatements, ironies, repetitions, formal descriptions, etc. A very elaborate analysis could be made in medieval terminology which would not, however, much benefit the student, though a few figures of speech are pointed out in the Commentary. The diction varies from the very formal and elaborate (as in the prologues, and the prayer at the very end) to the simple and homely.

Recognition of the artistic elaboration and formality of the style should not obscure two characteristics more familiar to and better liked by modern readers: first, a kind of spontaneity or casualness and, second, a vivid realism. The sense of spontaneity or casualness arises from the vigour of the style; from the poet's expression of his personal comments (sometimes ironical); from the sometimes cavalier treatment of the rules of grammar, a looseness of syntax, which occasionally allows him (like Shakespeare) to say literally the opposite of what it is clearly his intention to say (e.g. II, 627–30); and sometimes even from the touches of homely realism.

The realism of Chaucer's style is a part of his rhetoric, but deserves special emphasis. By realism is meant here 'a plausible representation of ordinary appearances'. The poem gives us many details of ordinary life (mostly drawn from medieval London), like the chains across the streets, II, 617–18, or the arrangements in Pandarus's house. Although the realism is conveyed only in brief touches, we get a lively sense of physical circumstance, social life, and consequently of real existence in the world. The supreme realism is perhaps in dialogue. Another kind of realism occurs in the deflating or homely comparisons, especially in contrast with more formal or idealistic expressions, as when Troilus is compared with a fresh horse (I, 218 ff.). In admiring the realism, however, we do not look for it in inappropriate places, e.g. in Troilus's songs, or in Troilus's long soliloquy on the problem of free will (IV, 958 ff., not in present selection).

The relation between realism and the general rhetorical ideal of pattern and beauty (which includes realism, but which does not make a realistic imitation of life its primary aim) is parallel to the general idea underlying the poem: that ordinary life (comparable to 'realism') is only part of a fuller reality, whose laws ultimately control even the ordinary life under Fortune and Nature, the ordinary life of the world beneath the moon, where joy and woe, and therefore tragedy, are to be found.

7

TRAGEDY

Chaucer calls his poem 'my little tragedy' (V, 1786). The 'little' is deliberately depreciatory and self-mocking, appropriate in its modesty for the poet, but not for us. It is a tragedy because it records a fall from high to low, which is the medieval definition of tragedy. This definition is found in a gloss included by Chaucer in his translation of Boethius's *Consolation*, Book II, prose 2, and repeated in *The Canterbury Tales*, 'Prologue to the Monk's Tale', VII, 1973–7. Tragedy is caused by Fortune, as Boethius makes clear. Nature creates a man. Fortune gives him gifts. These gifts are never his rightful possessions, and they may be withdrawn, just as, within the realm of Nature, he must die. We do not like giving up Fortune's gifts, or indeed Nature's, and we tend to rely on them. But they must perish, both the body (from Nature) and its raiment (from Fortune). The tragedy arises from our sorrow, misunderstanding, wrong attitudes, and the waste that is caused. If we love the world, which is natural enough, we find that tragedy is part of its nature. The whole creation groans in travail.

The tragedy of Fortune is secular, and concludes with death. This is an entirely sensible view for either atheist or Christian. If you are an atheist you believe you cease entirely to exist after death, and therefore nothing matters any more to you. If you are a Christian you believe that through death you in some way confront the ultimate reality behind the world of Fortune and Nature, and that this reality is the ultimate justice and goodness that mysteriously surround and support earthly existence. In either case it is ridiculous to mourn the dead, though we may mourn for ourselves, and Troilus after death rightly laughs at such mourning (V, 1821–2).

Excessive concern with earthly affairs and with our own suffering is absurd either in the light of what really matters or in the context of ultimate meaninglessness. But in no case can we avoid pain. If we behave with 'truth', loyalty, faith, honesty in worldly matters we may well find that such behaviour increases our suffering. There is no guarantee in worldly affairs that 'truth' will bring love, success, riches, prestige, comfort. It may bring some of these good things. But its opposite may well bring more, as we see daily. What 'truth' will bring is the capacity, the ending of *Troilus* seems to say, to endure ultimate reality. The poet does not commit himself to an opinion about Troilus's ultimate destination. It would be as impertinent to advise Eternal Justice as it would be to argue about its dispositions.

The tragedy of Fortune is thus Christian tragedy, which means a tragedy of choice. To call it so is to remember that we, with the poet, stand outside the action. Troilus may not be perfect but he is a good man; he is obviously not a Christian. To Troilus himself, an unfortunate pagan, his personal tragedy is a tragedy of necessity. As his soliloquy (IV, 953–1082, discussed below, p. xxxviii) makes clear, he thinks he is pre-ordained to suffer. This was the view of the philosopher Boethius before the Lady Philosophy corrected him and showed that men have free will. But to us the tragedy of Troilus is a tragedy of choice. As W. H. Auden has written: 'Greek Tragedy is the tragedy of necessity: i.e. the feeling aroused in the spectator is "What a pity it had to be this way"; Christian Tragedy is the tragedy of possibility, "What a pity it was this way when it might have been otherwise".' Of Captain Ahab in *Moby Dick* Auden writes, as one might of Troilus, that he has 'an opportunity to choose; by making the wrong choice and continuing to make it, Ahab punishes himself' ('The Christian Tragic Hero', *The New York Times Book Review*, 16 December 1945, quoted by W. K. Wimsatt, Jr, and Cleanth Brooks, *Literary Criticism: A Short History*, New York, 1957).

The medieval tragedy of Fortune confronts the suffering of the world unblinkingly, though not unsympathetically. It is unsentimental. It implies that if we refuse to lend ourselves to the uses of this world we could not so much avoid suffering as be morally superior to it. It says that in the end, if we are honest, we see that we need not have taken misfortune so seriously. It also says that though the world is a mixture of good and bad both in its physical and moral nature, it is possible so to pass through things temporal that we may not lose the things eternal. The temporal is 'surrounded' by a mystery; the limits of temporality are those of life on this earth, but even the humblest or worst parts of the temporal are in some way penetrated, even sustained, by ultimate values, as the universe was considered to be 'surrounded' by unconditioned divinity.

For this reason the medieval tragedy of Fortune, though full of suffering and dismay, is not pessimistic. Since mid-twentieth-century literature at its most characteristic is almost totally pessimistic in its assertion of the utter meaninglessness of experience (and, of course, may be right), we do well to notice consciously here the moral optimism that informs great tragedy (including Shakespeare's) in earlier English literature. Much English writing in the fourteenth century – for example,

Piers Plowman, Sir Gawain and the Green Knight, Pearl – says, in effect, 'If you keep your nerve, if you don't give in, you'll be all right'. There is some of this spirit in *Troilus and Criseyde*.

On this view the 'truth' or integrity that a man or woman preserves in life is one of the chief connections between ultimate values (i.e. for medieval Christians, God) and the world God has made. In twentieth-century terms perhaps we may say that it is personal integrity which makes us fully human, even if, paradoxically, we die for it, as so many have, and even if so many more fail to achieve or, like Diomede, do not wish to achieve, 'truth'.

In the medieval view of the world the moral and physical structures of the world were closely linked, as they are not in modern thought. The physical passion of sex, for example, was largely controlled by the stars, which in their turn were ultimately the instruments of God's Providence.

We must now turn to what the poem says about, or how it uses, certain major topics which are all interrelated: Love; Astrology; Destiny, Fate and Fortune; Mythology. As always, what is said here is designed to be helpful and suggestive, rather than authoritative and exhaustive.

8

LOVE – *FINE AMOUR*

So much has been written about love in the Middle Ages and misapplied to *Troilus and Criseyde*, that the first advice to a reader interested in what Chaucer has to say about love (as indeed about anything else) is *look and see*. Historical connections are important and can improve our insight, but here must come second.

The way Troilus falls in love is entirely natural, though a modern explanation of the mechanism differs from the medieval. His absorption in Criseyde is equally natural. It is sexual, but also involves a total orientation of the personality (e.g. III, 1716 ff.), and concerns far more than sex. Such love can probably only exist with some restraint of sexuality. Promiscuity either fragments the personality or largely removes sex from its realm, as with Diomede; marriage also changes the quality of romantic love.

Troilus's extreme shyness sometimes seems to modern readers exaggerated. In one sense no doubt it is, since Troilus is exceptional in personality and gifts, and since his high social position gives him a freedom to indulge his feelings largely unrestrained. But the misery of shyness endured by him is familiar still. That the middle-aged poet – and so the reader of any age – is also a little amused by Troilus's self-pitying misery does not mean it is any the less natural, or that it is satirized or sneered at as a whole.

Troilus, already a good and brave young man, becomes even better through love. The security, happiness, energy and warmth generated by loving and being loved are a commonplace of modern psychology, and of ageless common sense. Similarly Troilus's incapacity for action, his misery, and, at the end, his anger, are the natural product of not being loved. His deference to Criseyde, his respect for her wishes, are part of a desire to please the beloved, natural in a sensitive, intelligent, decent young man, in an aristocratic society where women were socially if not legally equal with men.

Reference to society, however, reminds us that all feelings, however universally and everlastingly common to mankind, can only be expressed in ways that are to some extent historically conditioned. The vocabulary of love used about and by Troilus is partly conditioned by a feudal society. He is her 'man'; he will 'serve' her, etc. It is the language of feudal obligation. Much of the value and veneration given to the beloved person was modelled on the dominant medieval social bond, which was obligation to the feudal superior.

The main flow of obligation was from inferior to superior, and thus the lady is regarded as the lover's superior, and he will obey her. Nevertheless, a superior person has a natural social obligation to his inferiors (at least according to medieval Christian thought, as in Chaucer's *Parson's Tale*), and a lover always feels that his beloved *ought* to love him in return, simply because he loves her so much. This is also a natural though illogical human feeling. But because the true lover is humble he expresses his sense of the lady's obligation to love him in return as a wish for her to 'pity him', or to give him her 'grace'. All such terms are part of the medieval language of love, which is unfamiliar to us, even if the basic emotions are not.

The word 'grace' introduces another pattern of love – that of religion; for the Christian hopes that God will grant him grace. In I, 15 of *Troilus and Criseyde* the God of Love is mentioned, in a parodic phrase that reminds us of the title of the Pope. This is clearly meant to be slightly amusing. In line 31 the words 'love' and 'heaven' are ambiguous, while in the following lines God, the real Christian God, is invoked in relation to Love. The God of Love who strikes Troilus with his arrow, I, 206–9, is plainly a mythological person, Cupid, the classical and medieval personification of some aspects of love. But the Love that can bind all things, because no man can destroy the law of Nature, in I, 237–8, seems to be that Love which knits together the whole universe and is later hymned by Troilus, III, 1744 ff. The poet insists this love is virtuous (I, 254). Of course, the poet may be ironical in Book I, while Troilus's hymn in Book III is only Troilus's opinion, as it were, and Troilus may be as mistaken about love as he is about free will in Book IV, 953–1082 (see below, p. xxxviii). What seems to be established in these early comments in Book I is an ambiguous relationship between secular, sexual love and the religious love of God. This is the basis of a general concern of the poem to suggest a puzzling, teasing relationship between the ups and downs of earthly experience and the surrounding mystery of Divine values.

The irresistibility of love is insisted on by the poet in these early parts of the poem. That love is irresistible does not resolve the ambiguity between earthly and heavenly love, for while men cannot avoid loving, they *can* choose *whom* they shall primarily love – God or a girl. As Pandarus casually remarks to Troilus later (I, 979, not in the present selection), everybody is bound to love, either 'love celestial or love of kind', that is, must direct their love either religiously or naturally. Such a remark establishes clearly the two loves, though it does not clarify the ambiguous relationship between them.

Troilus chooses natural love, and though it is painful at times it is not in itself condemned by the poet. Indeed it brings supreme joy to Troilus. Moreover, Troilus feels that it is holy. He expresses the wish that it may be part of the Love that binds the universe. Troilus may be mistaken, but he is, so to say, honestly mistaken. He suffuses his love and to some extent his language with religious feeling (e.g. III, 712, his prayer to

Venus). The difficulty with natural love is that it is settled upon unstable human beings, as Criseyde's actions demonstrate. Even if Criseyde had not betrayed Troilus, she would have died and so left him. In this rather severe sense, implied at the end of the poem, all human love is 'fained love' (V, 1848). Celestial love, the love of God, is invoked at the end of the poem, in contradistinction to natural love. Natural love passes as this world, vanity fair, passes away, like a flower. Love of God, by definition, lasts for ever.

Yet still the ambiguous relationship between the two loves haunts us, and we are troubled by a question deep in the heart of the poem, which perhaps Chaucer could not even quite formulate, but is at the source of the beauty and pathos. Why must natural and heavenly love be in conflict? Are we not told to love God *and* our neighbour? Why could not Troilus love God through Criseyde? Was he so very much mistaken? Natural love is validated at least to this extent in Troilus, that he is granted after death apparently some understanding of the true nature of things, perhaps because he was a true lover, even though he set his heart on the wrong object of love, or loved it wrongly. Perhaps we may say, in the jargon of today, that he got his priorities wrong, as most of us do, but was essentially right.

Within Troilus's natural love two questions arise. Why did Troilus not marry Criseyde? And what is meant by the 'craft' of love (I, 379)? A number of answers to the question of marriage suggest themselves. First, it was historically not a story about marriage. It is a story about love; specifically, about love betrayed. Basically, the story is of a hot-blooded princeling who takes a mistress and is jilted. Have the morals of the aristocracy ever been such as to make this unrealistic? Marriage is a public, social, legal, financial act; it involves responsibilities towards families present and to come, towards society at large. For princes it involves problems of ranks, inheritances, dynasties, countries, government. It is an institution in human relationships where personal likes and dislikes, though important, have to take their place among many other factors. Marriage thus conceived is one of the great stabilizers of personal and social life. It is a very appropriate end to a successful love affair, and its breakdown is a tragedy, but it is a more complex business than love, and not Chaucer's subject. Furthermore, if

Troilus *had* married Criseyde she could not have betrayed him in the way she did. Her marriage would have been public, or would not have been truly marriage, and the Trojan parliament could not have separated her from her husband. If Troilus had married Criseyde he would have saved himself a lot of trouble; though to think of the poem as a tract in favour of marriage would be rather too explicit! (And of course the point that *all* earthly experience is inevitably compounded of both joy and sorrow would apply equally to marriage, were that the subject.) It is true that, in his agony at the decree that Criseyde must be exchanged, Troilus has contemplated asking his father for her in marriage, as he tells Pandarus. But it is too late. It would merely reveal that she is his mistress, which would shame her, while Priam could not rescind the decree on such grounds (IV, 554–60). One may notice in this connection some illogicality in Troilus. Love is essentially for him private, and therefore secret; not a public or social act. Yet he feels, rightly we may think, according to the great Boethian hymn to love at the end of Book III, that his love should be part of that greater love that moves the sun and stars, 'that impels all thinking things, all objects of all thought, and rolls through all things'. As is characteristic of a young man, he wants the benefits of the private world and the cosmos, and disregards the demands of society. But because his love is private, the pressures of society, which both he and Criseyde accept almost unquestioningly, divide them. (This is not to say that society is necessarily right.)

The problem chiefly arises because Troilus is presented as so idealistic, decent, loving, and loyal that marriage, a public declaration, would seem as natural a conclusion of his private passion as it is (contrary to the impression sometimes given by critics) for *all* other English medieval romances, Chaucerian and other, apart from the story of Lancelot. In *Troilus and Criseyde*, in this respect we find a certain difference (which is not an artistic flaw) between what the character is and what he does (cf. above, p. xix). Chaucer also reminds us that there are different conventions of love in different ages, and that we are not to judge the way Troilus went on, in secrecy, by our standards of 'open visiting', etc., II, 29–49. Chaucer is keenly aware of historical change and distance, though there may be a touch of irony here.

Chaucer, therefore, invokes a sort of historical relativism to account for Troilus's (or perhaps rather Pandarus's) conduct of the love affair. The way Troilus wins Criseyde's love is very deceitful, and the whole affair is furtive, but Chaucer never condemns the affair because of its immorality. Immorality is not as much the point as the *naturalness* of the affair, and consequently its joy and its pain. One is the inevitable accompaniment of the other, because that is what the world is like. 'Such is this world', says Chaucer, for those who have the nerve to look at it steadily. 'God grant us for to take it for the best!' (cf. V, 1748–50). The poem, one can hardly say too often, is primarily about joy and sorrow, not about good and bad morals.

Many critics have assumed that Troilus practises 'the code of courtly love', which is said to be essentially adulterous. This is nonsense, though like most errors it has a grain of truth. Troilus cannot commit adultery because neither he nor Criseyde is married. They commit the simpler sin of fornication, less harmful to other people.

The 'code of courtly love' is a modern notion, based on what Chaucer elsewhere calls the 'law of love' (*Envoy to Scogan*, 17), i.e. the obligation to remain faithful to one's promises of love; and on 'the art and craft of fine loving' (*Prologue to the Legend of Good Women*, F 544). The 'craft', as Chaucer calls it in *Troilus and Criseyde*, I, 379, is the art of pleasing the beloved by behaving well in all respects, from personal cleanliness through good manners to complete moral integrity. It is natural that the details of behaviour vary according to historical circumstances, though the amount of difference can be exaggerated. Young people dance and sing, struggle and fight, and pray, with, about, and for each other, in most periods. A good medieval account of the craft of love, well known to Chaucer, is in the thirteenth-century French poem *Le Roman de la Rose* (ll. 2145 ff. in the Chaucerian English translation). Accounts of young men in love were fairly stylized in medieval literature, but the impression occasionally given by critics that at every stage of his love Troilus consulted 'the code of courtly love' in order to know what to do next does not arise from the poem. The phrase 'courtly love' has now become so misleading that it is better abandoned in favour of 'love', or, with more historical reference, in favour of the medieval French term *fine amour*, 'refined love'.

The historical significance of *fine amour* is great indeed, and its full complexity cannot be dealt with here. Men and women have lusted for each other, as they have also loved and cherished each other, in all ages and countries, but the particular form of love called *fine amour*, caused by a particular conjunction of economic, social, religious, literary, and foreign causes, seems to have begun about the eleventh century in Provence. From there it spread to all European countries and has powerfully influenced human feeling even to the present day. Over such a range of time and place it has naturally taken many differing forms, but a few essential characteristics may be noted. (*a*) The initiative lies with the man, though women do indeed love in return, as Antigone's song (II, 827–75), and Criseyde's actions, indicate; (*b*) sexual desire is the basis, and sexual fulfilment is the aim; (*c*) the total emotion is much more than merely sexual: the beloved becomes a symbol of inexpressible and almost transcendental longings and satisfactions; (*d*) the lover feels the superiority of his beloved to himself, and ardently as he desires her feels that he can only ask her to condescend to him; (*e*) the pattern of the lover's whole personality is affected by his love, as iron filings by a magnet, and the whole personality is made finer; (*f*) the feeling is intensely personal and therefore private and secret – it is much too deep, and part of both the lovers' intimate selfhood, to be lightly discussed or displayed. This is why it is not the same as marriage; it usually leads to marriage, but it is essentially pre-marital and may be adulterous. To summarize, then, *fine amour* may be said to be essentially (*a*) masculine, (*b*) sexual, (*c*) symbolical, (*d*) humble, (*e*) improving, (*f*) private. Other elements were often associated: notably joy, bravery, courtesy, eloquence, kindness, such as may be seen in the description of Troilus, III, 1772 ff.

The total effect may be described as the personalization, and even the consecration, of sex. The movement is a very familiar one in human psychology, whereby a means becomes treated as an end. Sex is a biological means for continuing the species, and partly functions so in marriage. But *fine amour* took sex as a feeling in its own right; sex was built into the personality and gave it more fire and light, while through personalization desire itself was made more gentle and loyal. It was inevitable that in such circumstances, and under the influence of Christianity, the religion of love, *fine amour*, should itself take on 'the holiness of the heart's affections'. The paradox follows that *fine amour* then easily became not only a part of holiness, but a rival to holiness.

This happened the more easily because of the early Christian Church's distrust of sex, and predominant distrust of the world. Such distrust is not unreasonable in technologically primitive communities. Sex is closely linked in nature with aggressiveness, misery, and death, as any day's news in a popular newspaper and many films will show. But of course in our view early Christian asceticism was sometimes crazily or morbidly exaggerated; and in the Middle Ages an ascetic ideal of real value, suited in its full rigour to only a chosen few, was often recommended to all. *Troilus and Criseyde* is remarkably free from any morbidity or exaggeration, and though the poem implies a distrust of 'natural' love, it is because of its instability rather than its sensuality.

This is a highly simplified view of a very complicated and varied mass of interrelated thoughts and feelings. *Fine amour* deserves our interest because of its own attractiveness and complexity, and also because, though it has been the mainspring of so much European literature and life for a thousand years, it may be that we are at the end of its influence, and are entering a period such as that described in Aldous Huxley's *Brave New World*. If, as seems possible, sex becomes a promiscuous, pleasant sporting activity, played between pairs, rather like tennis, and about as public, it will have no significant relation to personality, and will become completely trivial. It will give far less pain than it did, and by the inexorable law that action equals reaction, will give far less joy. The feelings of a Troilus or a Romeo, incomprehensible now to the complete extrovert or boor, will then have become as remote even to the imaginative as the scientific concepts, to which we now turn.

9

ASTROLOGY

Science offers us a model of 'reality' and an explanation of how things happen. Fourteenth-century science was largely wrong, but it offered a quite reasonable model of reality on the information and assumptions that were then available. The master science was astrology, a mixture of what we would think of as 'pure science', i.e. astronomy, and of moral, religious, philosophical notions, which was developed to great complexity. Chaucer himself was something of an adept, and was well up with the most modern scientific thought. He often uses astrological references to indicate the season, and for learned poetic decoration (e.g. II, 54–6). Troilus is not a very highly educated young man, but Pandarus, like the normal fourteenth-century intellectual, understands astrology very well. He does not move in Troilus's love affair until he has consulted the stars (II, 74). The rain which kept Criseyde in Pandarus's house was caused by a very rare conjunction of stars (III, 624, n.), which Pandarus seems to have foreseen, though the stars are not specifically mentioned (III, 519–21, not in present selection). That Criseyde stayed in his house is attributed to the influence of the stars, not her own will (III, 621–3). Astrology provided at least a partial theory of cause and effect for actions in the world. To make this clear, a brief description of the picture of the universe may help.

To an ordinary observer the earth is motionless, and the sun, moon, and other stars appear to move round it at varying speeds. Most stars appear to be set in fixed patterns (the Plough, Orion, etc.), and these are called the fixed stars. They move slowly all together from east to west. Until the sixteenth century everybody believed that the earth was the centre of a huge hollow sphere, and these stars were fixed as it were on the inside lining. The sun, the moon, and (to ordinary observation) five other bright stars, have obviously different movements from the fixed stars. These seven are the planets, and each was thought to have a hollow transparent sphere of its own to which it was attached. The moon is nearest, and all things beneath the moon (i.e. the earth) were thought to be changeable, perishable, corrupt. Hell was at the very centre of the earth. Above the moon each successive planet was attached to its own hollow transparent sphere, in the order of Mercury, Venus, the Sun, Mars, Jupiter, Saturn. Then came the fixed stars. Each sphere moved independently, so producing the heavenly harmony, 'the music of the spheres', which Troilus heard (V, 1812). Above the moon all was perfection and incorruptibility. Outside these eight spheres was a ninth, the

Primum Mobile, whose function was to transform the love of God into the energy that moves the stars and ultimately, through them, controls the earth. The stars, themselves perfect, transmitted the 'influences' (a technical word) that, for example, control the force of gravity, the weather, the crops, and the passions of men, including love. Some planets were mainly favourable, 'benefic', others were mainly unfavourable, 'malefic', but the total effect depended also on the interrelationships of the planets with each other and to certain of the fixed stars, which appear to an observer on earth to be behind the planets.

The paths that the planets appear to take round the earth in the course of a year pass in front of a band of fixed stars. This band is called the Zodiac. If the whole universe of nine concentric spheres is thought of as a cricket ball, the Zodiac is the band formed by the ball's broad seam, and the planets are inside, while the earth is of course a tiny point at the very centre of the ball. The band of the Zodiac was divided into twelve sections, each given a particular name, and these are called the signs of the Zodiac. 'And in the Zodiac been the 12 signs that have names of beasts . . .', writes Chaucer in his *Treatise on the Astrolabe* (an astrological work written for his little son Lewis), either because, 'when the sun entreth into any of the signs he taketh the property [quality] of such beasts, or else for [because] the stars that been there fixed been disposed in signs of beasts, or shape like beasts, or else when the planets been under thilk [those] signs they cause us by their influence operations and effects like to the operations of beasts' (Part I, 60–70). Each sign also has particular influence over a part of the body, Taurus, the bull, for example, over neck and throat.

The band of the Zodiac, being part of the fixed stars, moved slowly round the earth during the course of the year, a new sign rising in the east roughly just before the middle of each month. The signs of the Zodiac thus helped to mark the seasons. (In modern times the positions have slightly changed.) The most significant position for a sign of the Zodiac was when it was just moving up past the eastern horizon, when it was said to be in the ascendant. Other positions were also significant, but less powerful.

Each planet had an influence on men and affairs; for

example, Venus encouraged love, Mars war. The relationship of a planet to other planets and to the fixed stars strengthened or weakened its influence. Thus when Criseyde first saw Troilus, Venus was in a strong position (II, 680–3). The seventh 'house of heaven' seems to signify the seventh of twelve equal divisions into which the fixed stars were sometimes divided, and to be just above the western horizon. (Usually 'house' means that sign of the Zodiac in which the planet exerts its strongest influence, but that is not meant here.) Venus helps Troilus from this position. The poet goes on to refer to her partial favour in Troilus's nativity (III, 685). This refers to the total pattern of the sky at his birth, which was called the horoscope. The horoscope was believed to foretell, perhaps control, a man's whole future.

Since current religion and philosophy normally emphasized personal responsibility before God, which implied human free will, there was clearly a problem raised by such predictive or 'judicial' astronomy, and Chaucer himself condemns judicial astronomy in his astrological work, *Treatise on the Astrolabe* (Part II, Section 4). Briefly, however, the general solution was that the stars do indeed control physical existence of all kinds on earth, including men in their animal natures, and passions. But the mind of man could, if he wished, rise above such control. It was frequently said that 'the wise man controls the stars' – not the other way round. Troilus is good, brave, young, true – but he is not wise. So he suffers experience of the world, which is notoriously painful, though like all young persons he thinks it ought not to be. Yet there is another paradox here. If normal experience is governed by the stars, then the stars cause much evil as well as good. But *ultimately* the stars are controlled by God, who is good. So not only are many obviously good things good; all obviously bad things must also ultimately in some way turn to some kind of good. This takes us away from astrology to more general problems. It is sufficient that astrology helped to rationalize men's sense of ultimate and mysterious cause and effect, of general inevitability, and yet of some possibility of personal choice, of mixed good and bad in the world. The stars are the mechanism of 'destiny'.

10
DESTINY, FATE AND FORTUNE

For Chaucer 'destiny' was the interlocked series of events in the world, the same as *wyrdes* (see note to III, 617), 'the way things are', full of ups and downs, but ultimately under the guidance of God. *Destiny* and *wyrdes* are thoroughly 'Christian', or at least 'medieval Christian', words and ideas. Chaucer uses the word *fate* with a classical flavour, once as poetic mythology (V, 1550, not in present selection), but otherwise only twice, in Book V, 209, and at 1552 (not in present selection), as a synonym for Troilus's personal destiny. The notion of Fate as a hostile or indifferent or impersonal universe is not present.

Within the general scheme of destiny arose the problem particularly of free will. The most influential general discussion of this for Chaucer was the famous *De Consolatione Philosophiae*, written by Boethius while awaiting death in prison in the fifth century, and very well known throughout the Middle Ages and later. Chaucer translated it, and references in the present selections are made to his translation as the *Consolation*. Boethius sees the ordinary physical world of experience as furthest away from God. His message, at its most general, is that the mind is the measure of all things. The body is conditioned; but the mind *can* be free, and it is through his mind that man can know and love God.

Troilus in the long soliloquy on free will at IV, 953–1082 (not in the present selection) reproduces Boethius's first argument that because God has foreseen everything that will happen, everything is determined in advance and man is in no way free. Troilus does not reproduce Boethius's counter-argument and conclusion that God's foreknowledge need not destroy our free will, though the poet himself of course knew it. Troilus paradoxically chooses to have no choice, because he follows his passions, not his mind. If we live in the world we are bound by its laws, which are of change, of joy after woe, and woe after joy – the inevitable ups and downs of life.

The ups and downs are poetically represented as the turns

of Fortune's wheel. Fortune was a late classical goddess; Boethius popularized the image of her wheel and made her a personification of 'the way the world is'. It is thus that she can be thought of as controlling events (III, 617) which are the effects of the stars (III, 618). (See the notes to these lines.) But her control, like 'Nature's' (another poetic personification), extends only over the world. When we die we escape from transience into permanence.

II

THE MYTHOLOGY

Fortune is a poetic personification for 'the way the world is', and thus for the underlying astrological truth. Fortune is therefore part of the mythology of the poem. There are also many other references to the mythological stories of classical gods and other personages, well known to medieval men from Ovid, Virgil and other poets, and from handbooks. These references serve several purposes. First, they offer a familiar adornment and variety to the texture of the poem. Second, they supply local colour for a pagan and classical story, since the characters can invoke them. Third, they, like Fortune, are a convenient poetical fiction with which in many cases to represent a scientific astrological truth. The references to Venus in particular do this, since 'she' is an important planet who helps to control love-affairs, as well as a particularly interesting goddess. Fourth, the use of classical mythology allows Chaucer to invoke not only scientific but also religious notions. Venus the planet may be a vehicle for the love of God. *Jove* (*Joves*, or *Jupiter*) may refer to the planet, or the classical god of well-known amatory disposition, but for centuries before Chaucer, as for centuries after, Christian poets also referred to God himself as Jove or Jupiter. It was a well-known convention; and the inconsistencies of references, by the same name, to God, to the planet, and to the heathen deity, need trouble no experienced reader of literature.

Chaucer is thus able, in one mythological name, to hint at the triple cord of religion, science, and poetic mythology. Such a use may stand as an emblem of the poetic richness and inclusiveness of the poem, and the poet's mind.

12

CHAUCER'S LIFE

The remarkable mind partially revealed by the poem speaks well for the culture of the late fourteenth-century English court, and for English medieval culture in general. No later poet, not even Shakespeare, displays in totality such variety of poetic form and material, with such sensitive awareness of the latest intellectual developments, and with such an interesting combination of religious piety and scepticism. Genius as Chaucer was, he must also have been helped by education, experience, family, friends, and general culture. But though many records of his official life survive they tell us little of his personal life.

Chaucer was born some time between 1340 and 1345, the son of a rich wine-merchant, prominent in the City of London, and with connections with the royal court. We know nothing personal about his family, nor, most regrettably, about his education, which must have been crucial, and which must have been good. In 1357 he appears as page in the household of a great lady, the Countess Elizabeth of Ulster. In 1359 he went to the war in France, was captured and ransomed. We next see him as a 'valectus' or yeoman of the King's Household in 1367, and with a wife. He may have had some part-time education at one of the Inns of Court – the only source of a liberal education in those days, though meant chiefly to give a legal training. The old King Edward III died in 1377, and his little grandson Richard II became king. Under both kings the court was one of the most brilliant and efficient courts in Europe, and Chaucer's positions in the Household, though never great, put him in the centre of courtly life. He had a busy career as courtier, diplomatic envoy, Customs official (a sort of high civil servant), Clerk of the King's Works, and doubtless (though no document says so) public entertainer. He tells us in *The House of Fame* that he spends half the night reading after his day's work at the office, and never meets anyone. But obviously his experience of men and affairs, as of books, was wide and deep. In December 1399 he took a house in the garden of Westminster Abbey, in which church he was buried, as a mark of distinction, when he died in the following October, 1400.

13

THE DATE OF 'TROILUS' AND THE MANUSCRIPTS

Chaucer is usually thought to have finished the poem about 1385, a date arrived at by consideration of a number of inter-related factors. The reference to 'our first letter' being now an A (I, 171) is almost certainly to Queen Anne, married in January 1382. The planetary situation described in III, 624 ff., actually occurred for the first time in over 600 years in 1385. In *The Prologue to the Legend of Good Women*, F 332-5, probably written about 1386, there is a reference to *Troilus and Criseyde*, which therefore must have been finished by then. How long Chaucer took to write the poem is not known; presumably it occupied his leisure from about 1382 to 1385.

The poem must have been copied many times, sometimes by Adam the scribe, to whom Chaucer wrote an irritable little poem blaming him for mistakes in copying. Today some seventeen manuscripts and early printed texts survive, besides a number of fragments.

14

THE AUDIENCE

The brilliantly colourful frontispiece (many times reproduced, e.g. in Brewer, *Chaucer in His Time*) of the best manuscript of *Troilus and Criseyde*, in Corpus Christi College, Cambridge, shows Chaucer reading the poem to the assembled court of often youthful lords and ladies, including King Richard himself, who was eighteen (little younger than Troilus) in 1385, and his even younger wife, Queen Anne. No doubt here is the primary audience, and Chaucer addresses it at V, 1783, in Prologue, Epilogue and elsewhere. The picture also reminds us of the vivid if enigmatic presence of the poet telling his poem, and of the oral nature of the poetry. Oral poetry is looser knit, warmer, more direct in its relationship to the hearer, than printed poetry or the printed novel.

At the same time the very survival of the poem in manuscripts shows that it was not purely oral, and was meant to be read. There are addresses to the reader (cf. I, 7, n.) as well as to the hearer. Written poetry is more precise, rich, and dense in meaning than purely oral poetry. Chaucer is half-way between 'oral culture' and 'print culture'; we may call it manuscript culture. The readers Chaucer had in mind were to some extent learned middle-aged friends, like Gower and Strode (cf. V, 1856, 1857, and notes), to whom the philosophical tone might be expected to appeal.

15

LANGUAGE

The unfamiliarity in spelling and the apparent quaintness of Chaucer's language soon wear off. Chaucer's order of words is not usually difficult for a modern English speaker – less difficult, often, than Shakespeare's or Milton's. There are a number of words now unfamiliar or with meanings different from their modern ones; but careful attention to the context, and to the guidance of teachers, commentary, and glossary, will soon reduce the difficulties.

Chaucer's English is called Middle English. It is part of the historical development of English from Old English (sometimes called Anglo-Saxon), which lasts till roughly 1150, through Middle English (roughly 1150–1500), to modern. Many modern words are descended from Old English, but during the Middle English period many French and Latin words were also adopted. Chaucer had a vocabulary of about 8,000 words, of which about 4,000 were from French or Latin. Of these latter, about 1,000 are first recorded in literary English in Chaucer's own work. In his own time his language was very fresh and modern, but also often stately and polite and learned. At the same time, in appropriate places it was more lively, informal, and realistic than any English written before him.

Chaucer was very conscious of the changes in English, and wrote in *Troilus and Criseyde*:

> Ye knowe ek that in forme of speche is chaunge
> Withinne a thousand yeer, and wordes tho
> That hadden pris, now wonder nyce and straunge
> Us thinketh hem, and yet thei spake hem so.

II, 22–5

This is a request not to think that words are quaint or silly, merely because they are unfamiliar, but to use your literary and historical imagination. In this quotation the spelling is a little strange, but most of the words are recognizable. Some are both more and less familiar than they at first seem. Thus *pris* is 'price' and *nyce* is 'nice', but their meanings are different from the modern meanings, though historically connected. *Pris* means 'value', hence 'high value'; *nyce* means, as it usually does in Shakespeare, 'foolish'. The phrase *us thinketh hem* means literally 'it seems to us about them', because *thinketh* is an impersonal verb (with the subject *it* omitted) meaning 'seems', and the whole phrase should be translated 'they seem to us'. The whole quotation is an example of the kind of linguistic difficulty the poem offers.

Vocabulary

The commentary points out words that may mislead by a familiar appearance with an unusual meaning, though such words are included in the Glossary. Unfamiliar words and meanings are also noted in the Glossary. A careful reader will also learn the special qualities of words by paying attention to their contexts in the poem, which reveal subtleties that no glossary can render. Thus a key-notion in the poem is *trouthe*, modern 'truth'. It refers to an ideal of integrity, honesty, goodness, faithfulness. In the short poem called *Trouthe* Chaucer even uses *trouthe* as a synonym for God. One can only translate it by the modern word *truth*, but the modern word has few of these associations, while the modern word has also associations with 'what is accurate, correct', which hardly appear in Chaucer's word; he used *sooth* for such senses. (We might also note that Pandarus, an arrant deceiver, often swears by his 'truth', while Troilus, who is 'true as steel', hardly ever does.) Words like *vertu* (e.g. III), *wyrdes* (III, 617), *Fortune*, *serve*, *sterve*, *gentillesse*, and many more have varying differences from modern meanings. While a glossary and commentary can help, only a sensitive reaction to the words as poetry can really lead to appreciation of the full meaning, and of the artistry of the style.

Sounds

The reader's guide to the sounds is the spelling, which is un-fortunately variable. Experience helps greatly, but the best way of starting to pronounce Chaucer is to listen to a modern recording of some of his poetry in the original sounds, then to plunge in boldly oneself. A rough approximation (basing the vowels on modern French, Italian or German, for example) is better than a feeble refusal to make an attempt. The frequent final -*e* of many spellings (often the remains of a fuller final inflection in Old English and so called 'etymological final -*e*') should be pronounced or not according to the requirements of the metre. Scholarship has re-created the sounds of Chaucer's English, of which the following account is a summary and an approximation.

(i) *Vowels in stressed syllables.* There were fewer diphthongs in Chaucer than in modern English, so that the language was more mellifluous, varied, and 'fresher' than modern English. Vowels were clearly pronounced, and did not, as so often in modern English, become blurred. The obscure vowel (pro-nounced like the final sound in *banana*) was used only for final -*e*.

Short vowels:

a	between modern *bun* and *ban* e.g. (M.E.)	als, am
e	as in *bed*	bed, serv(en)
i (or *y*)	*sit*	list, nyst(e)
o	*box*	of, for

(But note that in the words *companye, love, come(n), konne, sonne, moche* (much), *yong* the letter *o* was written instead of *u* to prevent the confusion possible in the Gothic script with the letters *m, n,* or *u* (*v* in modernized spelling), and therefore the vowel in such words should actually be pronounced as *u*. The vowel in *worth* and *world* should also be sounded as in modern English.)

u	as in modern *full*	e.g. (M.E.) ful, but.

Long vowels:

a, aa	as in modern	*father*	e.g. (M.E.) caas, fac(e)
e, ee, ie		*fate*	wep(en), sweet(e), ek, chier(e)

(this is close $\bar{e}$ discussed below)

e, ee	as in modern	*where*	e.g. (M.E.) ther, feer(e), deed (meaning *dead*), pees (peace)

(this is open $\bar{e}$ discussed below)

i, y	as in modern	*machine*	e.g. (M.E.) write, nyce
o, oo		*so*	do, good, blood

(this is close $\bar{o}$ discussed below)

o, oo	as in modern	*saw*	e.g. (M.E.) fro, wo, goon

(this is open $\bar{o}$ discussed below)

u	as in modern	*pew*	e.g. (M.E.) vertu, nature, fortune

Open and close $\bar{e}$ and $\bar{o}$:

Chaucer differentiated in rhyme between open and close forms of $\bar{e}$ and $\bar{o}$. A rough guide is that the close $\bar{e}$ (roughly as in modern *fate*) is normally spelt in the equivalent modern word with *e* or *ee*, e.g. *be, sweet*, etc. Words which in Chaucer's language had open $\bar{e}$ (pronounced roughly as in modern English *there*) are normally spelt in modern English with *ea*, as in *peace, dream, clean, great, dead*, etc. The few exceptions are not important.

Close $\bar{o}$ (roughly as in modern *so*) is normally found in words whose vowels in modern English equivalents are pronounced like *blood*, or *food*, or *other*, whether spelt with *o* or *oo*. Open $\bar{o}$ (as in modern *saw*) should be used for those words in Chaucer where the modern equivalent vowel is sounded like *throat, most*.

Diphthongs:

ai, ay, ei, ey   between modern
           day and *aisle*   e.g. (M.E.) availle, payne,
                                         seye

(But note that M.E. *eye*, sometimes spelt *ye*, is always pronounced 'eeyer', and M.E. *deye* is sometimes pronounced to rhyme with this.)

au, aw   as in modern *bounce*   e.g. (M.E.) cause, lawe

(But dauncen, chaumbre, straunge, etc., may have been pronounced with a long *ā*.)

eu, ew   as in modern   *new*   e.g. (M.E.) newe, trewe,
                                          seur

(But notice that M.E. *fewe, lewed, shewe*, were pronounced with short *ē* (as in bed) followed by *u*.)

ou, ow,   as in modern *boot* if   e.g. these same words in
     the vowel in the equivalent   M.E., and M.E. proud,
     modern word is sounded like   trouthe, how
     house, or *through*

ou, ow, ough   as in modern   e.g. (M.E.) boughten,
     grow if the vowel in the equi-   soule, knowe
     valent   modern   word   is
     sounded like *grow* or like
     thought.

(ii) *Vowels in unstressed syllables.* Probably unstressed vowels already showed a tendency towards the neutral or 'obscure' vowel sound already mentioned, though occasionally noun or verbal inflections were stressed in rhyme or because of the metrical accent, and so were sounded more fully. Apart from such exceptions, they can be pronounced as in modern English. Etymological final *-e* already noted has the neutral vowel sound.

(iii) *Consonants.* Most consonants were pronounced as in modern English, but *r* was trilled as in modern Scots, and some consonants or consonant-groups that have fallen silent in English were still pronounced. Thus the initial *k, g, w*, of

knyght, *gnawe*, *write* and other words with these initial consonants were pronounced, as well as the consonant following;
gh was pronounced as in German *ich* in *knyght*, *ybought*, etc.;
l was pronounced before *f*, *v*, *k*, *m*, as in *half*, *walk*, etc.

Note further that *ch* is always pronounced as in *church*; *ng*
when stressed (as in *thinges*, *singen*) is pronounced as in *finger*,
though the ending *-ing* or *-yng* is pronounced as in modern
English; *-gn-* in French words (e.g. digne) is pronounced *-n-*.

Dialectal variation

Chaucer notes ruefully the 'great diversity / In English and in
writing of our tongue' (V, 1793–4). Different parts of the
country spoke, and wrote, in different dialects. Chaucer wrote
in the dialect of London and the Court, which was predomin-
antly that of the East Midlands, and destined to become the
standard English of modern England. In Chaucer's English a
few dialectal variations appear, often deliberately employed, it
would seem, to help with a rhyme. Most notably, beside the
East Midland form *list* (both noun and verb) appear Kentish
lest and Western *lust*; beside East Midland *fir* (fire), Kentish
afere (afire); Chaucer's own form *myrie* (merry) is found within
the line, but *merye*, the Kentish form, which of course has
survived in Modern English, is twice used for the rhyme in the
present selection.

Grammar

(No attempt is made at a full sketch of the grammar. The following notes point out some principal elements.)

(i) *Inflections of nouns.* Most nouns in the genitive singular and
in the plural end in *-es*. A few nouns may have an uninflected
genitive singular: *herte*, *hevene*, *lady*. Some nouns and names
ending in *-s* in the nominative singular remain unchanged in
the genitive singular and in the plural, as occasionally do *yeer*,
thing. Some nouns make their plural in *-en* or *-n*, e.g. *yen* (eyes),
foon (foes). There are remnants of inflection of nouns in the
dative case; e.g. *lif* (life), but *on lyve*, where the final *-e* represents an older fuller inflection and *f* between two vowels has
become *v*; and *bed*, but *to bedde*.

(ii) *Pronouns*. As in modern English, except that *it* is *hit*, *hyt*, with genitive singular *his*, and the oblique cases of *they* are genitive *hir(e)*, accusative, and dative *hem*. (The forms *its*, *their*, *them* do not appear in Chaucer.) There is an important difference in usage between the singular forms of the second personal pronoun and the plural, comparable to what is still common practice in Continental languages, but lost to modern standard English. The singular is familiar and intimate, hence used between friends, to inferiors, in prayer, or (possibly) in contempt. For all his passionate devotion, Troilus never uses the second person singular to Criseyde. The plural is polite and respectful. The second singular is sometimes combined with the verb, e.g. *saistow* (sayest thou) V, 1161.

The indefinite pronoun *men* or *me* (one) occasionally occurs, e.g. II, 189.

(iii) *Adjectives*. If they are monosyllables ending in a consonant, adjectives are inflected by the addition of final -*e* in the plural, and also on those occasions in the singular when they precede the noun they qualify, and follow *the*, *this*, *that*, *my*, *your* (and other possessives), *o* (signifying address), and a noun in the genitive case.

There are a few exceptions. When in doubt pronounce the final -*e* or not according to the requirements of the metre.

(iv) *Verbs*. Where the structure of the verb offers difficulty consult the glossary. The endings of the present *indicative* are: singular, 1st person -*e*, 2nd, -(*e*)*st*, 3rd, -(*e*)*th*; plural, all persons -*e*(*n*).

It is very important to recognize the *subjunctive* whose endings in all persons are in the present tense singular, -(*e*); plural -*e*(*n*); indicating a wish, a hope, etc., without certainty. See, e.g., *Bynd*, III, 1750 n.

'Weak' verbs are those which form their past tense and past participle by the addition of -(*e*)*d*, or -*t*, and offer no difficulty. The past participle may or may not have the prefix *y*-, remnant of Old English *ge*-. 'Strong' verbs form their past tense by changing the stem vowel, and a few verbs now weak in modern English were still strong in Chaucer, e.g. helpen, past participle *holpen*. The past participle of a strong verb is either uninflected, or ends in -*en* or -*e*, and has occasionally the prefix *y*-, e.g. *ybought*, beside *bought*.

Impersonal verbs are fairly common, with the subject, *hit*, often omitted; e.g. *liketh*, it pleases; *list* (*lest*, *lust*), it pleases; *thinketh*, it seems.

(v) *Conjunctions, prepositions, adverbs.* These are familiar in form. The reader should regard the context carefully before assuming that a modern meaning is necessarily the same as Chaucer's; often it is not. The Commentary and Glossary will give a guide.

Syntax

In general Chaucer's syntax is that of modern English, except that it is rather freer, less formal and more tolerant – like speech – of broken or apparently illogical constructions. A few characteristic differences from modern English are noted here. There may be change of tense or construction within the sentence; occasional lack of agreement between subject and verb; omission of subject pronoun, of *to* as sign of the infinitive, and of *of* in various constructions. Constructions with *that* as a relative, or in which *that* is redundant, are frequent. Among verbs impersonal constructions have already been noted. More verbs are used reflexively than in modern English. Occasionally an infinitive is used where we should use a present participle, and a past participle where we should use an infinitive. Adverbs vary more widely in position than in modern English, and there is frequent use of *as, so,* as intensives, and of *as, so,* and *ther* (especially frequent) to introduce a wish or a curse. Such usages are untranslatable, but sometimes suitable modern equivalents can be found.

16

VERSIFICATION

The line

For enjoyment of the poetry the metre is even more important than historically accurate sounds. Chaucer earnestly hoped that none will 'mis-metre' the poem 'for default of tongue' (V, 1796). As in all English verse except Old English and modern free verse, there are two underlying principles. The first is that the line has a basically repetitive rhythmic pattern; in this case five heavy stresses alternating with five light stresses, sometimes called the iambic pentameter, thus:

$$\overset{\times}{\text{Help}} \overset{/}{\text{me}} // \text{that } \overset{\times}{\text{am}} \overset{/}{\text{the}} \overset{\times}{\text{sor}}\overset{/}{\text{wful}} \text{ in}\overset{\times}{\text{stru}}\overset{/}{\text{ment}} \qquad \text{(I, 10)}$$

The pause may occur anywhere in the line, and some lines have either no pause or two slight ones. (The variation of the pause is one of the secrets of the perpetual freshness and vigour of Chaucer's verse.)

The second principle is that the *actual movement* of any given line depends on the *normal speech-rhythm* (as determined by the sense) and normal stress *in conjunction with the basic pattern*. The pleasure of reading this kind of verse derives largely from the tension and reconcilement between the regularity of the basic rhythm and the irregularity of normal speech-rhythms. Too complete regularity would be monotonous; complete irregularity would lose the musical pleasure of a regular beat, and the satisfying effects of a combination of regular rhythm with good sense. Therefore one needs to have the beat in one's head, and yet be prepared to recognize a thousand obvious or subtle variations from it: a lightening or weighting of individual stresses; inversions; elisions; omissions of syllables; extra syllables – all may be found. Very occasionally Chaucer seems not quite to have reconciled the twofold demands of speech-rhythm and metre, but normally he does so triumphantly. Outstanding in this respect are the speeches of Pandarus in Book II.

The most important linguistic fact from the point of view of the metre is the remains in many words of the older full inflection, represented in writing by the etymological final -*e*, noted above, p. xliv. Thus the final -*e* of *sothe* in the following line must be pronounced.

$$\text{For } \overset{\times}{\text{wel}} \overset{/}{\text{sit}} \overset{\times}{\text{it}} // \overset{\times}{\text{the}} \overset{/}{\text{so}}\overset{\times}{\text{the}} \overset{/}{\text{for}} \overset{\times}{\text{to}} \overset{/}{\text{sey}}\overset{\times}{\text{ne}} \qquad \text{(I, 12)}$$

It will be noticed that in this line the final -*e* of *seyne* is also to be lightly pronounced, though less harm is done if it is omitted than when a metrically necessary final -*e* within the line is omitted, which sounds horrible.

In some words the final -*e* is merely 'scribal', i.e. a spelling convention, as so often in modern English, and does not represent an independent sound; e.g. *evere* (I, 9) which would normally be two syllables like modern English *ever*, though in this particular case, by a familiar English verse convention, it is pronounced as one syllable, *ev'r* or *e'er*.

The situation is a little complicated because Chaucer himself occasionally varies his practice for metrical convenience. He sometimes suppresses the etymological final *-e* in very common words, e.g. *hire* (*their*):

$$\overset{\times}{\text{And}}\ \overset{/}{\text{sende}}\ \overset{\times}{\text{hem}}\ \overset{/}{\text{myght}}\ //\ \overset{\times}{\text{hire}}\ \overset{/}{\text{ladies}}\ \overset{\times}{\text{so}}\ \overset{/}{\text{to}}\ \overset{\times}{\text{plese}} \qquad \text{(I, 45)}$$

Note that the final *-e* of *sende* is not pronounced, because the following word is one syllable beginning with *h* (itself probably not pronounced).

In the last resort one may say that final *-e* is pronounced or suppressed according to the requirements of the metre. The same is true for some other endings, e.g. the ending of the third person singular, *-eth*, sometimes a full syllable, sometimes not. It should also be remembered that normally the genitive singular and the plural inflection *-es* is sounded as a syllable. The ending *-ioun*, corresponding to modern *-ion*, is two syllables; the word *creature* (I, 104, n.) is four syllables. Some words have variable stress, and others have their stress on a different syllable from their modern descendant, e.g. $\overset{\times}{\text{ma}}\overset{/}{\text{tere}}$, 'matter'. In all these cases the reader's own experience and ear will be his guide.

The stanza

The seven-line stanza is the so-called rhyme-royal, first used in English by Chaucer in *The Parlement of Foules*. It is a splendid instrument for narrative poetry, flexible, with a good forward movement, but musical and capable of containing a full unit of meaning within its own bounds. Chaucer only occasionally runs on the sense from one stanza to the next.

BIBLIOGRAPHICAL NOTE

Important critical commentary on *Troilus and Criseyde* will be found in D. Everett, *Essays on Middle English Literature*,

Clarendon Press, Oxford, 1955; C. Muscatine, *Chaucer and the French Tradition*, University of California Press, Berkeley, 1957, etc.; R. O. Payne, *The Key of Remembrance*, New Haven, Conn., and London, Yale University Press, 1963; G. T. Shepherd in *Chaucer and Chaucerians*, ed. D. S. Brewer, Nelson, London, 1966; Mrs E. Salter in *Patterns of Love and Courtesy*, ed. J. Lawlor, Edward Arnold, London, 1967. Other valuable essays will be found in *Chaucer Criticism*, Vol. II (*Troilus and Criseyde and the Minor Poems*), eds. R. J. Schoeck and J. Taylor, University of Notre Dame Press, Notre Dame, Indiana; and *Chaucer: Modern Essays in Criticism*, ed. E. Wagenknecht, Oxford University Press, New York, 1959. (A number of these books are published in paperback.) The edition by E. T. Donaldson, *Chaucer's Poetry: An Anthology for the Modern Reader*, The Ronald Press, New York, 1958, has a very stimulating and valuable Commentary. Cf. also the essay on *Troilus and Criseyde* by D. S. Brewer in *A History of Literature in the English Language*, Vol. I, The Middle Ages, ed. W. F. Bolton, Sphere Books, London, 1970.

A general survey of Chaucer's life, times, and work may be found in D. S. Brewer, *Chaucer*, 2nd rev. edn, Longmans, London, 1961; and an account of his general culture in D. S. Brewer, *Chaucer in his Time*, Nelson, London, 1964. There are numerous other good accounts. Gervase Mathew, *The Court of Richard II*, John Murray, London, 1968, discusses background, while a splendidly sympathetic and illuminating discussion of medieval and Renaissance men's thoughts and feelings is by C. S. Lewis, *The Discarded Image*, Cambridge University Press, Cambridge, 1964. Surveys of the latest developments in criticism and scholarship will be found in *A Companion to Chaucer Studies*, ed. B. Rowland, Oxford University Press, New York, 1968, and in *Chaucer's Mind and Art*, ed. A. C. Cawley, Oliver and Boyd, Edinburgh, 1969.

The complete text of *Troilus and Criseyde*, with brief notes, is in *Chaucer's Major Poetry*, ed. A. C. Baugh, Routledge & Kegan Paul, London, 1963, and in the edition by E. T. Donaldson noted above. For a complete edition of all Chaucer's works, with notes, etc., see *The Works of Geoffrey Chaucer*, 2nd edn, ed. F. N. Robinson, Oxford University Press, London, 1957. A text of Chaucer's poem, together with a translation of Boccaccio's *Il Filostrato* and some translated extracts from Benoît, will be found in *The Story of Troilus*, ed. R. K. Gordon, Dutton Paperbacks, New York, Toronto and London, 1964.

Students wishing to explore further in medieval romance and literature will enjoy Dante's *Divine Comedy*, of which the most useful and agreeable translation is by Dorothy Sayers and Barbara Reynolds in Penguin Books. Canto XVIII of *Purgatory* discusses love and free will, and the *Purgatory* in general does much to clarify and enhance *Troilus and Criseyde*. The French poet Chrestien of Troyes, whose works are translated in Everyman's Library, is very different from Dante; he gives a vivid picture of love and chivalry in the late twelfth century. Of Chaucer's own English contemporaries the remarkable poems *Sir Gawain and the Green Knight* and Langland's *Piers Plowman* and some of Gower's poetry are translated in Penguin Books. The most convenient and up-to-date surveys of medieval English literature in general are D. M. Zesmer and S. B. Greenfield, *Guide to English Literature from Beowulf through Chaucer and Medieval Drama*, Barnes & Noble, New York, 1961; and Margaret Schlauch, *English Medieval Literature and its Social Foundations*, Oxford University Press, London, 1967; W. P. Ker's much older and shorter *English Literature: Medieval*, Home University Library, Oxford University Press, London, 1912, etc., is very readable and still valuable.

A recording of an abridged text of *Troilus and Criseyde* in the original pronunciation has been made for the Argo Record Company, 115 Fulham Road, London, S.W.3, in association with the British Council, in their series *The English Poets, Chaucer to Yeats*. It will be issued, together with a broadsheet of the text used, with glosses, in early 1970.

TROILUS AND CRISEYDE

Book I

PROLOGUE

The double sorwe of Troilus to tellen,
That was the kyng Priamus sone of Troye,
In lovynge, how his aventures fellen
Fro wo to wele, and after out of joie,
My purpos is, er that I parte fro ye.　　　　　5
Thesiphone, thow help me for t'endite
Thise woful vers, that wepen as I write.

To the clepe I, thow goddesse of torment,
Thow cruwel Furie, sorwynge evere yn peyne,
Help me, that am the sorwful instrument,　　　　10
That helpeth loveres, as I kan, to pleyne.
For wel sit it, the sothe for to seyne,
A woful wight to han a drery feere,
And to a sorwful tale, a sory chere.

For I, that God of Loves servantz serve,　　　　15
Ne dar to Love, for myn unliklynesse,
Preyen for speed, al sholde I therfore sterve,
So fer am I from his help in derknesse.
But natheles, if this may don gladnesse
To any lovere, and his cause availle,　　　　20
Have he my thonk, and myn be this travaille!

But ye loveres, that bathen in gladnesse,
If any drope of pyte in yow be,
Remembreth yow on passed hevynesse
That ye han felt, and on the adversite　　　　25

Of othere folk, and thynketh how that ye
Han felt that Love dorste yow displese,
Or ye han wonne hym with to grete an ese.

And preieth for hem that ben in the cas
Of Troilus, as ye may after here,   30
That Love hem brynge in hevene to solas.
And ek for me preieth to God so dere
That I have myght to shewe, in som manere,
Swich peyne and wo as Loves folk endure,
In Troilus unsely aventure.   35

And biddeth ek for hem that ben despeired
In love, that nevere nyl recovered be,
And ek for hem that falsly ben apeired
Thorugh wikked tonges, be it he or she;
Thus biddeth God, for his benignite,   40
So graunte hem soone owt of this world to pace,
That ben despeired out of Loves grace.

And biddeth ek for hem that ben at ese,
That God hem graunte ay good perseveraunce,
And sende hem myght hire ladies so to plese   45
That it to Love be worship and plesaunce.
For so hope I my sowle best avaunce,
To prey for hem that Loves servauntz be,
And write hire wo, and lyve in charite,

And for to have of hem compassioun,   50
As though I were hire owne brother dere.
Now herkneth with a good entencioun,
For now wil I gon streght to my matere,
In which ye may the double sorwes here
Of Troilus, in lovynge of Criseyde,   55
And how that she forsook hym er she deyde.

THE STORY

Yt is wel wist how that the Grekes, stronge
In armes, with a thousand shippes, wente

To Troiewardes, and the cite longe
Assegeden, neigh ten yer er they stente, 60
And in diverse wise and oon entente,
The ravysshyng to wreken of Eleyne,
By Paris don, they wroughten al hir peyne.

Now fel it so that in the town ther was
Dwellynge a lord of gret auctorite, 65
A gret devyn, that clepid was Calkas,
That in science so expert was that he
Knew wel that Troie sholde destroied be,
By answere of his god, that highte thus,
Daun Phebus or Appollo Delphicus. 70

So whan this Calkas knew by calkulynge,
And ek by answer of this Appollo,
That Grekes sholden swich a peple brynge,
Thorugh which that Troie moste ben fordo,
He caste anon out of the town to go; 75
For wel wiste he by sort that Troye sholde
Destroyed ben, ye, wolde whoso nolde.

For which for to departen softely
Took purpos ful this forknowynge wise,
And to the Grekes oost ful pryvely 80
He stal anon; and they, in curteys wise,
Hym diden bothe worship and servyse,
In trust that he hath konnynge hem to rede
In every peril which that is to drede.

The noise up ros, whan it was first aspied 85
Thorugh al the town, and generaly was spoken,
That Calkas traitour fled was and allied
With hem of Grece, and casten to be wroken
On hym that falsly hadde his feith so broken,
And seyden he and al his kyn at-ones 90
Ben worthi for to brennen, fel and bones.

Now hadde Calkas left in this meschaunce,
Al unwist of this false and wikked dede,
His doughter, which that was in gret penaunce,

For of hire lif she was ful sore in drede,   95
As she that nyste what was best to rede;
For bothe a widewe was she and allone
Of any frend to whom she dorste hir mone.

Criseyde was this lady name al right.
As to my doom, in al Troies cite   100
Nas non so fair, for passynge every wight
So aungelik was hir natif beaute,
That lik a thing inmortal semed she,
As doth an hevenyssh perfit creature,
That down were sent in scornynge of nature.   105

This lady, which that alday herd at ere
Hire fadres shame, his falsnesse and tresoun,
Wel neigh out of hir wit for sorwe and fere,
In widewes habit large of samyt broun,
On knees she fil biforn Ector adown;   110
With pitous vois, and tendrely wepynge,
His mercy bad, hirselven excusynge.

Now was this Ector pitous of nature,
And saugh that she was sorwfully bigon,
And that she was so fair a creature;   115
Of his goodnesse he gladede hire anon,
And seyde, 'Lat youre fadres treson gon
Forth with meschaunce, and ye youreself in joie
Dwelleth with us, whil yow good list, in Troie.

'And al th'onour that men may don yow have,   120
As ferforth as youre fader dwelled here,
Ye shul have, and youre body shal men save,
As fer as I may ought enquere or here.'
And she hym thonked with ful humble chere,
And ofter wolde, and it hadde ben his wille,   125
And took hire leve, and hom, and held hir stille.

And in hire hous she abood with swich meyne
As til hire honour nede was to holde;
And whil she was dwellynge in that cite,
Kepte hir estat, and both of yonge and olde   130

Ful wel biloved, and wel men of hir tolde.
But wheither that she children hadde or noon,
I rede it naught, therfore I late it goon.

The thynges fellen, as they don of werre,
Bitwixen hem of Troie and Grekes ofte;   135
For som day boughten they of Troie it derre,
And eft the Grekes founden nothing softe
The folk of Troie; and thus Fortune on lofte,
And under eft, gan hem to whielen bothe
Aftir hir cours, ay whil that thei were wrothe.   140

But how this town com to destruccion
Ne falleth naught to purpos me to telle;
For it were here a long digression
Fro my matere, and yow to long to dwelle.
But the Troian gestes, as they felle,   145
In Omer, or in Dares, or in Dite,
Whoso that kan may rede hem as they write.

But though that Grekes hem of Troie shetten,
And hir cite bisegede al aboute,
Hire olde usage nolde they nat letten,   150
As for to honoure hir goddes ful devoute;
But aldirmost in honour, out of doute,
Thei hadde a relik, heet Palladion,
That was hire trist aboven everichon.

And so bifel, whan comen was the tyme   155
Of Aperil, whan clothed is the mede
With newe grene, of lusty Veer the pryme,
And swote smellen floures white and rede,
In sondry wises shewed, as I rede,
The folk of Troie hire observaunces olde,   160
Palladiones feste for to holde.

And to the temple, in al hir beste wise,
In general ther wente many a wight,
To herknen of Palladion the servyse;
And namely, so many a lusty knyght,   165
So many a lady fressh and mayden bright,

Ful wel arayed, bothe meste and leste,
Ye, bothe for the seson and the feste.

Among thise othere folk was Criseyda,
In widewes habit blak; but natheles,   170
Right as oure firste lettre is now an A,
In beaute first so stood she, makeles.
Hire goodly lokyng gladed al the prees.
Nas nevere yet seyn thyng to ben preysed derre,
Nor under cloude blak so bright a sterre   175

As was Criseyde, as folk seyde everichone
That hir behelden in hir blake wede.
And yet she stood ful lowe and stille allone,
Byhynden other folk, in litel brede,
And neigh the dore, ay under shames drede,   180
Simple of atire and debonaire of chere,
With ful assured lokyng and manere.

This Troilus, as he was wont to gide
His yonge knyghtes, lad hem up and down
In thilke large temple on every side,   185
Byholding ay the ladyes of the town,
Now here, now there; for no devocioun
Hadde he to non, to reven hym his reste,
But gan to preise and lakken whom hym leste.

And in his walk ful faste he gan to wayten   190
If knyght or squyer of his compaignie
Gan for to syke, or lete his eighen baiten
On any womman that he koude espye,
He wolde smyle and holden it folye,
And seye hym thus, 'God woot, she slepeth softe   195
For love of the, whan thow turnest ful ofte!

'I have herd told, pardieux, of youre lyvynge,
Ye loveres, and youre lewede observaunces,
And which a labour folk han in wynnynge
Of love, and in the kepyng which doutaunces;   200
And whan youre prey is lost, woo and penaunces.

O veray fooles, nyce and blynde be ye!
Ther nys nat oon kan war by other be.'

And with that word he gan caste up the browe,
Ascaunces, 'Loo! is this naught wisely spoken?'   205
At which the God of Love gan loken rowe
Right for despit, and shop for to ben wroken.
He kidde anon his bowe nas naught broken,
For sodeynly he hitte hym atte fulle;
And yet as proud a pekok kan he pulle.   210

O blynde world, O blynde entencioun!
How often falleth al the effect contraire
Of surquidrie and foul presumpcioun;
For kaught is proud, and kaught is debonaire.
This Troilus is clomben on the staire,   215
And litel weneth that he moot descenden;
But alday faileth thing that fooles wenden.

As proude Bayard gynneth for to skippe
Out of the weye, so pryketh hym his corn,
Til he a lasshe have of the longe whippe;   220
Than thynketh he, 'Though I praunce al byforn
First in the trays, ful fat and newe shorn,
Yet am I but an hors, and horses lawe
I moot endure, and with my feres drawe';

So ferde it by this fierse and proude knyght: 225
Though he a worthy kynges sone were,
And wende nothing hadde had swich myght
Ayeyns his wille that shuld his herte stere,
Yet with a look his herte wax a-fere,
That he that now was moost in pride above,   230
Wax sodeynly moost subgit unto love.

Forthy ensample taketh of this man,
Ye wise, proude, and worthi folkes alle,
To scornen Love, which that so soone kan
The fredom of youre hertes to hym thralle;   235
For evere it was, and evere it shal byfalle,

That Love is he that alle thing may bynde,
For may no man fordon the lawe of kynde.

That this be soth, hath preved and doth yit.
For this trowe I ye knowen alle or some,   240
Men reden nat that folk han gretter wit
Than they that han be most with love ynome;
And strengest folk ben therwith overcome,
The worthiest and grettest of degree:
This was, and is, and yet men shal it see.   245

And trewelich it sit wel to be so.
For alderwisest han therwith ben plesed;
And they that han ben aldermost in wo,
With love han ben comforted moost and esed;
And ofte it hath the cruel herte apesed,   250
And worthi folk maad worthier of name,
And causeth moost to dreden vice and shame.

Now sith it may nat goodly ben withstonde,
And is a thing so vertuous in kynde,
Refuseth nat to Love for to ben bonde,   255
Syn, as hymselven liste, he may yow bynde.
The yerde is bet that bowen wole and wynde
Than that that brest; and therfore I yow rede
To folowen hym that so wel kan yow lede.

But for to tellen forth in special   260
As of this kynges sone of which I tolde,
And leten other thing collateral,
Of hym thenke I my tale forth to holde,
Bothe of his joie and of his cares colde;
And al his werk, as touching this matere,   265
For I it gan, I wol therto refere.

Withinne the temple he wente hym forth pleyinge,
This Troilus, of every wight aboute,
On this lady, and now on that, lokynge,
Wher so she were of town or of withoute;   270
And upon cas bifel that thorugh a route

His eye percede, and so depe it wente,
Til on Criseyde it smot, and ther it stente.

And sodeynly he wax therwith astoned,
And gan hir bet biholde in thrifty wise. 275
'O mercy, God,' thoughte he, 'wher hastow woned,
That art so feyr and goodly to devise?'
Therwith his herte gan to sprede and rise,
And softe sighed, lest men myghte hym here,
And caught ayeyn his firste pleyinge chere. 280

She nas nat with the leste of hire stature,
But alle hire lymes so wel answerynge
Weren to wommanhode, that creature
Was nevere lasse mannyssh in semynge.
And ek the pure wise of hire mevynge 285
Shewed wel that men myght in hire gesse
Honour, estat, and wommanly noblesse.

To Troilus right wonder wel with alle
Gan for to like hire mevynge and hire chere,
Which somdel deignous was, for she let falle 290
Hire look a lite aside in swich manere,
Ascaunces, 'What! may I nat stonden here?'
And after that hir lokynge gan she lighte,
That nevere thoughte hym seen so good a syghte.

And of hire look in him ther gan to quyken 295
So gret desir and such affeccioun,
That in his hertes botme gan to stiken
Of hir his fixe and depe impressioun.
And though he erst hadde poured up and down,
He was tho glad his hornes in to shrinke; 300
Unnethes wiste he how to loke or wynke.

Lo, he that leet hymselven so konnynge,
And scorned hem that Loves peynes dryen,
Was ful unwar that Love hadde his dwellynge
Withinne the subtile stremes of hir yën; 305
That sodeynly hym thoughte he felte dyen,

Right with hire look, the spirit in his herte.
Blissed be Love, that kan thus folk converte!

She, this in blak, likynge to Troilus
Over al thing, he stood for to biholde;   310
Ne his desir, ne wherfore he stood thus,
He neither chere made, ne worde tolde;
But from afer, his manere for to holde,
On other thing his look som tyme he caste,
And eft on hire, while that the servyse laste.   315

And after this, nat fullich al awhaped,
Out of the temple al esilich he wente,
Repentynge hym that he hadde evere ijaped
Of Loves folk, lest fully the descente
Of scorn fille on hymself; but what he mente,   320
Lest it were wist on any manere syde,
His woo he gan dissimulen and hide.

Whan he was fro the temple thus departed,
He streght anon unto his paleys torneth,
Right with hire look thorugh-shoten and thorugh-
    darted,   325
Al feyneth he in lust that he sojorneth;
And al his chere and speche also he borneth,
And ay of Loves servantz every while,
Hymself to wrye, at hem he gan to smyle,

And seyde, 'Lord, so ye lyve al in lest,   330
Ye loveres! for the konnyngeste of yow,
That serveth most ententiflich and best,
Hym tit as often harm therof as prow.
Youre hire is quyt ayeyn, ye, God woot how!
Nought wel for wel, but scorn for good servyse.   335
In feith, youre ordre is ruled in good wise!

'In nouncerteyn ben alle youre observaunces,
But it a sely fewe pointes be;
Ne no thing asketh so gret attendaunces
As doth youre lay, and that knowe alle ye;   340
But that is nat the worste, as mote I the!

But, tolde I yow the worste point, I leve,
Al seyde I soth, ye wolden at me greve.

'But take this: that ye loveres ofte eschuwe,
Or elles doon, of good entencioun,   345
Ful ofte thi lady wol it mysconstruwe,
And deme it harm in hire oppynyoun;
And yet if she, for other enchesoun,
Be wroth, than shaltow have a groyn anon.
Lord, wel is hym that may ben of yow oon!'   350

But for al this, whan that he say his tyme,
He held his pees; non other boote hym gayned;
For love bigan his fetheres so to lyme,
That wel unnethe until his folk he fayned
That other besy nedes hym destrayned;   355
For wo was hym, that what to doon he nyste,
But bad his folk to gon wher that hem liste.

And whan that he in chambre was allone,
He doun upon his beddes feet hym sette,
And first he gan to sike, and eft to grone,   360
And thought ay on hire so, withouten lette,
That, as he sat and wook, his spirit mette
That he hire saugh a-temple, and al the wise
Right of hire look, and gan it newe avise.

Thus gan he make a mirour of his mynde,   365
In which he saugh al holly hire figure;
And that he wel koude in his herte fynde,
It was to hym a right good aventure
To love swich oon, and if he dede his cure
To serven hir, yet myghte he falle in grace,   370
Or ellis for oon of hire servantz pace;

Imaginynge that travaille nor grame
Ne myghte for so goodly oon be lorn
As she, ne hym for his desir no shame,
Al were it wist, but in pris and up-born   375
Of alle lovers wel more than biforn.

Thus argumented he in his gynnynge,
Ful unavysed of his woo comynge.

Thus took he purpos loves craft to suwe,
And thoughte he wolde werken pryvely,   380
First to hiden his desir in muwe
From every wight yborn, al-outrely,
But he myghte ought recovered be therby;
Remembryng hym that love to wide yblowe
Yelt bittre fruyt, though swete seed be sowe.   385

Troilus falls deeper and deeper in love, so that he is quite ill, but he does not tell anyone, and is too shy to approach Criseyde. His friend Pandarus wheedles his secret out of him, and promises to help.

Book II

PROLOGUE

Owt of thise blake wawes for to saylle,
O wynd, o wynd, the weder gynneth clere;
For in this see the boot hath swych travaylle,
Of my connyng, that unneth I it steere.
This see clepe I the tempestous matere   5
Of disespeir that Troilus was inne;
But now of hope the kalendes bygynne.

O lady myn, that called art Cleo,
Thow be my speed fro this forth, and my Muse,
To ryme wel this book til I have do;   10
Me nedeth here noon other art to use.
Forwhi to every lovere I me excuse,
That of no sentement I this endite,
But out of Latyn in my tonge it write.

Wherfore I nyl have neither thank ne blame   15
Of al this werk, but prey yow mekely,
Disblameth me, if any word be lame,

For as myn auctour seyde, so sey I.
Ek though I speeke of love unfelyngly,
No wondre is, for it nothyng of newe is;   20
A blynd man kan nat juggen wel in hewis.

Ye knowe ek that in forme of speche is chaunge
Withinne a thousand yeer, and wordes tho
That hadden pris, now wonder nyce and straunge
Us thinketh hem, and yet thei spake hem so,   25
And spedde as wel in love as men now do;
Ek for to wynnen love in sondry ages,
In sondry londes, sondry ben usages.

And forthi if it happe in any wyse,
That here be any lovere in this place   30
That herkneth, as the storie wol devise,
How Troilus com to his lady grace,
And thenketh, 'so nold I nat love purchace,'
Or wondreth on his speche or his doynge,
I noot; but it is me no wonderynge.   35

For every wight which that to Rome went
Halt nat o path, or alwey o manere;
Ek in som lond were al the game shent,
If that they ferde in love as men don here,
As thus, in opyn doyng or in chere,   40
In visityng, in forme, or seyde hire sawes;
Forthi men seyn, ecch contree hath his lawes.

Ek scarsly ben ther in this place thre
That have in love seid lik, and don, in al;
For to thi purpos this may liken the,   45
And the right nought, yet al is seid or schal;
Ek som men grave in tree, some in ston wal,
As it bitit; but syn I have bigonne,
Myn auctour shal I folwen, if I konne.

THE STORY

In May, that moder is of monthes glade,   50
That fresshe floures, blew and white and rede,
Ben quike agayn, that wynter dede made,
And ful of bawme is fletyng every mede;
Whan Phebus doth his bryghte bemes sprede,
Right in the white Bole, it so bitidde,   55
As I shal synge, on Mayes day the thrydde,

That Pandarus, for al his wise speche,
Felt ek his part of loves shotes keene,
That, koude he nevere so wel of lovyng preche,
It made his hewe a-day ful ofte greene.
So shop it that hym fil that day a teene   60
In love, for which in wo to bedde he wente,
And made, er it was day, ful many a wente.

The swalowe Proigne, with a sorowful lay,
Whan morwen com, gan make hire waymentynge,   65
Whi she forshapen was; and ever lay
Pandare abedde, half in a slomberynge,
Til she so neigh hym made hire cheterynge
How Tereus gan forth hire suster take,
That with the noyse of hire he gan awake,   70

And gan to calle, and dresse hym up to ryse,
Remembryng hym his erand was to doone
From Troilus, and ek his grete emprise;
And caste and knew in good plit was the moone
To doon viage, and took his weye ful soone   75
Unto his neces palays ther biside.
Now Janus, god of entree, thow hym gyde!

Whan he was come unto his neces place,
'Wher is my lady?' to hire folk quod he;
And they hym tolde, and he forth in gan pace,   80
And fond two othere ladys sete, and she,
Withinne a paved parlour, and they thre

Herden a mayden reden hem the geste
Of the siege of Thebes, while hem leste.

Quod Pandarus, 'Madame, God yow see,   85
With al youre book, and al the compaignie!'
'Ey, uncle myn, welcome iwys,' quod she;
And up she roos, and by the hond in hye
She took hym faste, and seyde, 'This nyght thrie,
To goode mot it turne, of yow I mette.'   90
And with that word she doun on bench hym sette.

'Ye, nece, yee shal faren wel the bet,
If God wol, al this yeer,' quod Pandarus;
'But I am sory that I have yow let
To herken of youre book ye preysen thus.   95
For Goddes love, what seith it? telle it us!
Is it of love? O, som good ye me leere!'
'Uncle,' quod she, 'youre maistresse is nat here.'

With that thei gonnen laughe, and tho she seyde,
'This romaunce is of Thebes that we rede;   100
And we han herd how that kyng Layus deyde
Thorough Edippus his sone, and al that dede;
And here we stynten at thise lettres rede,
How the bisshop, as the book kan telle,
Amphiorax, fil thorugh the ground to helle.'   105

Quod Pandarus, 'Al this knowe I myselve,
And al th'assege of Thebes and the care;
For herof ben ther maked bookes twelve.
But lat be this, and telle me how ye fare.
Do wey youre barbe, and shewe youre face bare;   110
Do wey youre book, rys up, and lat us daunce,
And lat us don to May som observaunce.'

'I? God forbede!' quod she, 'be ye mad?'
Is that a widewes lif, so God yow save?
By God, ye maken me ryght soore adrad!   115
Ye ben so wylde, it semeth as ye rave
It sate me wel bet ay in a cave

To bidde and rede on holy seyntes lyves;
Lat maydens gon to daunce, and yonge wyves.'

'As evere thryve I,' quod this Pandarus,   120
'Yet koude I telle a thyng to doon yow pleye.'
'Now, uncle deere,' quod she, 'telle it us
For Goddes love; is than th'assege aweye?
I am of Grekes so fered that I deye.'
'Nay, nay,' quod he, 'as evere mote I thryve,   125
It is a thing wel bet than swyche fyve.'

'Ye, holy God,' quod she, 'what thyng is that?
What! bet than swyche fyve? I! nay, ywys!
For al this world ne kan I reden what
It sholde ben; som jape, I trowe, is this;   130
And but youreselven telle us what it is,
My wit is for t'arede it al to leene.
As help me God, I not nat what ye meene.'

'And I youre borugh, ne nevere shal, for me,
This thyng be told to yow, as mote I thryve!'   135
'And whi so, uncle myn? whi so?' quod she.
'By God,' quod he, 'that wol I telle as blyve!
For prouder womman is ther noon on lyve,
And ye it wist, in al the town of Troye.
I jape nought, as evere have I joye!'   140

Tho gan she wondren moore than biforn
A thousand fold, and down hire eyghen caste;
For nevere, sith the tyme that she was born,
To knowe thyng desired she so faste;
And with a syk she seyde hym atte laste,   145
'Now, uncle myn, I nyl yow nought displese,
Nor axen more that may do yow disese.'

So after this, with many wordes glade,
And frendly tales, and with merie chiere,
Of this and that they pleide, and gonnen wade   150
In many an unkouth glad and dep matere,
As frendes doon whan thei ben mette yfere,

Tyl she gan axen hym how Ector ferde,
That was the townes wal and Grekes yerde.

'Ful wel, I thonk it God,' quod Pandarus,   155
'Save in his arm he hath a litel wownde;
And ek his fresshe brother Troilus,
The wise, worthi Ector the secounde,
In whom that alle vertu list habounde,
As alle trouth and alle gentilesse,   160
Wisdom, honour, fredom, and worthinesse.'

'In good feith, em,' quod she, 'that liketh me;
Thei faren wel, God save hem bothe two!
For trewelich I holde it gret deynte,
A kynges sone in armes wel to do,   165
And ben of goode condiciouns therto;
For gret power and moral vertu here
Is selde yseyn in o persone yfere.'

'In good faith, that is soth,' quod Pandarus.
'But, by my trouthe, the kyng hath sones tweye –   170
That is to mene, Ector and Troilus –
That certeynly, though that I sholde deye,
Thei ben as voide of vices, dar I seye,
As any men that lyven under the sonne
Hire myght is wyde yknowe, and what they konne.   175

'Of Ector nedeth it namore for to telle:
In al this world ther nys a bettre knyght
Than he, that is of worthynesse welle;
And he wel moore vertu hath than myght.
This knoweth many a wis and worthi wight.   180
The same pris of Troilus I seye;
God help me so, I knowe nat swiche tweye.'

'By God,' quod she, 'of Ector that is sooth.
Of Troilus the same thyng trowe I;
For, dredeles, men tellen that he doth   185
In armes day by day so worthily,
And bereth hym here at hom so gentily

To every wight, that alle pris hath he
Of hem that me were levest preysed be.'

'Ye sey right sooth, ywys,' quod Pandarus;   190
'For yesterday, whoso hadde with hym ben,
He myghte han wondred upon Troilus;
For nevere yet so thikke a swarm of been
Ne fleigh, as Grekes fro hym gonne fleen,
And thorugh the feld, in everi wightes eere,   195
There nas no cry but "Troilus is there!"

'Now here, now ther, he hunted hem so faste,
Ther nas but Grekes blood – and Troilus.
Now hym he hurte, and hym al down he caste;
Ay wher he wente, it was arayed thus: 200
He was hir deth, and sheld and lif for us;
That, as that day, ther dorste non withstonde,
Whil that he held his blody swerd in honde.

'Therto he is the friendlieste man
Of gret estat, that evere I saugh my lyve,   205
And wher hym lest, best felawshipe kan
To swich as hym thynketh able for to thryve.'
And with that word tho Pandarus, as blyve,
He took his leve, and seyde, 'I wol gon henne.'
'Nay, blame have I, myn uncle,' quod she thenne.   210

'What aileth yow to be thus wery soone,
And namelich of wommen? wol ye so?
Nay, sitteth down; by God, I have to doone
With yow, to speke of wisdom er ye go.'
And everi wight that was aboute hem tho,   215
That herde that, gan fer awey to stonde,
Whil they two hadde al that hem liste in honde.

Whan that hire tale al brought was to an ende,
Of hire estat and of hire governaunce,
Quod Pandarus, 'Now is it tyme I wende.   220
But yet, I say, ariseth, lat us daunce,
And cast youre widewes habit to mischaunce!

What list yow thus youreself to disfigure,
Sith yow is tid thus fair an aventure?'

'A! wel bithought! for love of God,' quod she,   225
'Shal I nat witen what ye meene of this?'
'No, this thing axeth leyser,' tho quod he,
'And eke me wolde muche greve, iwys,
If I it tolde, and ye it toke amys.
Yet were it bet my tonge for to stille   230
Than seye a soth that were ayeyns youre wille.

'For, nece, by the goddesse Mynerve,
And Jupiter, that maketh the thondre rynge,
And by the blisful Venus that I serve,
Ye ben the womman in this world lyvynge,   235
Withouten paramours, to my wyttynge,
That I best love, and lothest am to greve,
And that ye weten wel yourself, I leve.'

'Iwis, myn uncle,' quod she, 'grant mercy.
Youre frendshipe have I founden evere yit;   240
I am to no man holden, trewely,
So muche as yow, and have so litel quyt;
And with the grace of God, emforth my wit,
As in my gylt I shal yow nevere offende;
And if I have er this, I wol amende.   245

'But, for the love of God, I yow biseche,
As ye ben he that I love moost and triste,
Lat be to me youre fremde manere speche,
And sey to me, youre nece, what yow liste.'
And with that word hire uncle anoon hire kiste,   250
And seyde, 'Gladly, leve nece dere!
Tak it for good, that I shal sey yow here.'

With that she gan hire eighen down to caste,
And Pandarus to coghe gan a lite,
And seyde, 'Nece, alwey, lo! to the laste,   255
How so it be that som men hem delite
With subtyl art hire tales for to endite,

Yet for al that, in hire entencioun,
Hire tale is al for som conclusioun.

'And sithen th'ende is every tales strengthe,   260
And this matere is so bihovely,
What sholde I peynte or drawen it on lengthe
To yow, that ben my frend so feythfully?'
And with that word he gan right inwardly
Byholden hire and loken on hire face,   265
And seyde, 'On swiche a mirour goode grace!'

Than thought he thus: 'If I my tale endite
Aught harde, or make a proces any whyle,
She shal no savour have therin but lite,
And trowe I wolde hire in my wil bigyle;   270
For tendre wittes wenen al be wyle
Thereas thei kan nought pleynly understonde;
Forthi hire wit to serven wol I fonde' –

And loked on hire in a bysi wyse,
And she was war that he byheld hire so,   275
And seyde, 'Lord! so faste ye m'avise!
Sey ye me nevere er now – What sey ye, no?'
'Yis, yis,' quod he, 'and bet wole er I go!
But, be my trouthe, I thoughte, now if ye
Be fortunat, for now men shal it se.   280

'For to every wight som goodly aventure
Som tyme is shape, if he it kan receyven;
And if that he wol take of it no cure,
Whan that it commeth, but wilfully it weyven,
Lo, neyther cas ne fortune hym deceyven,   285
But ryght his verray slouthe and wrecchednesse;
And swich a wight is for to blame, I gesse.

'Good aventure, o beele nece, have ye
Ful lightly founden, and ye konne it take;
And, for the love of God, and ek of me,   290
Cache it anon, lest aventure slake!
What sholde I lenger proces of it make?

Yif me youre hond, for in this world is noon,
If that yow list, a wight so wel bygon.

'And sith I speke of good entencioun,   295
As I to yow have told wel here-byforn,
And love as wel youre honour and renoun
As creature in al this world yborn,
By alle the othes that I have yow sworn,
And ye be wrooth therfore, or wene I lye,   300
Ne shal I nevere sen yow eft with yë.

'Beth naught agast, ne quaketh naught! Wherto?
Ne chaungeth naught for fere so youre hewe!
For hardely the werst of this is do,
And though my tale as now be to yow newe,   305
Yet trist alwey ye shal me fynde trewe;
And were it thyng that me thoughte unsittynge,
To yow wolde I no swiche tales brynge.'

'Now, my good em, for Goddes love, I preye,'
Quod she, 'come of, and telle me what it is!   310
For both I am agast what ye wol seye,
And ek me longeth it to wite, ywys;
For whethir it be wel or be amys,
Say on, lat me nat in this feere dwelle.'
'So wol I doon; now herkeneth! I shal telle: 315

'Now, nece myn, the kynges deere sone,
The goode, wise, worthi, fresshe, and free –
Which alwey for to don wel is his wone –
The noble Troilus, so loveth the,
That, but ye helpe, it wol his bane be.   320
Lo, here is al! What sholde I moore seye?
Do what yow lest, to make hym lyve or deye.

'But if ye late hym deye, I wol sterve –
Have here my trouthe, nece, I nyl nat lyen –
Al sholde I with this knyf my throte kerve.'   325
With that the teris breste out of his yën,
And seide, 'If that ye don us bothe dyen,

Thus gilteles, than have ye fisshed fayre!
What mende ye, though that we booth appaire?

'Allas! he which that is my lord so deere,   330
That trewe man, that noble gentil knyght,
That naught desireth but youre frendly cheere,
I se hym deyen, ther he goth upryght,
And hasteth hym with al his fulle myght
For to ben slayn, if his fortune assente.   335
Allas, that God yow swich a beaute sente!

'If it be so that ye so cruel be,
That of his deth yow liste nought to recche,
That is so trewe and worthi, as ye se,
Namoore than of a japer or a wrecche –   340
If ye be swich, youre beaute may nat strecche
To make amendes of so cruel a dede.
Avysement is good byfore the nede.

'Wo worth the faire gemme vertulees!
Wo worth that herbe also that dooth no boote!   345
Wo worth that beaute that is routheles!
Wo worth that wight that tret ech undir foote!
And ye, that ben of beaute crop and roote,
If therwithal in yow ther be no routhe,
Than is it harm ye lyven, by my trouthe!   350

'And also think wel that this is no gaude;
For me were levere thow and I and he
Were hanged, than I sholde ben his baude,
As heigh as men myghte on us alle ysee!
I am thyn em; the shame were to me,   355
As wel as the, if that I sholde assente,
Thorugh myn abet, that he thyn honour shente.

'Now understonde, for I yow nought requere
To bynde yow to hym thorugh no byheste,
But only that ye make hym bettre chiere   360
Than ye han doon er this, and moore feste,
So that his lif be saved atte leeste:

This al and som, and pleynly oure entente.
God help me so, I nevere other mente!

'Lo, this requeste is naught but skylle, ywys,   365
Ne doute of reson, pardee, is ther noon.
I sette the worste, that ye dreden this:
Men wolde wondren sen hym come or goon.
Ther-ayeins answere I thus anoon,
That every wight, but he be fool of kynde,   370
Wol deme it love of frendshipe in his mynde.

'What? who wol demen, though he se a man
To temple go, that he th'ymages eteth?
Thenk ek how wel and wisely that he kan
Governe hymself, that he no thyng foryeteth,   375
That where he cometh, he pris and thank hym
    geteth;
And ek therto, he shal come here so selde,
What fors were it though al the town byhelde?

'Swych love of frendes regneth al this town;
And wry yow in that mantel evere moo;   380
And, God so wys be my savacioun,
As I have seyd, youre beste is to do soo.
But alwey, goode nece, to stynte his woo,
So lat youre daunger sucred ben a lite,
That of his deth ye be naught for to wite.'   385

Criseyde, which that herde hym in this wise,
Thoughte, 'I shal felen what he meneth, ywis.'
'Now em,' quod she, 'what wolde ye devise?
What is youre reed I sholde don of this?'
'That is wel seyd,' quod he, 'certein, best is   390
That ye hym love ayeyn for his lovynge,
As love for love is skilful guerdonynge.

'Thenk ek how elde wasteth every houre
In eche of yow a partie of beautee;
And therfore, er that age the devoure,   395
Go love; for olde, ther wol no wight of the.
Lat this proverbe a loore unto yow be:

"To late ywar, quod beaute, whan it paste";
And elde daunteth daunger at the laste.

'The kynges fool is wont to crien loude,　　　　400
Whan that hym thinketh a womman berth hire hye,
"So longe mote ye lyve, and alle proude,
Til crowes feet be growen under youre yë,
And sende yow than a myrour in to prye,
In which that ye may se youre face a-morwe!"
Nece, I bidde wisshe yow namore sorwe.'　　　　405

With this he stynte, and caste adown the heed,
And she began to breste a-wepe anoon,
And seyde, 'Allas, for wo! Why nere I deed?
For of this world the feyth is al agoon.　　　　410
Allas! what sholden straunge to me doon,
When he, that for my beste frend I wende,
Ret me to love, and sholde it me defende?

'Allas! I wolde han trusted, douteles,
That if that I, thorugh my disaventure,　　　　415
Hadde loved outher hym or Achilles,
Ector, or any mannes creature,
Ye nolde han had no mercy ne mesure
On me, but alwey had me in repreve.
This false world, allas! who may it leve?　　　　420

'What! is this al the joye and al the feste?
Is this youre reed? Is this my blisful cas?
Is this the verray mede of youre byheeste?
Is al this paynted proces seyd, allas!
Right for this fyn? O lady myn, Pallas!　　　　425
Thow in this dredful cas for me purveye,
For so astoned am I that I deye.'

Wyth that she gan ful sorwfully to syke.
'A! may it be no bet?' quod Pandarus;
'By God, I shal namore come here this wyke,　　　　430
And God toforn, that am mystrusted thus!
I se ful wel that ye sette lite of us,

Or of oure deth! allas, I, woful wrecche!
Might he yet lyve, of me is nought to recche.

'O cruel god, O dispitouse Marte,   435
O Furies thre of helle, on yow I crye!
So lat me nevere out of this hous departe,
If that I mente harm or vilenye!
But sith I se my lord mot nedes dye,
And I with hym, here I me shryve, and seye   440
That wikkedly ye don us bothe deye.

'But sith it liketh yow that I be ded,
By Neptunus, that god is of the see,
Fro this forth shal I nevere eten bred
Til I myn owen herte blood may see;   445
For certeyn I wol deye as soone as he.'
And up he sterte, and on his wey he raughte,
Til she agayn hym by the lappe kaughte.

Criseyde, which that wel neigh starf for feere,
So as she was the ferfulleste wight   450
That myghte be, and herde ek with hire ere
And saugh the sorwful ernest of the knyght,
And in his preier ek saugh noon unryght,
And for the harm that myghte ek fallen moore,
She gan to rewe, and dredde hire wonder soore,   455

And thoughte thus: 'Unhappes fallen thikke
Alday for love, and in swych manere cas
As men ben cruel in hemself and wikke;
And if this man sle here hymself, allas!
In my presence, it wol be no solas.   460
What men wolde of hit deme I kan nat seye:
It nedeth me ful sleighly for to pleie.'

And with a sorowful sik she sayde thrie,
'A! Lord! what me is tid a sory chaunce!
For myn estat lith now in jupartie,   465
And ek myn emes lif is in balaunce;
But natheles, with Goddes governaunce,

I shal so doon, myn honour shal I kepe,
And ek his lif' – and stynte for to wepe.

'Of harmes two, the lese is for to chese;   470
Yet have I levere maken hym good chere
In honour, than myn emes lyf to lese.
Ye seyn, ye nothyng elles me requere?'
'No, wis,' quod he, 'myn owen nece dere.'
'Now wel,' quod she, 'and I wol doon my peyne;   475
I shal myn herte ayeins my lust constreyne.

'But that I nyl nat holden hym in honde;
Ne love a man ne kan I naught, ne may,
Ayeins my wyl; but elles wol I fonde,
Myn honour sauf, plese hym fro day to day.   480
Therto nolde I nat ones han seyd nay,
But that I dredde, as in my fantasye;
But cesse cause, ay cesseth maladie.

'And here I make a protestacioun,
That in this proces if ye depper go,   485
That certeynly, for no salvacioun
Of yow, though that ye sterven bothe two,
Though al the world on o day be my fo,
Ne shal I nevere of hym han other routhe.'
'I graunte wel,' quod Pandare, 'by my trowthe.   490

'But may I truste wel therto,' quod he,
'That of this thyng that ye han hight me here,
Ye wole it holden trewely unto me?'
'Ye, doutelees,' quod she, 'myn uncle deere.'
'Ne that I shal han cause in this matere,'   495
Quod he, 'to pleyne, or ofter yow to preche?'
'Why, no, parde; what nedeth moore speche?'

Tho fillen they in other tales glade,
Tyl at the laste, 'O good em,' quod she tho,
'For his love, which that us bothe made,   500
Tel me how first ye wisten of his wo.
Woot noon of it but ye?' He seyde, 'No.'

'Kan he wel speke of love?' quod she; 'I preye
Tel me, for I the bet me shal purveye.'

Tho Pandarus a litel gan to smyle,   505
And seyde, 'By my trouthe, I shal yow telle.
This other day, naught gon ful longe while,
In-with the paleis gardyn, by a welle,
Gan he and I wel half a day to dwelle,
Right for to speken of an ordinaunce,   510
How we the Grekes myghten disavaunce.

'Soon after that bigonne we to lepe,
And casten with oure dartes to and fro,
Tyl at the laste he seyde he wolde slepe,
And on the gres adoun he leyde hym tho;   515
And I afer gan romen to and fro,
Til that I herde, as that I welk alone,
How he bigan ful wofully to grone.

'Tho gan I stalke hym softely byhynde,
And sikirly, the soothe for to seyne,   520
As I kan clepe ayein now to my mynde,
Right thus to Love he gan hym for to pleyne:
He seyde, "Lord, have routhe upon my peyne,
Al have I ben rebell in myn entente;
Now, *mea culpa*, lord, I me repente!   525

'"O god, that at thi disposicioun
Ledest the fyn, by juste purveiaunce,
Of every wight, my lowe confessioun
Accepte in gree, and sende me swich penaunce
As liketh the, but from disesperaunce,   530
That may my goost departe awey fro the,
Thow be my sheld, for thi benignite.

'"For certes, lord, so soore hath she me wounded,
That stood in blak, with lokyng of hire eyen,
That to myn hertes botme it is ysounded,   535
Thorough which I woot that I moot nedes deyen.
This is the werste, I dar me nat bywreyen;

And wel the hotter ben the gledes rede,
That men hem wrien with asshen pale and dede."

'Wyth that he smot his head adown anon,   540
And gan to motre, I noot what, trewely.
And I with that gan stille awey to goon,
And leet therof as nothing wist had I,
And com ayein anon, and stood hym by,
And seyde, "awake, ye slepen al to longe!   545
It semeth nat that love doth yow longe,

'"That slepen so that no man may yow wake.
Who sey evere or this so dul a man?"
"Ye, frend," quod he, "do ye youre hedes ake
For love, and lat me lyven as I kan."   550
But though that he for wo was pale and wan,
Yet made he tho as fressh a countenaunce
As though he sholde have led the newe daunce.

'This passed forth til now, this other day,
It fel that I com romyng al allone   555
Into his chaumbre, and fond how that he lay
Upon his bed; but man so soore grone
Ne herde I nevere, and what that was his mone
Ne wist I nought; for, as I was comynge,
Al sodeynly he lefte his complaynynge.   560

'Of which I took somwat suspecioun,
And ner I com, and fond he wepte soore;
And God so wys be my savacioun,
As nevere of thyng hadde I no routhe moore.
For neither with engyn, ne with no loore,   565
Unnethes myghte I fro the deth hym kepe,
That yet fele I myn herte for hym wepe.

'And God woot, nevere, sith that I was born,
Was I so besy no man for to preche,
Ne nevere was to wight so depe isworn,   570
Or he me told who myghte ben his leche.
But now to yow rehercen al his speche,

Or alle his woful wordes for to sowne,
Ne bid me naught, but ye wol se me swowne.

'But for to save his lif, and elles nought,   575
And to noon harm of yow, thus am I dryven;
And for the love of God, that us hath wrought,
Swich cheer hym dooth, that he and I may lyven!
Now have I plat to yow myn herte shryven;
And sith ye woot that myn entent is cleene,   580
Take heede therof, for I non yvel meene.

'And right good thrift, I prey to God, have ye,
That han swich oon ykaught withouten net!
And, be ye wis as ye be fair to see,
Wel in the ryng than is the ruby set.   585
Ther were nevere two so wel ymet,
Whan ye ben his al hool, as he is youre:
Ther myghty God yet graunte us see that houre!'

'Nay, therof spak I nought, ha, ha!' quod she;
'As helpe me God, ye shenden every deel!'   590
'O, mercy, dere nece,' anon quod he,
'What so I spak, I mente naught but wel,
By Mars, the god that helmed is of steel!
Now beth naught wroth, my blood, my nece dere.'
'Now wel,' quod she, 'foryeven be it here!'   595

With this he took his leve, and home he wente;
And, Lord, so he was glad and wel bygon!
Criseyde aros, no lenger she ne stente,
But streght into hire closet wente anon,
And set hire doun as stylle as any ston,   600
And every word gan up and down to wynde
That he had seyd, as it com hire to mynde;

And was somdel astoned in hire thought,
Right for the newe cas; but whan that she
Was ful avysed, tho fond she right nought   605
Of peril, why she ought afered be.
For man may love, of possibilite,

A womman so, his herte may tobreste,
And she naught love ayein, but if hire leste.

But as she sat allone and thoughte thus,   610
Ascry aros at scarmuch al withoute,
And men cride in the strete, 'Se, Troilus
Hath right now put to flighte the Grekes route!'
With that gan al hire meyne for to shoute,
'A, go we se! cast up the yates wyde!   615
For thorwgh this strete he moot to paleys ride;

'For other wey is fro the yate noon
Of Dardanus, there opyn is the cheyne.'
With that com he and al his folk anoon
An esy pas rydyng, in routes tweyne,   620
Right as his happy day was, sooth to seyne,
For which, men seyn, may nought destourbed be
That shal bityden of necessitee.

This Troilus sat on his baye steede,
Al armed, save his hed, ful richely;   625
And wownded was his hors, and gan to blede,
On which he rood a pas ful softely.
But swich a knyghtly sighte, trewely,
As was on hym, was nought, withouten faille,
To loke on Mars, that god is of bataille.   630

So lik a man of armes and a knyght
He was to seen, fulfilled of heigh prowesse;
For bothe he hadde a body and a myght
To don that thing, as wel as hardynesse;
And ek to seen hym in his gere hym dresse,   635
So fressh, so yong, so weldy semed he,
It was an heven upon hym for to see.

His helm tohewen was in twenty places,
That by a tyssew heng his bak byhynde;
His sheeld todasshed was with swerdes and maces,   640
In which men myghte many an arwe fynde
That thirled hadde horn and nerf and rynde;

And ay the peple cryde, 'Here cometh oure joye,
And, next his brother, holder up of Troye!'

For which he wex a litel reed for shame,   645
Whan he the peple upon hym herde cryen,
That to byholde it was a noble game,
How sobrelich he caste down his yën.
Criseyda gan al his chere aspien,
And leet it so softe in hire herte synke,   650
That to hireself she seyde, 'Who yaf me drynke?'

For of hire owen thought she wex al reed,
Remembryng hire right thus, 'Lo, this is he
Which that myn uncle swerith he moot be deed,
But I on hym have mercy and pitee.'   655
And with that thought, for pure ashamed, she
Gan in hire hed to pulle, and that as faste,
Whil he and alle the peple forby paste;

And gan to caste and rollen up and down
Withinne hire thought his excellent prowesse,   660
And his estat, and also his renown,
His wit, his shap, and ek his gentilesse;
But moost hir favour was, for his distresse
Was al for hire, and thoughte it was a routhe
To sleen swich oon, if that he mente trouthe.   665

Now myghte som envious jangle thus:
'This was a sodeyn love; how myght it be
That she so lightly loved Troilus,
Right for the firste syghte, ye, parde?'
Now whoso seith so, mote he nevere ythe!   670
For every thyng, a gynnyng hath it nede
Er al be wrought, withowten any drede.

For I sey nought that she so sodeynly
Yaf hym hire love, but that she gan enclyne
To like hym first, and I have told yow whi;   675
And after that, his manhod and his pyne
Made love withinne hire herte for to myne,

For which, by proces and by good servyse,
He gat hire love, and in no sodeyn wyse.

And also blisful Venus, wel arrayed,   680
Sat in hire seventhe hous of hevene tho,
Disposed wel, and with aspectes payed,
To helpe sely Troilus of his woo.
And, soth to seyne, she nas not al a foo
To Troilus in his nativitee;   685
God woot that wel the sonner spedde he.

Now lat us stynte of Troilus a throwe,
That rideth forth, and lat us torne faste
Unto Criseyde, that heng hire hed ful lowe,
Ther as she sat allone, and gan to caste   690
Where on she wolde apoynte hire atte laste,
If it so were hire em ne wolde cesse
For Troilus upon hire for to presse.

And, Lord! so she gan in hire thought argue
In this matere of which I have yow told,   695
And what to doone best were, and what eschue,
That plited she ful ofte in many fold.
Now was hire herte warm, now was it cold;
And what she thoughte, somwhat shal I write,
As to myn auctour listeth for t'endite.   700

She thoughte wel that Troilus persone
She knew by syghte, and ek his gentilesse,
And thus she seyde, 'Al were it nat to doone
To graunte hym love, yet for his worthynesse
It were honour, with pley and with gladnesse,   705
In honestee with swich a lord to deele,
For myn estat, and also for his heele.

'Ek wel woot I my kynges sone is he;
And sith he hath to se me swich delit,
If I wolde outreliche his sighte flee,   710
Peraunter he myghte have me in dispit,
Thorugh whicch I myghte stonde in worse plit.

Now were I wis, me hate to purchace,
Withouten nede, ther I may stonde in grace?

'In every thyng, I woot, there lith mesure.   715
For though a man forbede dronkenesse,
He naught forbet that every creature
Be drynkeles for alwey, as I gesse.
Ek sith I woot for me is his destresse,
I ne aughte nat for that thing hym despise,   720
Sith it is so, he meneth in good wyse.

'And eke I knowe, of longe tyme agon,
His thewes goode, and that he is nat nyce.
N'avantour, seith men, certein, he is noon;
To wis is he to doon so gret a vice;   725
Ne als I nyl hym nevere so cherice
That he may make avaunt, by juste cause,
He shal me nevere bynde in swich a clause.

'Now sette a caas: the hardest is, ywys,
Men myghten demen that he loveth me.   730
What dishonour were it unto me, this?
May ich hym lette of that? Why, nay, parde!
I knowe also, and alday heere and se,
Men loven wommen al biside hire leve;
And whan hem leste namore, lat hem byleve!   735

'I thenke ek how he able is for to have
Of al this noble town the thriftieste,
To ben his love, so she hire honour save.
For out and out he is the worthieste,
Save only Ector, which that is the beste;   740
And yet his lif al lith now in my cure.
But swich is love, and ek myn aventure.

'Ne me to love, a wonder is it nought;
For wel woot I myself, so God me spede,
Al wolde I that noon wiste of this thought,   745
I am oon the faireste, out of drede,
And goodlieste, whoso taketh hede,

And so men seyn, in al the town of Troie.
What wonder is though he of me have joye?

'I am myn owene womman, wel at ese,   750
I thank it God, as after myn estat,
Right yong, and stonde unteyd in lusty leese,
Withouten jalousie or swich debat.
Shal noon housbonde seyn to me "chek mat!"
For either they ben ful of jalousie,   755
Or maisterfull, or loven novelrie.

'What shal I doon? To what fyn lyve I thus?
Shal I nat love, in cas if that me leste?
What, par dieux! I am naught religious.
And though that I myn herte sette at reste   760
Upon this knyght, that is the worthieste,
And kepe alwey myn honour and my name,
By alle right, it may do me no shame.'

But right as when the sonne shyneth brighte
In March, that chaungeth ofte tyme his face,   765
And that a cloude is put with wynd to flighte,
Which oversprat the sonne as for a space,
A cloudy thought gan thorugh hire soule pace,
That overspradde hire brighte thoughtes alle,
So that for feere almost she gan to falle.   770

That thought was this: 'Allas! syn I am free,
Sholde I now love, and put in jupartie
My sikernesse, and thrallen libertee?
Allas! how dorst I thenken that folie?
May I naught wel in other folk aspie   775
Hire dredfull joye, hire constreinte, and hire peyne?
Ther loveth noon, that she nath why to pleyne.

'For love is yet the mooste stormy lyf,
Right to hymself, that evere was bigonne;
For evere som mystrust or nice strif   780
Ther is in love, som cloude is over that sonne.
Therto we wrecched wommen nothing konne,

Whan us is wo, but wepe and sitte and thinke;
Oure wrecche is this, oure owen wo to drynke.

'Also thise wikked tonges ben so prest   785
To speke us harm, ek men ben so untrewè,
That, right anon as cessed is hire lest,
So cesseth love, and forth to love a newe.
But harm ydoon is doon, whoso it rewe;
For though thise men for love hem first torende,   790
Ful sharp bygynnyng breketh ofte at ende.

'How ofte tyme hath it yknowen be,
The tresoun that to wommen hath ben do!
To what fyn is swich love I kan nat see,
Or wher bycometh it, whan it is ago.   795
Ther is no wight that woot, I trowe so,
Where it bycometh; lo, no wight on it sporneth:
That erst was nothing, into nought it torneth.

'How bisy, if I love, ek most I be
To plesen hem that jangle of love, and dremen,   800
And coye hem, that they seye noon harm of me!
For though ther be no cause, yet hem semen
Al be for harm that folk hire frendes quemen;
And who may stoppen every wikked tonge,
Or sown of belles whil that thei ben ronge?'   805

And after that, hire thought gan for to clere,
And seide, 'He which that nothing undertaketh,
Nothyng n'acheveth, be hym looth or deere.'
And with an other thought hire herte quaketh;
Than slepeth hope, and after drede awaketh;   810
Now hoot, now cold; but thus, bitwixen tweye,
She rist hire up, and went here for to pleye.

Adown the steyre anon-right tho she wente
Into the garden, with hire neces thre,
And up and down ther made many a wente,   815
Flexippe, she, Tharbe, and Antigone,
To pleyen, that it joye was to see;

And other of hire wommen, a gret route,
Hire folowede in the garden al abowte.

This yerd was large, and rayled alle th' aleyes,   820
And shadewed wel with blosmy bowes grene,
And benched newe, and sonded alle the weyes,
In which she walketh arm in arm bitwene,
Til at the laste Antigone the shene
Gan on a Troian song to singen cleere,   825
That it an heven was hire vois to here.

She seyd: 'O Love, to whom I have and shal
Ben humble subgit, trewe in myn entente,
As I best kan, to yow, lord, yeve ich al,
For everemo, myn hertes lust to rente.   830
For nevere yet thi grace no wight sente
So blisful cause as me, my lif to lede
In alle joie and seurte, out of drede.

'Ye, blisful god, han me so wel byset
In love, iwys, that al that bereth lif   835
Ymagynen ne koude how to be bet;
For, lord, withouten jalousie or strif,
I love oon which that is moost ententif
To serven wel, unweri or unfeyned,
That evere was, and leest with harm desteyned.   840

'As he that is the welle of worthynesse,
Of trouthe grownd, mirour of goodlihed,
Of wit Apollo, stoon of sikernesse,
Of vertu roote, of lust fynder and hed,
Thorugh which is alle sorwe fro me ded,   845
Iwis, I love hym best, so doth he me;
Now good thrift have he, wherso that he be!

'Whom shulde I thanken but yow, god of Love,
Of al this blisse, in which to bathe I gynne?
And thanked be ye, lord, for that I love!   850
This is the righte lif that I am inne,
To flemen alle manere vice and synne:

This dooth me so to vertu for t'entende,
That day by day I in my wille amende.

'And whoso seith that for to love is vice, 855
Or thraldom, though he feele in it destresse,
He outher is envyous, or right nyce,
Or is unmyghty, for his shrewednesse,
To loven; for swich manere folk, I gesse,
Defamen Love, as nothing of him knowe: 860
Thei speken, but thei benten nevere his bowe!

'What is the sonne wers, of kynde right,
Though that a man, for feeblesse of his yën,
May nought endure on it to see for bright?
Or love the wers, though wrecches on it crien? 865
No wele is worth that may no sorwe dryen.
And forthi, who that hath an hed of verre,
Fro caste of stones war hym in the werre!

'But I with al myn herte and al my myght,
As I have seyd, wol love unto my laste, 870
My deere herte, and al myn owen knyght,
In which myn herte growen is so faste,
And his in me, that it shal evere laste.
Al dredde I first to love hym to bigynne,
Now woot I wel, ther is no peril inne.' 875

And of hir song right with that word she stente,
And therwithal, 'Now nece' quod Cryseyde,
'Who made this song now with so good entente?'
Antygone answerde anoon and seyde,
'Madame, iwys, the goodlieste mayde 880
Of gret estat in al the town of Troye,
And let hire lif in moste honour and joye.'

'Forsothe, so it semeth by hire song,'
Quod tho Criseyde, and gan therwith to sike,
And seyde, 'Lord, is ther swych blisse among 885
Thise loveres, as they konne faire endite?'
'Yes, wis,' quod fresshe Antigone the white,

'For alle the folk that han or ben on lyve
Ne konne wel the blisse of love discryve.

'But wene ye that every wrecche woot   890
The parfite blisse of love? Why, nay, iwys!
They wenen all be love, if oon be hoot.
Do wey, do wey, they woot no thyng of this!
Men mosten axe at seyntes if it is
Aught fair in hevene (why? for they kan telle),   895
And axen fendes is it foul in helle.'

Criseyde unto that purpos naught answerde,
But seyde, 'Ywys, it wol be nyght as faste.'
But every word which that she of hire herde,
She gan to prenten in hire herte faste,   900
And ay gan love hire lasse for t'agaste
Than it dide erst, and synken in hire herte,
That she wex somwhat able to converte.

The dayes honour, and the hevenes yë,
The nyghtes foo – al this clepe I the sonne –   905
Gan westren faste, and downward for to wrye,
As he that hadde his dayes cours yronne;
And white thynges wexen dymme and donne
For lakke of lyght, and sterres for t'apere,
That she and alle hire folk in went yfeere.   910

So whan it liked hire to go to reste,
And voided weren thei that voiden oughte,
She seyde that to slepen wel hire leste.
Hire wommen soone til hire bed hire broughte.
Whan al was hust, than lay she stille and thoughte   915
Of al this thing; the manere and the wise
Reherce it nedeth nought, for ye ben wise.

A nyghtyngale, upon a cedre grene,
Under the chambre wal ther as she ley,
Ful loude song ayein the moone shene,   920
Peraunter, in his briddes wise, a lay
Of love, that made hire herte fressh and gay.

That herkned she so longe in good entente,
Til at the laste the dede slep hire hente.

And as she slep, anon-right tho hire mette   925
How that an egle, fethered whit as bon,
Under hire brest his longe clawes sette,
And out hire herte he rente, and that anon,
And dide his herte into hire brest to gon,
Of which she nought agroos, ne nothyng smerte;   930
And forth he fleigh, with herte left for herte.

Pandarus arranges a correspondence and finally Criseyde is
tricked into meeting Troilus at the house of his brother,
Deiphebus, where Troilus is feigning sickness. After the
meeting Pandarus has some misgiving about having acted as a
bawd, but Troilus assures him that he will always be faithful to
Criseyde, and as a sign of his gratitude offers to procure for
Pandarus Helen herself, or any of his own sisters if Pandarus
likes. Pandarus then arranges for Criseyde to come to supper in
his house, assuring her that Troilus is out of town, though the
poet will not guarantee that she believed him.

Book III

Whan al was wel, he roos and took his leve,
And she to soper com, whan it was eve,   595

With a certein of hire owen men,
And with hire faire nece Antigone,
And other of hire wommen nyne or ten.
But who was glad now, who, as trowe ye,
But Troilus, that stood and myght it se   600
Thorughout a litel wyndow in a stuwe,
Ther he bishet syn mydnyght was in mewe,

Unwist of every wight but of Pandare?
But to the point; now whan that she was come,
With alle joie and alle frendes fare,   605

Hire em anon in armes hath hire nome,
And after to the soper, alle and some,
Whan tyme was, ful softe they hem sette.
God woot, ther was no deynte for to fette!

And after soper gonnen they to rise,   610
At ese wel, with hertes fresshe and glade,
And wel was hym that koude best devyse
To liken hire, or that hire laughen made.
He song; she pleyde; he tolde tale of Wade.
But at the laste, as every thyng hath ende,
She took hire leve, and nedes wolde wende.   615

But O Fortune, executrice of wyrdes!
O influences of thise hevenes hye!
Soth is, that under God ye ben oure hierdes,
Though to us bestes ben the causes wrie.   620
This mene I now, for she gan homward hye,
But execut was al bisyde hire leve
The goddes wil; for which she moste bleve.

The bente moone with hire hornes pale,
Saturne, and Jove, in Cancro joyned were,   625
That swych a reyn from heven gan avale,
That every maner womman that was there
Hadde of that smoky reyn a verray feere;
At which Pandare tho lough, and seyde thenne,
'Now were it tyme a lady to gon henne!   630

'But goode nece, if I myghte evere plese
Yow any thyng, than prey ich yow,' quod he,
'To don myn herte as now so grete an ese
As for to dwelle here al this nyght with me,
For-whi this is youre owen hous, parde.   635
For, by my trouthe, I sey it nought a-game,
To wende as now, it were to me a shame.'

Criseyde, which that koude as muche good
As half a world, took hede of his preyere;
And syn it ron, and al was on a flod,   640
She thoughte, 'As good chepe may I dwellen here,
And graunte it gladly with a frendes chere,

And have a thonk, as grucche and thanne abide;
For hom to gon, it may nought wel bitide.'

'I wol,' quod she, 'myn uncle lief and deere;   645
Syn that yow list, it skile is to be so.
I am right glad with yow to dwellen here;
I seyde but a-game, I wolde go.'
'Iwys, graunt mercy, nece,' quod he tho,
'Were it a-game or no, soth for to telle,   650
Now am I glad, syn that yow list to dwelle.'

Thus al is wel; but tho bigan aright
The newe joie and al the feste agayn.
But Pandarus, if goodly hadde he myght,
He wolde han hyed hire to bedde fayn,   655
And seyde, 'Lord, this is an huge rayn!
This were a weder for to slepen inne;
And that I rede us soone to bygynne.

'And, nece, woot ye wher I wol yow leye,
For that we shul nat liggen far asonder,   660
And for ye neither shullen, dar I seye,
Heren noyse of reynes nor of thonder?
By God, right in my litel closet yonder.
And I wol in that outer hous allone
Be wardein of youre wommen everichone.   665

'And in this myddel chaumbre that ye se
Shul youre wommen slepen, wel and softe;
And there I seyde shal yourcselven be;
And if ye liggen wel to-nyght, com ofte,
And careth nought what weder is alofte.   670
The wyn anon! – and whan so that yow leste,
So go we slepe; I trowe it be the beste.'

Ther nys no more, but hereafter soone,
The voidë dronke, and travers drawe anon,
Gan every wight that hadde nought to done   675
More in the place out of the chaumbre gon.
And evere mo so sterneliche it ron,

And blew therwith so wondirliche loude,
That wel neigh no man heren other koude.

Tho Pandarus, hire em, right as hym oughte,   680
With wommen swiche as were hire most aboute,
Ful glad unto hire beddes syde hire broughte,
And took his leve, and gan ful lowe loute,
And seyde, 'Here at this closet dore withoute,
Right overthwart, youre wommen liggen alle,   685
That, whom yow list of hem, ye may here calle.'

So whan that she was in the closet leyd,
And alle hire wommen forth by ordinaunce
Abedde weren, ther as I have seyd,
There was nomore to skippen nor to traunce,   690
But boden go to bedde, with meschaunce,
If any wight was steryng anywhere,
And lat hem slepen that abedde were.

But Pandarus, that wel koude eche a deel
The olde daunce, and every point therinne,   695
Whan that he sey that alle thyng was wel,
He thought he wolde upon his werk bigynne,
And gan the stuwe doore al softe unpynne,
And stille as stoon, withouten lenger lette,
By Troilus adown right he hym sette.   700

And, shortly to the point right for to gon,
Of al this werk he tolde hym word and ende,
And seyde, 'Make the redy right anon,
For thow shalt into hevene blisse wende.'
'Now, blisful Venus, thow me grace sende!'   705
Quod Troilus, 'For nevere yet no nede
Hadde ich er now, ne halvendel the drede.'

Quod Pandarus, 'Ne drede the nevere a deel,
For it shal be right as thow wolt desire;
So thryve I, this nyght shal I make it weel,   710
Or casten al the gruwel in the fire.'
'Yet, blisful Venus, this nyght thow me enspire,'

Quod Troilus, 'As wys as I the serve,
And evere bet and bet shal, til I sterve.

'And if ich hadde, O Venus ful of myrthe,   715
Aspectes badde of Mars or of Saturne,
Or thow combust or let were in my birthe,
Thy fader prey al thilke harm disturne
Of grace, and that I glad ayein may turne,
For love of hym thow lovedest in the shawe,   720
I meene Adoun, that with the boor was slawe.

'O Jove ek, for the love of faire Europe,
The which in forme of bole awey thow fette,
Now help! O Mars, thow with thi blody cope,
For love of Cipris, thow me nought ne lette!   725
O Phebus, thynk whan Dane hireselven shette
Under the bark, and laurer wax for drede,
Yet for hire love, O help now at this nede!

'Mercurie, for the love of Hierse eke,
For which Pallas was with Aglawros wroth,   730
Now help! and ek Diane, I the biseke,
That this viage be nought to the looth.
O fatal sustren, which, er any cloth
Me shapen was, my destine me sponne,
So helpeth to this werk that is bygonne!'   735

Quod Pandarus, 'Thow wrecched mouses herte,
Artow agast so that she wol the bite?
Why, don this furred cloke upon thy sherte,
And folwe me, for I wol have the wite.
But bide, and lat me gon biforn a lite.'   740
And with that word he gan undon a trappe,
And Troilus he brought in by the lappe.

The sterne wynd so loude gan to route
That no wight oother noise myghte heere;
And they that layen at the dore withoute,   745
Ful sikerly they slepten alle yfere;
And Pandarus, with a ful sobre cheere,

Goth to the dore anon, withouten lette,
There as they laye, and softely it shette.

And as he com ayeynward pryvely,   750
His nece awook, and axed, 'Who goth there?'
'My dere nece,' quod he, 'it am I.
Ne wondreth nought, ne have of it no fere.'
And ner he com, and seyde hire in hire ere,
'No word, for love of God, I yow biseche!   755
Lat no wight risen and heren of oure speche.'

'What! which wey be ye comen, *benedicite*?'
Quod she, 'and how thus unwist of hem alle?'
'Here at this secre trappe-dore,' quod he.
Quod tho Criseyde, 'Lat me som wight calle!'   760
'I! God forbede that it sholde falle,'
Quod Pandarus, 'that ye swich folye wroughte!
They myghte demen thyng they nevere er thoughte.

'It is nought good a slepyng hound to wake,
Ne yeve a wight a cause to devyne.   765
Youre wommen slepen alle, I undertake,
So that, for hem, the hous men myghte myne,
And slepen wollen til the sonne shyne.
And whan my tale brought is to an ende,
Unwist, right as I com, so wol I wende.   770

'Now, nece myn, ye shul wel understonde,'
Quod he, 'so as ye wommen demen alle,
That for to holde in love a man in honde,
And hym hire lief and deere herte calle,
And maken hym an howve above a calle,   775
I meene, as love another in this while,
She doth hireself a shame, and hym a gyle.

'Now, wherby that I telle yow al this:
Ye woot youreself, as wel as any wight,
How that youre love al fully graunted is   780
To Troilus, the worthieste knyght
Oon of this world, and therto trouthe yplight,

That, but it were on hym along, ye nolde
Hym nevere falsen while ye lyven sholde.

'Now stant it thus, that sith I fro yow wente,   785
This Troilus, right platly for to seyn,
Is thorugh a goter, by a pryve wente,
Into my chaumbre come in al this reyn,
Unwist of every manere wight, certeyn,
Save of myself, as wisly have I joye,   790
And by that feith I shal Priam of Troie.

'And he is come in swich peyne and distresse
That, but he be al fully wood by this,
He sodeynly mot falle into wodnesse,
But if God helpe; and cause whi this is,   795
He seith hym told is of a frend of his
How that ye sholden love oon hatte Horaste;
For sorwe of which this nyght shal ben his laste.'

Criseyde, which that al this wonder herde,
Gan sodeynly aboute hire herte colde,   800
And with a sik she sorwfully answerde,
'Allas! I wende, whoso tales tolde,
My deere herte wolde me nought holde
So lightly fals! Allas! conceytes wronge,
What harm they don, for now lyve I to longe!   805

'Horaste! allas, and falsen Troilus?
I knowe hym nought, God helpe me so,' quod she.
'Allas, what wikked spirit tolde hym thus?
Now certes, em, tomorwe, and I hym se,
I shal therof as ful excusen me,   810
As evere dide womman, if hym like.'
And with that word she gan ful soore sike.

'O God!' quod she, 'so worldly selynesse,
Which clerkes callen fals felicitee,
Imedled is with many a bitternesse!   815
Ful angwissous than is, God woot,' quod she,
'Condicioun of veyn prosperitee;

For either joies comen nought yfeere,
Or elles no wight hath hem alwey here.

'O brotel wele of mannes joie unstable!   820
With what wight so thow be, or how thow pleye,
Either he woot that thow, joie, art muable,
Or woot it nought; it mot ben oon of tweye.
Now if he woot it nought, how may he seye
That he hath verray joie and selynesse,   825
That is of ignoraunce ay in derknesse?

'Now if he woot that joie is transitorie,
As every joie of worldly thyng mot flee,
Than every tyme he that hath in memorie,
The drede of lesyng maketh hym that he   830
May in no perfit selynesse be;
And if to lese his joie he sette a myte,
Than semeth it that joie is worth ful lite.

'Wherfore I wol diffyne in this matere,
That trewely, for aught I kan espie,   835
Ther is no verray weele in this world heere.
But O thow wikked serpent, jalousie,
Thow mysbyleved and envyous folie,
Why hastow Troilus mad to me untriste,
That nevere yet agylt hym, that I wiste?'   840

Quod Pandarus, 'Thus fallen is this cas.'
'Why, uncle myn,' quod she, 'who tolde hym this?
Why doth my deere herte thus, allas?'
'Ye woot, ye, nece myn,' quod he, 'what is.
I hope al shal be wel that is amys,   845
For ye may quenche al this, if that yow leste.
And doth right so, for I holde it the beste.'

'So shal I do to-morwe, ywys,' quod she,
'And God toforn, so that it shal suffise.'
'To-morwe? allas, that were a fair!' quod he.   850
'Nay, nay, it may nat stonden in this wise.
For, nece myn, thus writen clerkes wise,

That peril is with drecchyng in ydrawe;
Nay, swiche abodes ben nought worth an hawe.

'Nece, alle thyng hath tyme, I dar avowe,   855
For whan a chaumbre afire is, or an halle,
Wel more nede is, it sodeynly rescowe
Than to dispute and axe amonges alle
How is this candele in the straw i-falle.
A, *benedicite!* for al among that fare   860
The harm is don, and farewel feldefare!

'And nece myn – ne take it naught agrief –
If that ye suffre hym al nyght in this wo,
God help me so, ye hadde hym nevere lief;
That dar I seyn, now ther is but we two.   865
But wel I woot that ye wol nat do so;
Ye ben to wys to doon so gret folie,
To putte his lif al nyght in jupertie.'

'Hadde I hym nevere lief? by God, I weene
Ye hadde nevere thyng so lief!' quod she.   870
'Now by my thrift,' quod he, 'that shal be seene!
For syn ye make this ensaumple of me,
If ich al nyght wolde hym in sorwe se,
For al the tresour in the town of Troie,
I bidde God I nevere mote have joie.   875

'Now loke thanne, if ye that ben his love
Shul putte his lif al night in jupertie
For thyng of nought, now, by that God above,
Naught oonly this delay comth of folie,
But of malice, if that I shal naught lie.   880
What! platly, and ye suffre hym in destresse,
Ye neyther bounte don ne gentilesse.'

Quod tho Criseyde, 'Wol ye don o thyng,
And ye therwith shal stynte al his disese?
Have heere, and bereth hym this blewe ryng,   885
For ther is nothyng myghte hym bettre plese,
Save I myself, ne more hys herte apese;

And sey my deere herte, that his sorwe
Is causeles, that shal be sene to-morwe.'

'A ryng?' quod he, 'ye, haselwodes shaken!   890
Ye, nece myn, that ryng moste han a stoon
That myhte dede men alyve maken;
And swich a ryng trowe I that ye have non.
Discrecioun out of youre hed is gon;
That fele I now,' quod he, 'and that is routhe.   895
O tyme ilost, wel maistow corsen slouthe!

'Woot ye not wel that noble and heigh corage
Ne sorweth nought, ne stynteth ek, for lite?
But if a fool were in a jalous rage,
I nolde setten at his sorwe a myte,   900
But feffe hym with a fewe wordes white
Anothir day, whan that I myghte hym fynde;
But this thyng stant al in another kynde.

'This is so gentil and so tendre of herte,
That with his deth he wol his sorwes wreke;   905
For trusteth wel, how sore that hym smerte,
He wol to yow no jalous wordes speke.
And forthi, nece, er that his herte breke,
So speke youreself to hym of this matere;
For with o word ye may his herte stere.   910

'Now have I told what peril he is inne,
And his comynge unwist is to every wight;
Ne, parde, harm may ther be non, ne synne;
I wol myself be with yow al this nyght.
Ye knowe ek how it is youre owen knyght,   915
And that bi right ye moste upon hym triste,
And I al prest to fecche hym whan yow liste.'

This accident so pitous was to here,
And ek so like a sooth, at prime face,
And Troilus hire knyght to hir so deere,   920
His prive comyng, and the siker place,
That, though that she did hym as thanne a grace,

Considered alle thynges as they stoode,
No wonder is, syn she did al for goode.

Criseyde answerde, 'As wisly God at reste   925
My soule brynge, as me is for hym wo!
And, em, iwis, fayn wolde I don the beste,
If that ich hadde grace to do so.
But whether that ye dwelle or for hym go,
I am, til God me bettre mynde sende,   930
At dulcarnoun, right at my wittes ende.'

Quod Pandarus, 'Yee, nece, wol ye here?
Dulcarnoun called is "flemyng of wrecches."
It semeth hard, for wrecches wol nought lere,
For verray slouthe or other wilfull tecches;   935
This seyd by hem that ben nought worth two
    fecches.
But ye ben wis, and that we han on honde
Nis neither hard, ne skilful to withstonde.'

'Than, em,' quod she, 'doth herof as yow list.
But er he come, I wil up first arise,   940
And, for the love of God, syn al my trist
Is on yow two, and ye ben bothe wise,
So werketh now in so discret a wise
That I honour may have, and he plesaunce;
For I am here al in youre governaunce.'   945

'That is wel seyd,' quod he, 'my nece deere.
Ther good thrift on that wise gentil herte!
But liggeth stille, and taketh hym right here;
It nedeth nought no ferther for hym sterte.
And ech of yow ese otheres sorwes smerte,   950
For love of God; and Venus, I the herye;
For soone, hope I, we shul ben alle merye.'

This Troilus ful soone on knees hym sette
Ful sobrely, right be hyre beddes hed,
And in his beste wyse his lady grette.   955
But, Lord, so she wex sodeynliche red!
Ne though men sholde smyten of hire hed,

She kouthe nought a word aright out-brynge
So sodeynly, for his sodeyn comynge.

But Pandarus, that so wel koude feele   960
In every thyng, to pleye anon bigan,
And seyde, 'Nece, se how this lord kan knele!
Now, for youre trouthe, se this gentil man!'
And with that word he for a quysshen ran,
And seyde, 'Kneleth now, while that yow leste,   965
There God youre hertes brynge soone at reste!'

Kan I naught seyn, for she bad hym nought rise,
If sorwe it putte out of hire remembraunce,
Or elles that she took it in the wise
Of dewete, as for his observaunce;   970
But wel fynde I she dede hym this pleasaunce,
That she hym kiste, although she siked sore,
And bad hym sitte adown withouten more.

Quod Pandarus, 'Now wol ye wel bigynne.
Now doth hym sitte, goode nece deere,   975
Upon youre beddes syde al ther withinne,
That ech of yow the bet may other heere.'
And with that word he drow hym to the feere,
And took a light, and fond his contenaunce
As for to looke upon an old romaunce.   980

Criseyde, that was Troilus lady right,
And cler stood on a ground of sikernesse,
Al thoughte she hire servant and hire knyght
Ne sholde of right non untrouthe in hire gesse,
Yet natheles, considered his distresse,   985
And that love is in cause of swich folie,
Thus to hym spak she of his jalousie:

'Lo, herte myn, as wolde the excellence
Of love, ayeins the which that no man may
Ne oughte ek goodly make resistence;   990
And ek bycause I felte wel and say
Youre grete trouthe and servise every day,

And that youre herte al myn was, soth to seyne –
This drof me for to rewe upon youre peyne.

'And youre goodnesse have I founde alwey yit,   995
Of which, my deere herte and al my knyght,
I thonke it yow, as fer as I have wit,
Al kan I nought as muche as it were right;
And I, emforth my connyng and my might,
Have and ay shal, how sore that me smerte,   1000
Ben to yow trewe and hool with al myn herte;

'And dredeles, that shal be founde at preve.
But, herte myn, what al this is to seyne
Shal wel be told, so that ye nought yow greve,
Though I to yow right on youreself compleyne.   1005
For therwith mene I fynaly the peyne
That halt youre herte and myn in hevynesse
Fully to slen, and every wrong redresse.

'My goode myn, noot I for-why ne how
That jalousie, allas! that wikked wyvere,   1010
Thus causeles is cropen into yow,
The harm of which I wolde fayn delyvere.
Allas, that he, al hool, or of hym slyvere,
Shuld han his refut in so digne a place,
Ther Jove hym soone out of youre herte arace!   1015

'But O, thow Jove, O auctour of nature,
Is this an honour to thi deyte,
That folk ungiltif suffren hire injure,
And who that giltif is, al quyt goth he?
O, were it leful for to pleyn on the,   1020
That undeserved suffrest jalousie,
Of that I wolde upon the pleyne and crie!

'Ek al my wo is this, that folk now usen
To seyn right thus, "Ye, jalousie is love!"
And wolde a busshel venym al excusen,   1025
For that o greyn of love is on it shove.
But that woot heighe God that sit above,

If it be likkere love, or hate, or grame;
And after that, it oughte bere his name.

'But certeyn is, som manere jalousie   1030
Is excusable more than som, iwys;
As whan cause is, and som swich fantasie
With piete so wel repressed is
That it unnethe doth or seyth amys,
But goodly drynketh up al his distresse;   1035
And that excuse I, for the gentilesse.

'And som so ful of furie is and despit
That it sourmounteth his repressioun.
But, herte myn, ye be nat in that plit,
That thonke I God; for which youre passioun   1040
I wol nought calle it but illusioun,
Of habundaunce of love and besy cure,
That doth youre herte this disese endure.

'Of which I am right sory, but nought wroth;
But, for my devoir and youre hertes reste,   1045
Wherso yow list, by ordal or by oth,
By sort, or in what wise so yow leste,
For love of God, lat preve it for the beste;
And if that I be giltif, do me deye!
Allas, what myght I more don or seye?'   1050

With that a fewe brighte teris newe
Owt of hire eighen fille, and thus she seyde,
'Now God, thow woost, in thought ne dede untrewe
To Troilus was nevere yet Criseyde.'
With that here heed down in the bed she leyde,   1055
And with the sheete it wreigh, and sighte soore,
And held hire pees; nought o word spak she more.

But now help God to quenchen al this sorwe!
So hope I that he shal, for he best may.
For I have seyn, of a ful misty morwe   1060
Folowen ful ofte a myrie someris day;
And after wynter foloweth grene May.

Men sen alday, and reden ek in stories,
That after sharpe shoures ben victories.

This Troilus, whan he hire wordes herde,　　　　1065
Have ye no care, hym liste nought to slepe;
For it thought hym no strokes of a yerde
To heere or seen Criseyde, his lady, wepe;
But wel he felt about his herte crepe,
For everi tere which that Criseyde asterte,　　　　1070
The crampe of deth, to streyne hym by the herte.

And in his mynde he gan the tyme acorse
That he com there, and that he was born;
For now is wikke torned into worse,
And al that labour he hath don byforn,　　　　1075
He wende it lost; he thoughte he nas but lorn.
'O Pandarus,' thoughte he, 'allas, thi wile
Serveth of nought, so weylaway, the while!'

And therwithal he heng adown the heed,
And fil on knees, and sorwfully he sighte.　　　　1080
What myghte he seyn? He felte he nas but deed,
For wroth was she that sholde his sorwes lighte.
But natheles, whan that he speken myghte,
Than seyde he thus, 'God woot that of this game,
Whan al is wist, than am I nought to blame.'　　　　1085

Therwith the sorwe so his herte shette,
That from his eyen fil ther nought a tere,
And every spirit his vigour in-knette,
So they astoned or oppressed were.
The felyng of his sorwe, or of his fere,　　　　1090
Or of aught elles, fled was out of towne;
And down he fel al sodeynly aswowne.

This was no litel sorwe for to se;
But al was hust, and Pandare up as faste –
'O nece, pes, or we be lost!' quod he,　　　　1095
'Beth naught agast!' but certeyn, at the laste,
For this or that, he into bed hym caste,

And seyde, 'O thef, is this a mannes herte!'
And of he rente al to his bare sherte;

And seyde, 'Nece, but ye helpe us now,   1100
Allas, youre owen Troilus is lorn!'
'Iwis, so wolde I, and I wiste how,
Ful fayn,' quod she; 'Allas, that I was born!'
'Yee, nece, wol ye pullen out the thorn
That stiketh in his herte,' quod Pandare,   1105
'Sey "al foryeve," and stynt is al this fare!'

'Ye, that to me,' quod she, 'ful levere were
Than al the good the sonne aboute gooth.'
And therwithal she swor hym in his ere,
'Iwys, my deere herte, I am nought wroth,   1110
Have here my trouthe!' and many an other oth;
'Now speke to me, for it am I, Criseyde!'
But al for nought; yit myght he nought abreyde.

Therwith his pous and paumes of his hondes
They gan to frote, and wete his temples tweyne;   1115
And to deliveren hym fro bittre bondes,
She ofte hym kiste; and shortly for to seyne,
Hym to revoken she did al hire peyne.
And at the laste, he gan his breth to drawe,
And of his swough sone after that adawe,   1120

And gan bet mynde and reson to hym take,
But wonder soore he was abayst, iwis.
And with a sik, whan he gan bet awake,
He seyde, 'O mercy, God, what thyng is this?'
'Why do ye with youreselven thus amys?'   1125
Quod tho Criseyde; 'Is this a mannes game?
What, Troilus, wol ye do thus for shame?'

And therwithal hire arm over hym she leyde,
And al foryaf, and ofte tyme hym keste.
He thonked hire, and to hire spak, and seyde   1130
As fil to purpos for his hertes reste;
And she to that answerde hym as hire leste,

And with hire goodly wordes hym disporte
She gan, and ofte his sorwes to comforte.

Quod Pandarus, 'For aught I kan aspien,   1135
This light, nor I, ne serven here of nought.
Light is nought good for sike folkes yën!
But, for the love of God, syn ye ben brought
In thus good plit, lat now no hevy thought
Ben hangyng in the hertes of yow tweye' –   1140
And bar the candele to the chymeneye.

Soone after this, though it no nede were,
Whan she swiche othes as hire leste devyse
Hadde of hym take, hire thoughte tho no fere,
Ne cause ek non to bidde hym thennes rise.   1145
Yet lasse thyng than othes may suffise
In many a cas; for every wyght, I gesse,
That loveth wel, meneth but gentilesse.

But in effect she wolde wite anon
Of what man, and ek wheer, and also why   1150
He jalous was, syn ther was cause non;
And ek the sygne that he took it by,
She badde hym that to telle hire bisily;
Or elles, certeyn, she bar hym on honde
That this was don of malice, hire to fonde.   1155

Withouten more, shortly for to seyne,
He most obeye unto his lady heste;
And for the lasse harm, he moste feyne.
He seyde hire, whan she was at swiche a feste,
She myght on hym han loked at the leste –   1160
Noot I nought what, al deere ynough a rysshe,
As he that nedes most a cause fisshe.

And she answerde, 'Swete, al were it so,
What harm was that, syn I non yvel mene?
For, by that God that bought us bothe two,   1165
In alle thyng is myn entente cleene.
Swiche argumentes ne ben naught worth a beene.

Wol ye the childissh jalous contrefete?
Now were it worthi that ye were ybete.'

Tho Troilus gan sorwfully to sike;   1170
Lest she be wroth, hym thoughte his herte deyde;
And seyde, 'Allas, upon my sorwes sike
Have mercy, swete herte myn, Criseyde!
And if that in tho wordes that I seyde
Be any wrong, I wol no more trespace.   1175
Doth what yow list, I am al in youre grace.'

And she answerde, 'Of gilt misericorde!
That is to seyn, that I foryeve al this.
And evere more on this nyght yow recorde,
And beth wel war ye do namore amys.'   1180
'Nay, dere herte myn,' quod he, 'iwys!'
'And now,' quod she, 'that I have don yow smerte,
Foryeve it me, myn owene swete herte.'

This Troilus, with blisse of that supprised,
Putte al in Goddes hand, as he that mente   1185
Nothyng but wel; and sodeynly avysed,
He hire in armes faste to hym hente.
And Pandarus, with a ful good entente,
Leyde hym to slepe, and seyde, 'If ye be wise,
Swouneth nought now, lest more folk arise!'   1190

What myghte or may the sely larke seye,
Whan that the sperhauk hath it in his foot?
I kan namore, but of thise ilke tweye –
To whom this tale sucre be or soot –
Though that I tarie a yer, somtyme I moot,   1195
After myn auctour, tellen hire gladnesse,
As wel as I have told hire hevynesse.

Criseyde, which that felte hire thus itake,
As writen clerks in hire bokes olde,
Right as an aspes leef she gan to quake,   1200
Whan she hym felte hire in his armes folde.
But Troilus, al hool of cares colde,

Gan thanken tho the blisful goddes sevene.
Thus sondry peynes bryngen folk to hevene.

This Troilus in armes gan hire streyne,   1205
And seyde, 'O swete, as evere mot I gon,
Now be ye kaught, now is ther but we tweyne!
Now yeldeth yow, for other bote is non!'
To that Criseyde answerde thus anon,
'Ne hadde I er now, my swete herte deere,   1210
Ben yold, ywis, I were now nought heere!'

O, sooth is seyd, that heled for to be
As of a fevre, or other gret siknesse,
Men moste drynke, as men may ofte se,
Ful bittre drynke; and for to han gladnesse,   1215
Men drynken ofte peyne and gret distresse;
I mene it here, as for this aventure,
That thorugh a peyne hath founden al his cure.

And now swetnesse semeth more swete,
That bitternesse assaied was byforn;   1220
For out of wo in blisse now they flete;
Non swich they felten syn that they were born.
Now is this bet than bothe two be lorn.
For love of God, take every womman heede
To werken thus, if it comth to the neede.   1225

Criseyde, al quyt from every drede and tene,
As she that juste cause hadde hym to triste,
Made hym swich feste, it jóye was to scene,
Whan she his trouthe and clene entente wiste;
And as aboute a tree, with many a twiste,   1230
Bytrent and writh the swote wodebynde,
Gan eche of hem in armes other wynde.

And as the newe abaysed nyghtyngale,
That stynteth first whan she bygynneth to synge,
Whan that she hereth any herde tale,   1235
Or in the hegges any wyght stirynge,
And after siker doth hire vois out rynge.

Right so Criseyde, whan hire drede stente,
Opned hire herte, and tolde hym hire entente.

And right as he that seth his deth yshapen,   1240
And dyen mot, in ought that he may gesse,
And sodeynly rescous doth hym escapen,
And from his deth is brought in sykernesse,
For al this world, in swych present gladnesse
Was Troilus, and hath his lady swete.   1245
With worse hap God lat us nevere mete!

Hire armes smale, hire streghte bak and softe,
Hire sydes longe, flesshly, smothe, and white
He gan to stroke, and good thrift bad ful ofte
Hire snowisshe throte, hire brestes rounde and lite. 1250
Thus in this hevene he gan hym to delite,
And therwithal a thousand tyme hire kiste,
That what to don, for joie unnethe he wiste.

Than seyde he thus, 'O Love, O Charite!
Thi moder ek, Citherea the swete,   1255
After thiself next heried be she,
Venus mene I, the wel-willy planete!
And next that, Imeneus, I the grete;
For nevere man was to yow goddes holde
As I, which ye han brought fro cares colde.   1260

'Benigne Love, thow holy bond of thynges,
Whoso wol grace, and list the nought honouren,
Lo, his desir wol fle withouten wynges.
For noldestow of bownte hem socouren
That serven best and most alwey labouren,   1265
Yet were al lost, that dar I wel seyn certes,
But if thi grace passed oure desertes.

'And for thow me, that leest koude disserve
Of hem that noumbred ben unto thi grace,
Hast holpen, ther I likly was to sterve,   1270
And me bistowed in so heigh a place
That thilke boundes may no blisse pace,

I kan namore; but laude and reverence
Be to thy bounte and thyn excellence!'

And therwithal Criseyde anon he kiste,   1275
Of which certein she felte no disese.
And thus seyde he, 'Now wolde God I wiste,
Myn herte swete, how I yow myght plese!
What man,' quod he, 'was evere thus at ese
As I, on which the faireste and the beste   1280
That evere I say, deyneth hire herte reste?

'Here may men seen that mercy passeth right;
Th'experience of that is felt in me,
That am unworthi to so swete a wight.
But herte myn, of youre benignite,   1285
So thynketh, though that I unworthi be,
Yet mot I nede amenden in som wyse,
Right thorugh the vertu of youre heigh servyse.

'And for the love of God, my lady deere,
Syn God hath wrought me for I shall yow serve –   1290
As thus I mene, he wol ye be my steere,
To do me lyve, if that yow liste, or sterve –
So techeth me how that I may disserve
Youre thonk, so that I thorugh myn ignoraunce,
Ne do no thing that yow be displesaunce.   1295

'For certes, fresshe wommanliche wif,
This dar I scye, that trouth and diligence,
That shal ye fynden in me al my lif;
N'y wol nat, certein, breken youre defence;
And if I do, present or in absence,   1300
For love of God, lat sle me with the dede,
If that it like unto youre wommanhede.'

'Iwys,' quod she, 'myn owen hertes list,
My ground of ese, and al myn herte deere,
Gramercy, for on that is al my trist!   1305
But lat us falle awey fro this matere,
For it suffiseth, this that seyd is heere,

And at o word, withouten repentaunce,
Welcome, my knyght, my pees, my suffisaunce!'

Of hire delit, or joies oon the leeste,   1310
Were impossible to my wit to seye;
But juggeth ye that han ben at the feste
Of swich gladnesse, if that hem liste pleye!
I kan namore, but thus thise ilke tweye,
That nyght, bitwixen drede and sikernesse,   1315
Felten in love the grete worthynesse.

O blisful nyght, of hem so longe isought,
How blithe unto hem bothe two thow weere!
Why nad I swich oon with my soule ybought,
Ye, or the leeste joie that was theere?   1320
Awey, thow foule daunger and thow feere,
And lat hem in this hevene blisse dwelle,
That is so heigh that al ne kan I telle!

But soth is, though I kan nat tellen al,
As kan myn auctour, of his excellence,   1325
Yet have I seyd, and God toforn, and shal
In every thyng the grete of his sentence;
And if that ich, at Loves reverence,
Have any word in eched for the beste,
Doth therwithal right as youreselven leste.   1330

For myne wordes, heere and every part,
I speke hem alle under correccioun
Of yow that felyng han in loves art,
And putte it al in youre discrecioun
T' encresse or maken dymynucioun   1335
Of my langage, and that I yow biseche.
But now to purpos of my rather speche.

Thise ilke two, that ben in armes laft,
So loth to hem asonder gon it were,
That ech from other wenden ben biraft,   1340
Or elles, lo, this was hir mooste feere,
That al this thyng but nyce dremes were;

For which ful ofte ech of hem seyde, 'O swete,
Clippe ich yow thus, or elles I it meete?'

And Lord! so he gan goodly on hire se,   1345
That nevere his look ne bleynte from hire face,
And seyde, 'O deere herte, may it be
That it be soth, that ye ben in this place?'
'Yee, herte myn, God thank I of his grace,'
Quod tho Criseyde, and therwithal hym kiste,   1350
That where his spirit was, for joie he nyste.

This Troilus ful ofte hire eyen two
Gan for to kisse, and seyde, 'O eyen clere,
It weren ye that wroughte me swich wo,
Ye humble nettes of my lady deere!   1355
Though ther be mercy writen in youre cheere,
God woot, the text ful hard is, soth, to fynde!
How koude ye withouten bond me bynde?'

Therwith he gan hire faste in armes take,
And wel an hondred tymes gan he syke,   1360
Naught swiche sorwfull sikes as men make
For wo, or elles when that folk ben sike,
But esy sykes, swiche as ben to like,
That shewed his affeccioun withinne;
Of swiche sikes koude he nought bilynne.   1365

Soone after this they spake of sondry thynges,
As fel to purpos of this aventure,
And pleyinge entrechaungeden hire rynges,
Of whiche I kan nought tellen no scripture;
But wel I woot, a broche, gold and asure,   1370
In which a ruby set was lik an herte,
Criseyde hym yaf, and stak it on his sherte.

Lord, trowe ye a coveytous or a wrecche,
That blameth love, and halt of it despit,
That of tho pens that he kan mokre and crecche   1375
Was evere yit yyeven hym swich delit
As is in love, in o poynt, in som plit?

Nay, douteles, for also God me save,
So perfit joie may no nygard have.

They wol seyn 'yis,' but Lord! so that they lye,   1380
Tho besy wrecches, ful of wo and drede!
Thei callen love a woodnesse or folie,
But it shall falle hem as I shal yow rede;
They shal forgon the white and ek the rede,
And lyve in wo, ther God yeve hem meschaunce,   1385
And every lovere in his trouthe avaunce!

As wolde God tho wrecches that dispise
Servise of love hadde erys also longe
As hadde Mida, ful of coveytise,
And therto dronken hadde as hoot and stronge   1390
As Crassus dide for his affectis wronge,
To techen hem that coveytise is vice,
And love is vertu, though men holde it nyce.

Thise ilke two, of whom that I yow seye,
Whan that hire hertes wel assured were,   1395
Tho gonne they to speken and to pleye,
And ek rehercen how, and whan, and where
Thei knewe hem first, and every wo and feere
That passed was; but al swich hevynesse,
I thank it God, was torned to gladnesse.   1400

And evere mo, when that hem fel to speke
Of any wo of swich a tyme agoon,
With kissyng al that tale sholde breke,
And fallen in a newe joye anoon;
And diden al hire myght, syn they were oon,   1405
For to recoveren blisse and ben at eise,
And passed wo with joie contrepeise.

Resoun wol nought that I speke of slep,
For it acordeth nought to my matere.
God woot, they took of that ful litel kep!   1410
But lest this nyght, that was to hem so deere,
Ne sholde in veyn escape in no manere,

It was byset in joie and bisynesse
Of al that souneth into gentilesse.

But whan the cok, comune astrologer, 1415
Gan on his brest to bete and after crowe,
And Lucyfer, the dayes messager,
Gan for to rise, and out hire bemes throwe,
And estward roos, to hym that koude it knowe,
Fortuna Major, that anoon Criseyde, 1420
With herte soor, to Troilus thus seyde:

'Myn hertes lif, my trist, and my plesaunce,
That I was born, allas, what me is wo,
That day of us moot make disseveraunce!
For tyme it is to ryse and hennes go, 1425
Or ellis I am lost for evere mo!
O nyght, allas! why nyltow over us hove,
As longe as whan Almena lay by Jove?

'O blake nyght, as folk in bokes rede,
That shapen art by God this world to hide 1430
At certeyn tymes wyth thi derke wede,
That under that men myghte in reste abide,
Wel oughten bestes pleyne, and folk the chide,
That there as day wyth labour wolde us breste,
That thow thus fleest, and deynest us nought reste. 1435

'Thow doost, allas, to shortly thyn office,
Thow rakle nyght, ther God, maker of kynde,
The, for thyn haste and thyn unkynde vice,
So faste ay to oure hemysperie bynde,
That nevere more under the ground thow wynde! 1440
For now, for thow so hiest out of Troie,
Have I forgon thus hastili my joie!'

This Troilus, that with tho wordes felte,
As thoughte hym tho, for pietous distresse,
The blody teris from his herte melte, 1445
As he that nevere yet swich hevynesse
Assayed hadde, out of so gret gladnesse,

Gan therwithal Criseyde, his lady deere,
In armes streyne, and seyde in this manere:

'O cruel day, accusour of the joie   1450
That nyght and love han stole and faste iwryen,
Acorsed be thi comyng into Troye,
For every bore hath oon of thi bryghte yën!
Envyous day, what list the so to spien?
What hastow lost, why sekestow this place?   1455
Ther God thi light so quenche, for his grace!

'Allas! what have thise loveris the agylt,
Dispitous day? Thyn be the peyne of helle!
For many a lovere hastow slayn, and wilt;
Thy pourynge in wol nowher lat hem dwelle.   1460
What profrestow thi light here for to selle?
Go selle it hem that smale selys grave;
We wol the nought, us nedeth no day have.'

And ek the sonne, Titan, gan he chide,
And seyde, 'O fool, wel may men the dispise,   1465
That hast the Dawyng al nyght by thi syde,
And suffrest hire so soone up fro the rise,
For to disese loveris in this wyse.
What! holde youre bed ther, thow, and ek thi
    Morwe!
I bidde God, so yeve yow bothe sorwe!'   1470

Therwith ful soore he syghte, and thus he seyde:
'My lady right, and of my wele or wo
The welle and roote, O goodly myn, Criseyde,
And shal I rise, allas, and shal I so?
Now fele I that myn herte moot a-two.   1475
For how sholde I my lif an houre save,
Syn that with yow is al the lyf ich have?

'What shal I don? For, certes, I not how,
Ne whan, allas! I shal the tyme see
That in this plit I may ben eft with yow.   1480
And of my lif, God woot how that shal be,
Syn that desir right now so biteth me,

That I am ded anon, but I retourne.
How sholde I longe, allas, fro yow sojourne?

'But natheles, myn owen lady bright,   1485
Yit were it so that I wiste outrely
That I, youre humble servant and youre knyght,
Were in youre herte iset as fermely
As ye in myn, the which thyng, trewely,
Me levere were than thise worldes tweyne,   1490
Yet sholde I bet enduren al my peyne.'

To that Criseyde answerde right anon,
And with a sik she seyde, 'O herte deere,
The game, ywys, so ferforth now is gon,
That first shal Phebus fallen fro his spere,   1495
And everich egle ben the dowves feere,
And everi roche out of his place sterte,
Er Troilus out of Criseydes herte.

'Ye ben so depe in-with myn herte grave,
That, though I wolde it torne out of my thought,   1500
As wisly verray God my soule save,
To dyen in the peyne, I koude nought.
And, for the love of God that us hath wrought,
Lat in youre brayn non other fantasie
So crepe, that it cause me to dye!   1505

'And that ye me wolde han as faste in mynde
As I have yow, that wolde I yow biseche;
And if I wiste sothly that to fynde,
God myghte nought a poynt my joies eche.
But herte myn, withouten more speche,   1510
Beth to me trewe, or ellis were it routhe;
For I am thyn, by God and by my trouthe!

'Beth glad, forthy, and lyve in sikernesse!
Thus seyde I nevere er this, ne shal to mo;
And if to yow it were a gret gladnesse   1515
To torne ayeyn soone after that ye go,
As fayn wolde I as ye that it were so,

As wisly God myn herte brynge at reste!'
And hym in armes tok, and ofte keste.

Agayns his wil, sith it mot nedes be,   1520
This Troilus up ros, and faste hym cledde,
And in his armes took his lady free
An hondred tyme, and on his wey hym spedde;
And with swiche voys as though his herte bledde,
He seyde, 'Farewel, dere herte swete,   1525
Ther God us graunte sownde and soone to mete!'

To which no word for sorwe she answerde,
So soore gan his partyng hire distreyne;
And Troilus unto his paleys ferde,
As wo-bygon as she was, soth to seyne.   1530
So harde hym wrong of sharp desir the peyne,
For to ben eft there he was in plesaunce,
That it may nevere out of his remembraunce.

Retorned to his real paleys soone,
He softe into his bed gan for to slynke,   1535
To slepe longe, as he was wont to doone.
Bul al for nought; he may wel ligge and wynke,
But slep ne may ther in his herte synke,
Thynkyng how she, for whom desir hym brende,
A thousand fold was worth more than he wende.   1540

And in his thought gan up and down to wynde
Hire wordes alle, and every countenaunce,
And fermely impressen in his mynde
The leeste point that to him was plesaunce;
And verraylich, of thilke remembraunce,   1545
Desir al newe hym brende, and lust to brede
Gan more than erst, and yet took he non hede.

Criseyde also, right in the same wyse,
Of Troilus gan in hire herte shette
His worthynesse, his lust, his dedes wise,   1550
His gentilesse, and how she with hym mette,
Thonkynge Love he so wel hire bisette;

Desirying eft to han hire herte deere
In swich a plit, she dorste make hym cheere.

Pandare, o-morwe which that comen was   1555
Unto his nece and gan hire faire grete,
Seyde, 'Al this nyght so reyned it, allas,
That al my drede is that ye, nece swete,
Han litel laiser had to slepe and mete.
Al nyght,' quod he, 'hath reyn so do me wake,   1560
That som of us, I trowe, hire hedes ake.'

And ner he com, and seyde, 'How stant it now
This mury morwe? Nece, how kan ye fare?'
Criseyde answerde, 'Nevere the bet for yow,
Fox that ye ben! God yeve your herte kare!
God help me so, ye caused al this fare,   1565
Trowe I,' quod she, 'for al youre wordes white.
O, whoso seeth yow, knoweth yow ful lite.'

With that she gan hire face for to wrye
With the shete, and wax for shame al reed;   1570
And Pandarus gan under for to prie,
And seyde, 'Nece, if that I shal be ded,
Have here a swerd and smyteth of myn hed!'
With that his arm al sodeynly he thriste
Under hire nekke, and at the laste hire kyste.   1575

I passe al that which chargeth nought to seye.
What! God foryaf his deth, and she al so
Foryaf, and with here uncle gan to pleye,
For other cause was ther noon than so.
But of this thing right to the effect to go,   1580
Whan tyme was, hom to here hous she wente,
And Pandarus hath fully his entente.

Now torne we ayeyn to Troilus,
That resteles ful longe abedde lay,
And pryvely sente after Pandarus,   1585
To hym to com in al the haste he may.
He com anon, nought ones seyde he nay;

And Troilus ful sobrely he grette,
And down upon his beddes syde hym sette.

This Troilus, with al th'affeccioun   1590
Of frendes love that herte may devyse,
To Pandarus on knowes fil adown,
And er that he wolde of the place arise,
He gan hym thonken in his beste wise
An hondred sythe, and gan the tyme blesse   1595
That he was born, to brynge hym fro destresse.

He seyde, 'O frend of frendes the alderbeste
That evere was, the sothe for to telle,
Thow hast in hevene ybrought my soule at reste
Fro Flegetoun, the fery flood of helle;   1600
That, though I myght a thousand tymes selle,
Upon a day, my lif in thi servise,
It myghte naught a moote in that suffise.

'The sonne, which that al the world may se,
Saugh nevere yet my lif, that dar I leye,   1605
So inly fair and goodly as is she,
Whos I am al, and shal, tyl that I deye.
And that I thus am hires, dar I seye,
That thanked be the heighe worthynesse
Of Love, and ek thi kynde bysynesse.   1610

'Thus hastow me no litel thing yyive,
For which to the obliged be for ay
My lif, and whi? For thorugh thyn help I lyve,
Or elles ded hadde I ben many a day.'
And with that word down in his bed he lay,   1615
And Pandarus ful sobrely hym herde
Til al was seyd, and than he thus answerde:

'My deere frend, if I have don for the
In any cas, God wot, it is me lief;
And am as glad as man may of it be,   1620
God help me so; but tak it nat a-grief
That I shal seyn, be war of this meschief,

That, there as thow now brought art in thy blisse,
That thow thiself ne cause it nat to misse.

'For of fortunes sharpe adversitee   1625
The worste kynde of infortune is this,
A man to han ben in prosperitee,
And it remembren, whan it passed is.
Th'art wis ynough, forthi do nat amys:
Be naught to rakel, theigh thow sitte warme;   1630
For if thow be, certeyn, it wol the harme.

'Thow art at ese, and hold the wel therinne;
For also seur as reed is every fir,
As gret a craft is kepe wel as wynne.
Bridle alwey wel thi speche and thi desir,   1635
For worldly joie halt nought but by a wir.
That preveth wel it brest alday so ofte;
Forthi nede is to werken with it softe.'

Quod Troilus, 'I hope, and God toforn,
My deere frend, that I shal so me beere,   1640
That in my gylt ther shal nothyng be lorn,
N'y nyl nought rakle as for to greven heere.
It nedeth naught this matere ofte stere;
For wystestow myn herte wel, Pandare,
God woot, of this thow woldest litel care.'   1645

Tho gan he telle hym of his glade nyght,
And wherof first his herte dred, and how,
And seyde, 'Frend, as I am trewe knyght,
And by that feyth I shal to God and yow,
I hadde it nevere half so hote as now;   1650
And ay the more that desir me biteth
To love hire best, the more it me deliteth.

'I not myself naught wisly what it is;
But now I feele a newe qualitee,
Yee, al another than I dide er this.'   1655
Pandare answerd, and seyde thus, that he
That ones may in hevene blisse be –

'He feleth other weyes, dar I leye,
Than thilke tyme he first herde of it seye.'

This is o word for al; this Troilus   1660
Was nevere ful to speke of this matere,
And for to preisen unto Pandarus
The bounte of his righte lady deere,
And Pandarus to thanke and maken cheere.
This tale was ay span-newe to bygynne,   1665
Til that the nyght departed hem atwynne.

Soon after this, for that Fortune it wolde,
Icomen was the blisful tyme swete
That Troilus was warned that he sholde,
There he was erst, Criseyde his lady mete;   1670
For which he felte his herte in joie flete,
And feithfully gan alle the goddes herie;
And lat se now if that he kan be merie!

And holden was the forme and al the wise
Of hire commyng, and ek of his also,   1675
As it was erst, which nedeth nought devyse.
But pleynly to th'effect right for to go,
In joie and suerte Pandarus hem two
Abedde brought, whan that hem bothe leste,
And thus they ben in quyete and in reste.   1680

Nought nedeth it to yow, syn they ben met,
To axe at me if that they blithe were;
For if it erst was wel, tho was it bet
A thousand fold; this nedeth nought enquere.
Agon was every sorwe and every feere.   1685
And bothe, ywys, they hadde – and so they wende –
As muche joie as herte may comprende.

This is no litel thyng of for to seye;
This passeth every wit for to devyse;
For eche of hem gan otheres lust obeye.   1690
Felicite, which that thise clerkes wise
Comenden so, ne may nought here suffise;

This joie may nought writen be with inke;
This passeth al that herte may bythynke.

But cruel day, so wailaway the stounde!   1695
Gan for t'aproche, as they by sygnes knewe;
For which hem thoughte feelen dethis wownde.
So wo was hem that changen gan hire hewe,
And day they gonnen to despise al newe,
Callyng it traitour, envyous, and worse,   1700
And bitterly the dayes light thei corse.

Quod Troilus, 'Allas, now am I war
That Pirous and tho swifte steedes thre,
Which that drawen forth the sonnes char,
Han gon som bi-path in dispit of me;   1705
That maketh it so soone day to be;
And, for the sonne hym hasteth thus to rise,
Ne shal I nevere don him sacrifise.'

But nedes day departe hem moste soone,
And whan hire speche don was and hire cheere,   1710
They twynne anon, as they were wont to doone,
And setten tyme of metyng eft yfeere.
And many a nyght they wroughte in this manere,
And thus Fortune a tyme ledde in joie
Criseyde, and ek this kynges sone of Troie.   1715

In suffisaunce, in blisse, and in singynges,
This Troilus gan al his lif to lede.
He spendeth, jousteth, maketh festeynges;
He yeveth frely ofte, and chaungeth wede,
And held aboute hym alwey, out of drede,   1720
A world of folk, as com hym wel of kynde,
The fresshest and the beste he koude fynde;

That swich a vois was of hym and a stevene
Thorughout the world, of honour and largesse,
That it up rong unto the yate of hevene.   1725
And, as in love, he was in swich gladnesse,
That in his herte he demed, as I gesse,

That ther nys lovere in this world at ese
So wel as he; and thus gan love hym plese.

The goodlihede or beaute which that Kynde   1730
In any other lady hadde yset
Kan nought the montance of a knotte unbynde,
Aboute his herte, of al Criseydes net.
He was so narwe ymasked and yknet,
That it undon on any manere syde –   1735
That nyl naught ben, for aught that may bitide.

And by the hond ful ofte he wolde take
This Pandarus, and into gardyn lede,
And swich a feste and swich a proces make
Hym of Criseyde, and of hire womanhede,   1740
And of hire beaute, that, withouten drede,
It was an hevene his wordes for to here;
And thanne he wolde synge in this manere:

'Love, that of erthe and se hath governaunce,
Love, that his hestes hath in hevenes hye,   1745
Love, that with an holsom alliaunce
Halt peples joyned, as hym lest hem gye,
Love, that knetteth lawe of compaignie,
And couples doth in vertu for to dwelle,
Bynd this acord, that I have told and telle.   1750

'That that the world with feith, which that is stable,
Diverseth so his stowndes concordynge,
That elementz that ben so discordable
Holden a bond perpetuely durynge,
That Phebus mote his rosy day forth brynge,   1755
And that the mone hath lordshipe over the nyghtes –
Al this doth Love, ay heried be his myghtes!

'That that the se, that gredy is to flowen,
Constreyneth to a certeyn ende so
His flodes that so fiersly they ne growen   1760
To drenchen erthe and al for evere mo;
And if that Love aught lete his bridel go,

Al that now loveth asondre sholde lepe,
And lost were al that Love halt now to-hepe.

'So wolde God, that auctour is of kynde,   1765
That with his bond Love of his vertu liste
To cerclen hertes alle, and faste bynde,
That from his bond no wight the wey out wiste;
And hertes colde, hem wolde I that he twiste
To make hem love, and that hem liste ay rewe   1770
On hertes sore, and kepe hem that ben trewe!' –

In alle nedes, for the townes werre,
He was, and ay, the first in armes dyght,
And certeynly, but if that bokes erre,
Save Ector most ydred of any wight;   1775
And this encres of hardynesse and myght
Com hym of love, his ladies thank to wynne,
That altered his spirit so withinne.

In tyme of trewe, on haukyng wolde he ride,
Or elles honte boor, beer, or lyoun;   1780
The smale bestes leet he gon biside.
And whan that he com ridyng into town,
Ful ofte his lady from hire wyndow down,
As fressh as faukoun comen out of muwe,
Ful redy was hym goodly to saluwe.   1785

And moost of love and vertu was his speche,
And in despit hadde alle wrecchednesse;
And douteles, no nede was hym biseche
To honouren hem that hadde worthynesse,
And esen hem that weren in destresse.   1790
And glad was he if any wyght wel ferde,
That lovere was, whan he it wiste or herde.

For, soth to seyne, he lost held every wyght,
But if he were in Loves heigh servise –
I mene folk that oughte it ben of right.   1795
And over al this, so wel koude he devyse
Of sentement, and in so unkouth wise

Al his array, that every lovere thoughte
That al was wel, what so he seyde or wroughte.

And though that he be come of blood roial,   1800
Hym liste of pride at no wight for to chace;
Benigne he was to ech in general,
For which he gat hym thank in every place.
Thus wolde Love, yheried be his grace,
That pride, envye, and ire, and avarice   1805
He gan to fle, and everich other vice.

Thow lady bryght, the doughter to Dyone,
Thy blynde and wynged sone ek, daun Cupide,
Yee sustren nyne ek, that by Elicone
In hil Pernaso listen for t'abide,   1810
That ye thus fer han deyned me to gyde,
I kan namore, but syn that ye wol wende,
Ye heried ben for ay withouten ende!

Thorugh yow have I seyd fully in my song
Th'effect and joie of Troilus servise,   1815
Al be that ther was som disese among,
As to myn auctour listeth to devise.
My thridde bok now ende ich in this wyse,
And Troilus in luste and in quiete
Is with Criseyde, his owen herte swete.   1820

Book IV

PROLOGUE

But al to litel, weylaway the whyle,
Lasteth swich joie, ythonked be Fortune,
That semeth trewest whan she wol bygyle,
And kan to fooles so hire song entune,
That she hem hent and blent, traitour comune!   5
And whan a wight is from hire whiel ythrowe,
Than laugheth she, and maketh hym the mowe.

From Troilus she gan hire brighte face
Awey to writhe, and tok of hym non heede,
But caste hym clene out of his lady grace,   10
And on hire whiel she sette up Diomede;
For which right now myn herte gynneth blede,
And now my penne, allas! with which I write,
Quaketh for drede of that I moste endite.

For how Criseyde Troilus forsook,   15
Or at the leeste, how that she was unkynde,
Moot hennesforth ben matere of my book,
As writen folk thorugh which it is in mynde.
Allas! that they sholde evere cause fynde
To speke hire harm, and if they on hire lye,   20
Iwis, hemself sholde han the vilanye.

O ye Herynes, Nyghtes doughtren thre,
That endeles compleignen evere in pyne,
Megera, Alete, and ek Thesiphone;
Thow cruel Mars ek, fader to Quyryne,   25
This ilke ferthe book me helpeth fyne,
So that the losse of lyf and love yfeere
Of Troilus be fully shewed heere.

As the war proceeds prisoners are taken. Calchas asks the
Greeks to offer a prominent Trojan for his daughter, and the
Trojan Parliament agrees to exchange Criseyde for Antenor.
Troilus and Criseyde are in agony at the thought of separation.
No device that Troilus can think of is agreeable to Criseyde,
and in a long soliloquy he concludes he is fore-ordained to lose
her. Criseyde says she will go to the Greeks, but will return
secretly on her own through the enemy lines on the tenth day
after.

Book V

PROLOGUE

Aprochen gan the fatal destyne
That Joves hath in disposicioun,
And to yow, angry Parcas, sustren thre,
Committeth, to don execucioun;
For which Criseyde moste out of the town,   5
And Troilus shal dwellen forth in pyne
Til Lachesis his thred no lenger twyne.

The golde-tressed Phebus heighe on-lofte
Thries hadde alle with his bemes clene
The snowes molte, and Zepherus as ofte   10
Ibrought ayeyn the tendre leves grene,
Syn that the sone of Ecuba the queenc
Bigan to love hire first for whom his sorwe
Was al, that she departe sholde a-morwe.

THE STORY

Ful redy was at prime Diomede,   15
Criseyde unto the Grekis oost to lede,
For sorwe of which she felt hire herte blede,
As she that nyste what was best to rede.
And trewely, as men in bokes rede,
Men wiste nevere womman han the care,   20
Ne was so loth out of a town to fare.

This Troilus, withouten reed or loore,
As man that hath his joies ek forlore,
Was waytyng on his lady evere more
As she that was the sothfast crop and more   25
Of al his lust or joies here-bifore.
But Troilus, now far-wel al thi joie,
For shaltow nevere sen hire eft in Troie!

Soth is that while he bood in this manere,
He gan his wo ful manly for to hide, 30
That wel unnethe it sene was in his chere;
But at the yate ther she sholde out ride,
With certeyn folk he hoved hire t'abide,
So wo-bigon, al wolde he naught hym pleyne,
That on his hors unnethe he sat for peyne. 35

For ire he quook, so gan his herte gnawe,
Whan Diomede on horse gan hym dresse,
And seyde to hymself this ilke sawe:
'Allas!' quod he, 'thus foul a wrecchednesse,
Whi suffre ich it? Whi nyl ich it redresse? 40
Were it nat bet atones for to dye
Than evere more in langour thus to drye?

'Whi nyl I make atones riche and pore
To have inough to doone, er that she go?
Why nyl I brynge al Troie upon a roore? 45
Whi nyl I slen this Diomede also?
Why nyl I rather with a man or two
Stele hire away? Whi wol I this endure?
Whi nyl I helpen to myn owen cure?'

But why he nolde don so fel a dede, 50
That shal I seyn, and whi hym liste it spare:
He hadde in herte alweyes a manere drede
Lest that Criseyde, in rumour of this fare,
Sholde han ben slayn; lo, this was al his care.
And ellis, certeyn, as I seyde yore, 55
He hadde it don, withouten wordes more.

Criseyde, whan she redy was to ride,
Ful sorwfully she sighte, and seyde 'allas!'
But forth she moot, for aught that may bitide,
And forth she rit ful sorwfully a pas. 60
Ther is non other remedie in this cas.
What wonder is, though that hire sore smerte,
Whan she forgoth hire owen swete herte?

This Troilus, in wise of curteysie,
With hauke on honde, and with an huge route   65
Of knyghtes, rood and did hire companye,
Passyng al the valeye fer withoute;
And ferther wolde han riden, out of doute,
Ful fayn, and wo was hym to gon so sone;
But torne he moste, and it was ek to done.   70

And right with that was Antenor ycome
Out of the Grekis oost, and every wight
Was of it glad, and seyde he was welcome.
And Troilus, al nere his herte light,
He peyned hym with al his fulle myght   75
Hym to withholde of wepyng atte leeste,
And Antenor he kiste, and made feste.

And therwithal he moste his leve take,
And caste his eye upon hire pitously,
And neer he rood, his cause for to make,   80
To take hire by the honde al sobrely.
And Lord! so she gan wepen tendrely!
And he ful softe and sleighly gan hire seye,
'Now holde youre day, and do me nat to deye.'

With that his courser torned he aboute   85
With face pale, and unto Diomede
No word he spak, ne non of al his route;
Of which the sone of Tideus took hede,
As he that koude more than the crede
In swich a craft, and by the reyne hire hente;   90
And Troilus to Troie homward he wente.

This Diomede, that ledde hire by the bridel,
Whan that he saugh the folke of Troie aweye,
Thoughte, 'Al my labour shal nat ben on ydel,
If that I may, for somwhat shal I seye.   95
For at the werste it may yet shorte oure weye.
I have herd seyd ek tymes twyes twelve,
"He is a fool that wole foryete hymselve."''

But natheles, this thoughte he wel ynough,
That 'certeynlich I am aboute nought,   100
If that I speke of love, or make it tough;
For douteles, if she have in hire thought
Hym that I gesse, he may nat ben ybrought
So soon awey; but I shal fynde a meene,
That she naught wite as yet shal what I mene.'   105

This Diomede, as he that koude his good,
Whan this was don, gan fallen forth in speche
Of this and that, and axed whi she stood
In swich disese, and gan hire ek biseche,
That if that he encresse myghte or eche   110
With any thyng hire ese, that she sholde
Comaunde it hym, and seyde he don it wolde.

For treweliche he swor hire, as a knyght,
That ther nas thyng with which he myghte hire plese,
That he nolde don his peyne and al his myght   115
To don it, for to done hire herte an ese;
And preyede hire, she wolde hire sorwe apese,
And seyde, 'Iwis, we Grekis kan have joie
To honouren yow, as wel as folk of Troie.'

He seyde ek thus, 'I woot yow thynketh straunge –   120
Ne wonder is, for it is to yow newe –
Th'aquayntaunce of thise Troians to chaunge
For folk of Grece, that ye nevere knewe.
But wolde nevere God but if as trewe
A Grek ye sholde among us alle fynde   125
As any Troian is, and ek as kynde.

'And by the cause I swor yow right, lo, now,
To ben youre frend, and helply, to my myght,
And for that more aquayntaunce ek of yow
Have ich had than another straunger wight,   130
So fro this forth, I pray yow, day and nyght,
Comaundeth me, how soore that me smerte,
To don al that may like unto youre herte;

'And that ye me wolde as youre brother trete;
And taketh naught my frendshipe in despit;   135
And though youre sorwes be for thynges grete,
Not I nat whi, but out of more respit,
Myn herte hath for t'amende it gret delit.
And if I may youre harmes nat redresse,
I am right sory for youre hevynesse.   140

'For though ye Troians with us Grekes wrothe
Han many a day ben, alwey yet, parde,
O god of Love in soth we serven bothe.
And, for the love of God, my lady fre,
Whomso ye hate, as beth nat wroth with me;   145
For trewely, ther kan no wyght yow serve,
That half so loth youre wratthe wold disserve.

'And nere it that we ben so neigh the tente
Of Calcas, which that sen us bothe may,
I wolde of this yow telle al myn entente;   150
But this enseled til anothir day.
Yeve me youre hond; I am, and shal ben ay,
God helpe me so, while that my lyf may dure,
Youre owene aboven every creature.

'Thus seyde I nevere er now to womman born;   155
For, God myn herte as wisly glade so,
I loved never womman here-biforn
As paramours, ne nevere shal no mo.
And, for the love of God, beth nat my fo,
Al kan I naught to yow, my lady deere,   160
Compleyne aright, for I am yet to leere.

'And wondreth nought, myn owen lady bright,
Though that I speke of love to yow thus blyve;
For I have herd er this of many a wight,
Hath loved thyng he nevere saigh his lyve.   165
Ek I am nat of power for to stryve
Ayeyns the god of Love, but hym obeye
I wole awey; and mercy I yow preye.

'Ther ben so worthi knyghtes in this place,
And ye so fayr, that everich of hem alle   170
Wol peynen hym to stonden in youre grace.
But myghte me so faire a grace falle,
That ye me for youre servant wolde calle,
So lowely ne so trewely yow serve
Nil non of hem, as I shal, til I sterve.'   175

Criseyde unto that purpos lite answerde,
As she that was with sorwe oppressed so
That, in effect, she naught his tales herde
But her and ther, now here a word or two.
Hire thoughte hire sorwful herte brast a-two;   180
For whan she gan hire fader fer espie,
Wel neigh down of hire hors she gan to sye.

But natheles she thonked Diomede
Of al his travaile and his goode cheere,
And that hym list his frendshipe hire to bede;   185
And she accepteth it in good manere,
And wol do fayn that is hym lief and dere,
And trusten hym she wolde, and wel she myghte,
As seyde she; and from hire hors sh'alighte.

Hire fader hath hire in his armes nome,   190
And twenty tyme he kiste his doughter sweete,
And seyde, 'O deere doughter myn, welcome!'
She seyde ek, she was fayn with hym to mete,
And stood forth muwet, milde, and mansuete.
But here I leve hire with hire fader dwelle,   195
And forth I wol of Troilus yow telle.

To Troie is come this woful Troilus,
In sorwe aboven alle sorwes smerte,
With feloun look and face dispitous.
Tho sodeynly doun from his hors he sterte,   200
And thorugh his paleis, with a swollen herte,
To chaumbre he wente; of nothyng took he hede,
Ne non to hym dar speke a word for drede.

And ther his sorwes that he spared hadde
He yaf an issue large, and 'deth!' he criede;   205
And in his throwes frenetik and madde
He corseth Jove, Appollo, and ek Cupide,
He corseth Ceres, Bacus, and Cipride,
His burthe, hymself, his fate, and ek nature,
And, save his lady, every creature.   210

To bedde he goth, and walweth ther and torneth
In furie, as doth he Ixion in helle;
And in this wise he neigh til day sojorneth.
But tho bigan his herte a lite unswelle
Thorugh teris, which that gonnen up to welle;   215
And pitously he cryde upon Criseyde . . .

Troilus laments Criseyde's absence. Pandarus, not believing
that Criseyde will return, nevertheless encourages Troilus to
hope. Criseyde, 'With wommen fewe, among the Grekis
stronge' (V, 688), regrets her foolish decision to make her own
way back and pines for Troilus, but, the poet tells us, before
two months Troy and Troilus 'Shal knotteles thorughout
hire herte slide; / For she wol take a purpos for t'abyde'
(V, 769–70).

This Diomede, of whom yow telle I gan,
Goth now withinne hymself ay arguynge
With al the sleghte, and al that evere he kan,
How he may best, with shortest taryinge,
Into his net Criseydes herte brynge.   775
To this entent he koude nevere fyne;
To fisshen hire, he leyde out hook and lyne.

But natheles, wel in his herte he thoughte,
That she nas nat withoute a love in Troie;
For nevere, sythen he hire thennes broughte,   780
Ne koude he sen hire laughe or maken joie.
He nyst how best hire herte for t'acoye.
'But for t'asay,' he seyde, 'it naught ne greveth;
For he that naught n'asaieth, naught n'acheveth.'

Yet seide he to hymself upon a nyght,   785
'Now am I nat a fool, that woot wel how
Hire wo for love is of another wight,
And hereupon to gon assaye hire now?
I may wel wite, it nyl nat ben my prow.
For wise folk in bookes it expresse,   790
"Men shal nat wowe a wight in hevynesse."

'But whoso myghte wynnen swich a flour
From hym for whom she morneth nyght and day,
He myghte seyn he were a conquerour.'
And right anon, as he that bold was ay,   795
Thoughte in his herte, 'Happe how happe may,
Al sholde I dye, I wol hire herte seche!
I shal namore lesen but my speche.'

This Diomede, as bokes us declare,
Was in his nedes prest and corageous,   800
With sterne vois and myghty lymes square,
Hardy, testif, strong, and chivalrous
Of dedes, like his fader Tideus.
And som men seyn he was of tonge large;
And heir he was of Calydoigne and Arge.   805

Criseyde mene was of hire stature,
Therto of shap, of face, and ek of cheere,
Ther myghte ben no fairer creature.
And ofte tyme this was hire manere,
To gon ytressed with hire heres clere   810
Doun by hire coler at hire bak byhynde,
Which with a thred of gold she wolde bynde.

And, save hire browes joyneden yfere,
Ther nas no lak, in aught I kan espien.
But for to speken of hire eyen cleere,   815
Lo, trewely, they writen that hire syen,
That Paradis stood formed in hire yën.
And with hire riche beaute evere more
Strof love in hire ay, which of hem was more.

She sobre was, ek symple, and wys withal,   820
The best ynorisshed ek that myghte be,
And goodly of hire speche in general,
Charitable, estatlich, lusty, and fre;
Ne nevere mo ne lakked hire pite;
Tendre-herted, slydynge of corage;   825
But trewely, I kan nat telle hire age.

And Troilus wel woxen was in highte,
And complet formed by proporcioun
So wel that kynde it nought amenden myghte;
Young, fressh, strong, and hardy as lyoun;   830
Trewe as steel in ech condicioun;
Oon of the beste entecched creature
That is, or shal, whil that the world may dure.

And certeynly in storye it is yfounde,
That Troilus was nevere unto no wight,   835
As in his tyme, in no degree secounde
In durryng don that longeth to a knyght.
Al myghte a geant passen hym of myght,
His herte ay with the first and with the beste
Stood paregal, to durre don that hym leste.   840

But for to tellen forth of Diomede:
It fel that after, on the tenthe day
Syn that Criseyde out of the citee yede,
This Diomede, as fressh as braunche in May,
Com to the tente, ther as Calkas lay,   845
And feyned hym with Calkas han to doone;
But what he mente, I shal yow tellen soone.

Criseyde, at shorte wordes for to telle,
Welcomed hym, and down hym by hire sette;
And he was ethe ynough to maken dwelle!   850
And after this, withouten longe lette,
The spices and the wyn men forth hem fette;
And forth they speke of this and that yfeere,
As frendes don, of which som shal ye heere.

He gan first fallen of the werre in speche   855
Bitwixe hem and the folk of Troie town;
And of th'assege he gan hire ek biseche
To telle hym what was hire opynyoun.
Fro that demaunde he so descendeth down
To axen hire, if that hire straunge thoughte   860
The Grekis gise, and werkes that they wroughte;

And whi hire fader tarieth so longe
To wedden hire unto som worthy wight.
Criseyde, that was in hire peynes stronge
For love of Troilus, hire owen knyght,   865
As ferforth as she konnyng hadde or myght,
Answerde hym tho; but, as of his entente,
It semed nat she wiste what he mente.

But natheles, this ilke Diomede
Gan in hymself assure, and thus he seyde: 870
'If ich aright have taken of yow hede,
Me thynketh thus, O lady myn, Criscyde,
That syn I first hond on youre bridel leyde,
Whan ye out come of Troie by the morwe,
Ne koude I nevere sen yow but in sorwe.   875

'Kan I nat seyn what may the cause be,
But if for love of som Troian it were,
The which right sore wolde athynken me,
That ye for any wight that dwelleth there
Sholden spille a quarter of a tere,   880
Or pitously youreselven so bigile;
For dredeles, it is nought worth the while.

'The folk of Troie, as who seyth, alle and some
In prisoun ben, as ye youreselven se;
Nor thennes shal nat oon on-lyve come   885
For al the gold atwixen sonne and se.
Trusteth wel, and understondeth me,
Ther shal nat oon to mercy gon on-lyve,
Al were he lord of worldes twiës fyve!

'Swiche wreche on hem, for fecchynge of Eleyne,   890
Ther shal ben take, er that we hennes wende,
That Manes, which that goddes ben of peyne,
Shal ben agast that Grekes wol hem shende.
And men shul drede, unto the worldes ende,
From hennesforth to ravysshen any queene,   895
So cruel shal oure wreche on hem be seene.

'And but if Calkas lede us with ambages,
That is to seyn, with double wordes slye,
Swiche as men clepen a word with two visages,
Ye shal wel knowen that I naught ne lye,   900
And al this thyng right sen it with youre yë,
And that anon, ye nyl nat trowe how sone.
Now taketh hede, for it is for to doone.

'What! wene ye youre wise fader wolde
Han yeven Antenor for yow anon,   905
If he ne wiste that the cite sholde
Destroied ben? Whi, nay, so mote I gon!
He knew ful wel ther shal nat scapen oon
That Troian is; and for the grete feere,
He dorste nat ye dwelte lenger there.   910

'What wol ye more, lufsom lady deere?
Lat Troie and Troian fro youre herte pace!
Drif out that bittre hope, and make good cheere,
And clepe ayeyn the beaute of youre face,
That ye with salte teris so deface.   915
For Troie is brought in swich a jupartie,
That it to save is now no remedie.

'And thenketh wel, ye shal in Grekis fynde
A moore parfit love, er it be nyght,
Than any Troian is, and more kynde,   920
And bet to serven yow wol don his myght.
And if ye vouchesauf, my lady bright,
I wol ben he to serven yow myselve,
Yee, levere than be lord of Greces twelve!'

And with that word he gan to waxen red,   925
And in in his speche a litel wight he quok,
And caste asyde a litle wight his hed,
And stynte a while; and afterward he wok,
And sobreliche on hire he threw his lok,
And seyde, 'I am, al be it yow no joie,   930
As gentil man as any wight in Troie.

'For if my fader Tideus,' he seyde,
'Ilyved hadde, ich hadde ben, er this,
Of Calydoyne and Arge a kyng, Criseyde!
And so hope I that I shal yet, iwis.   935
But he was slayn, allas! the more harm is,
Unhappily at Thebes al to rathe,
Polymytes and many a man to scathe.

'But herte myn, syn that I am youre man –
And ben the first of whom I seche grace –   940
To serve yow as hertely as I kan,
And evere shal, whil I to lyve have space,
So, er that I departe out of this place,
Ye wol me graunte that I may to-morwe,
At bettre leyser, tellen yow my sorwe.'   945

What sholde I telle his wordes that he seyde?
He spak inough, for o day at the meeste.
It preveth wel, he spak so that Criseyde
Graunted, on the morwe, at his requeste,
For to speken with hym at the leeste,   950
So that he nolde speke of swich matere.
And thus to hym she seyde, as ye may here,

As she that hadde hire herte on Troilus
So faste, that ther may it non arace;
And strangely she spak, and seyde thus:
'O Diomede, I love that ilke place   955
Ther I was born; and Joves, for his grace,
Delyvere it soone of al that doth it care!
God, for thy myght, so leve it wel to fare!

'That Grekis wolde hire wrath on Troie wreke,   960
If that they myght, I knowe it wel, iwis.
But it shal naught byfallen as ye speke,
And God toforn! and forther over this,
I woot my fader wys and redy is;
And that he me hath bought, as ye me tolde,   965
So deere, I am the more unto hym holde.

'That Grekis ben of heigh condicioun,
I woot ek wel; but certeyn, men shal fynde
As worthi folk withinne Troie town,
As konnyng, and as parfit, and as kynde,   970
As ben bitwixen Orkades and Inde.
And that ye koude wel yowre lady serve,
I trowe ek wel, hire thank for to deserve.

'But as to speke of love, ywis,' she seyde,
'I hadde a lord, to whom I wedded was,   975
The whos myn herte al was, til that he deyde;
And other love, as help me now Pallas,
Ther in myn herte nys, ne nevere was.
And that ye ben of noble and heigh kynrede,
I have wel herd it tellen, out of drede.   980

'And that doth me to han so gret a wonder,
That ye wol scornen any womman so.
Ek, God woot, love and I ben fer ysonder!
I am disposed bet, so mot I go,
Unto my deth, to pleyne and maken wo.   985
What I shal after don, I kan nat seye;
But trewelich, as yet me list nat pleye.

'Myn herte is now in tribulacioun,
And ye in armes bisy day by day.
Herafter, whan ye wonnen han the town,   990
Peraunter, thanne so it happen may,
That whan I se that nevere yit I say,
Than wol I werke that I nevere wroughte!
This word to yow ynough suffisen oughte.

'To-morwe ek wol I speken with yow fayn,   995
So that ye touchen naught of this matere.
And whan yow list, ye may come here ayayn;
And er ye gon, thus muche I sey yow here:
As help me Pallas with hire heres clere,
If that I sholde of any Grek han routhe,   1000
It sholde be yourselven, by my trouthe!

'I say nat therfore that I wol yow love,
N'y say nat nay; but in conclusioun,
I mene wel, by God that sit above!'
And therwithal she caste hire eyen down,   1005
And gan to sike, and seyde, 'O Troie town,
Yet bidde I God, in quiete and in reste
I may yow sen, or do myn herte breste.'

But in effect, and shortly for to seye,
This Diomede al fresshly newe ayeyn   1010
Gan pressen on, and faste hire mercy preye;
And after this, the sothe for to seyn,
Hire glove he took, of which he was ful feyn.
And finaly, whan it was woxen eve,
And al was wel, he roos and tok his leve.   1015

The brighte Venus folwede and ay taughte
The wey ther brode Phebus down alighte;
And Cynthea hire char-hors overraughte
To whirle out of the Leoun, if she myghte;
And Signifer his candels sheweth brighte,   1020
Whan that Criseyde unto hire bedde wente
Inwith hire fadres faire brighte tente,

Retornyng in hire soule ay up and down
The wordes of this sodeyn Diomede,
His grete estat, and perel of the town,   1025
And that she was allone and hadde nede
Of frendes help; and thus bygan to brede
The cause whi, the sothe for to telle,
That she took fully purpos for to dwelle.

The morwen com, and gostly for to speke,   1030
This Diomede is come unto Criseyde;
And shortly, lest that ye my tale breke,
So wel he for hymselven spak and seyde,
That alle hire sikes soore adown he leyde.
And finaly, the sothe for to seyne,   1035
He refte hire of the grete of al hire peyne.

And after this the storie telleth us
That she hym yaf the faire baye-stede,
The which he ones wan of Troilus;
And ek a broche – and that was litel nede –   1040
That Troilus was, she yaf this Diomede.
And ek, the bet from sorwe hym to releve,
She made hym were a pencel of hire sleve.

I fynde ek in the stories elleswhere,
Whan thorugh the body hurt was Diomede   1045
Of Troilus, tho wepte she many a teere,
Whan that she saugh his wyde wowndes blede;
And that she took, to kepen hym, good hede;
And for to helen hym of his sorwes smerte,
Men seyn – I not – that she yaf hym hire herte.   1050

But trewely, the storie telleth us,
Ther made nevere woman moore wo
Than she, whan that she falsed Troilus.
She seyde, 'Allas! for now is clene ago
My name of trouthe in love, for everemo!   1055
For I have falsed oon the gentileste
That evere was, and oon the worthieste!

'Allas! of me, unto the worldes ende,
Shal neyther ben ywriten nor ysonge
No good word, for thise bokes wol me shende.   1060
O, rolled shal I ben on many a tonge!
Thoroughout the world my belle shal be ronge!
And wommen moost wol haten me of alle.
Allas, that swich a cas me sholde falle!

'Thei wol seyn, in as muche as in me is,   1065
I have hem don dishonour, weylaway!
Al be I nat the first that dide amys,
What helpeth that to don my blame awey?
But syn I se ther is no bettre way,
And that to late is now for me to rewe,   1070
To Diomede algate I wol be trewe.

'But, Troilus, syn I no bettre may,
And syn that thus departen ye and I,
Yet prey I God, so yeve yow right good day,
As for the gentileste, trewely,   1075
That evere I say, to serven feythfully,
And best kan ay his lady honour kepe' –
And with that word she brast anon to wepe.

'And certes, yow ne haten shal I nevere;
And frendes love, that shal ye han of me,   1080
And my good word, al sholde I lyven evere.
And, trewely, I wolde sory be
For to seen yow in adversitee;
And gilteles, I woot wel, I yow leve.
But al shal passe; and thus take I my leve.'   1085

But trewely, how longe it was bytwene
That she forsok hym for this Diomede,
Ther is non auctour telleth it, I wene.
Take every man now to his bokes hede;
He shal no terme fynden, out of drede.   1090
For though that he bigan to wowe hire soone,
Er he hire wan, yet was ther more to doone.

Ne me ne list this sely womman chyde
Forther than the storye wol devyse.
Hire name, allas! is punysshed so wide,   1095
That for hire gilt it oughte ynough suffise.
And if I myghte excuse hire any wise,
For she so sory was for hire untrouthe,
Iwis, I wolde excuse hire yet for routhe.

This Troilus, as I byfore have told,   1100
Thus driveth forth, as wel as he hath myght.
But often was his herte hoot and cold,
And namely that ilke nynthe nyght,
Which on the morwe she hadde hym bihight
To com ayeyn: God woot, ful litel reste   1105
Hadde he that nyght; nothyng to slepe hym leste.

The laurer-crowned Phebus, with his heete,
Gan, in his course ay upward as he wente,
To warmen of the est see the wawes weete,
And Nysus doughter song with fressh entente,   1110
Whan Troilus his Pandare after sente;
And on the walles of the town they pleyde,
To loke if they kan sen aught of Criseyde.

Tyl it was noon, they stoden for to se
Who that ther come; and every maner wight   1115
That com fro fer, they seyden it was she,
Til that thei koude knowen hym aright.
Now was his herte dul, now was it light.
And thus byjaped stonden for to stare
Aboute naught this Troilus and Pandare.   1120

To Pandarus this Troilus tho seyde,
'For aught I woot, byfor noon, sikirly,
Into this town ne comth nat here Criseyde.
She hath ynough to doone, hardyly,
To wynnen from hire fader, so trowe I.   1125
Hire olde fader wol yet make hire dyne
Er that she go; God yeve hys herte pyne!'

Pandare answerde, 'It may wel be, certeyn.
And forthi lat us dyne, I the byseche,
And after noon than maystow come ayeyn.'   1130
And hom they go, withoute more speche,
And comen ayeyn; but longe may they seche
Er that they fynde that they after gape.
Fortune hem bothe thenketh for to jape!

Quod Troilus, 'I se wel now that she   1135
Is taried with hire olde fader so,
That er she come, it wol neigh even be.
Com forth, I wole unto the yate go.
Thise porters ben unkonnyng evere mo,
And I wol don hem holden up the yate   1140
As naught ne were, although she come late.'

The day goth faste, and after that com eve,
And yet com nought to Troilus Criseyde.
He loketh forth by hegge, by tre, by greve,
And fer his hed over the wal he leyde,   1145
And at the laste he torned hym and seyde,
'By God, I woot hire menyng now, Pandare!
Almoost, ywys, al newe was my care.

'Now douteles, this lady kan hire good;
I woot, she meneth riden pryvely.   1150
I comende hire wisdom, by myn hood!
She wol nat maken peple nycely
Gaure on hire whan she comth; but softely
By nyghte into the town she thenketh ride.
And, deere brother, thynk not longe t'abide.   1155

'We han naught elles for to don, ywis.
And Pandarus, now woltow trowen me?
Have here my trouthe, I se hire! yond she is!
Heve up thyn eyen, man! maistow nat se?'
Pandare answerede, 'Nay, so mote I the!   1160
Al wrong, by God! What saistow, man, where arte?
That I se yond nys but a fare-carte.'

'Allas! thow seyst right soth,' quod Troilus.
'But, hardily, it is naught al for nought
That in myn herte I now rejoysse thus.   1165
It is ayeyns som good I have a thought.
Not I nat how, but syn that I was wrought,
Ne felte I swich a comfort, dar I seye;
She comth to-nyght, my lif that dorste I leye!'

Pandare answerde, 'It may be, wel ynough,'   1170
And held with hym of al that evere he seyde.
But in his herte he thoughte, and softe lough,
And to hymself ful sobreliche he seyde,
'From haselwode, there joly Robyn pleyde,
Shal come al that that thow abidest heere.   1175
Ye, fare wel al the snow of ferne yere!'

The warden of the yates gan to calle
The folk which that withoute the yates were,
And bad hem dryven in hire bestes alle,
Or al the nyght they moste bleven there.   1180
And fer withinne the nyght, with many a teere,
This Troilus gan homward for to ride;
For wel he seth it helpeth naught t'abide . . .

Troilus resists his growing realization of loss. He writes, and
Criseyde replies she will return as soon as she can. He dreams
he has lost her to a boar (symbol of Diomede), but writes many
times. Eventually she replies that she is sorry he is upset – but
she understands he is deceiving her – but she believes all
truth is in him – but truly, she will always be his friend. Troilus
thinks the letter strange.

But natheles, men seyen that at the laste,
For any thyng, men shal the soothe se.   · 1640
And swich a cas bitidde, and that as faste,
That Troilus wel understod that she
Nas nought so kynde as that hire oughte be.
And fynaly, he woot now, out of doute,
That al is lost that he hath ben aboute.   1645

Stood on a day in his malencolie
This Troilus, and in suspecioun
Of hire for whom he wende for to dye.
And so bifel that thorughout Troye town,
As was the gise, iborn was up and down   1650

A manere cote-armure, as seith the storie,
Byforn Deiphebe, in signe of his victorie;

The whiche cote, as telleth Lollius,
Deiphebe it hadde rent fro Diomede
The same day. And whan this Troilus   1655
It saugh, he gan to taken of it hede,
Avysyng of the lengthe and of the brede,
And al the werk; but as he gan byholde,
Ful sodeynly his herte gan to colde,

As he that on the coler fond withinne   1660
A broche, that he Criseyde yaf that morwe
That she from Troie moste nedes twynne,
In remembraunce of hym and of his sorwe.
And she hym leyde ayeyn hire feith to borwe
To kepe it ay! But now ful wel he wiste,   1665
His lady nas no lenger on to triste.

He goth hym hom, and gan ful soone sende
For Pandarus; and al this newe chaunce,
And of this broche, he tolde hym word and ende,
Compleynyng of hire hertes variaunce,   1670
His longe love, his trouthe, and his penaunce.
And after deth, withouten wordes moore,
Ful faste he cride, his reste hym to restore.

Than spak he thus, 'O lady myn, Criseyde,
Where is youre feith, and where is youre biheste?   1675
Where is youre love? where is youre trouthe?' he
     seyde.
'Of Diomede have ye now al this feeste!
Allas! I wolde han trowed atte leeste
That, syn ye nolde in trouthe to me stonde,
That ye thus nolde han holden me in honde!   1680

'Who shal now trowe on any othes mo?
Allas! I nevere wolde han wend, er this,
That ye, Criseyde, koude han chaunged so;
Ne, but I hadde agilt and don amys,
So cruel wende I nought youre herte, ywis,   1685

To sle me thus! Allas, youre name of trouthe
Is now fordon, and that is al my routhe.

'Was ther non other broche yow liste lete
To feffe with youre newe love,' quod he,
'But thilke broch that I, with teris wete,   1690
Yow yaf, as for a remembraunce of me?
Non other cause, allas, ne hadde ye
But for despit, and ek for that ye mente
Al outrely to shewen youre entente.

'Thorugh which I se that clene out of youre mynde 1695
Ye han me cast; and I ne kan nor may,
For al this world, withinne myn herte fynde
To unloven yow a quarter of a day!
In corsed tyme I born was, weilaway,
That yow, that doon me al this wo endure,   1700
Yet love I best of any creature!

'Now God,' quod he, 'me sende yet the grace
That I may meten with this Diomede!
And trewely, if I have myght and space,
Yet shal I make, I hope, his sydes blede.   1705
O God,' quod he, 'that oughtest taken heede
To fortheren trouthe, and wronges to punyce,
Whi nyltow don a vengeaunce of this vice?

'O Pandarus, that in dremes for to triste
Me blamed hast, and wont art oft upbreyde,   1710
Now maistow se thiself, if that the liste,
How trewe is now thi nece, bright Criseyde!
In sondry formes, God it woot,' he seyde,
'The goddes shewen bothe joie and tene
In slep, and by my drem it is now sene.   1715

'And certeynly, withouten moore speche,
From hennesforth, as ferforth as I may,
Myn owen deth in armes wol I seche.
Irecche nat how soone be the day!
But trewely, Criseyde, swete may,   1720

Whom I have ay with al my myght yserved,
That ye thus doon, I have it nat deserved.'

This Pandarus, that al thise thynges herde,
And wiste wel he seyde a soth of this,
He nought a word ayeyn to hym answerde;   1725
For sory of his frendes sorwe he is,
And shamed for his nece hath don amys,
And stant, astoned of thise causes tweye,
As stille as ston; a word ne kowde he seye.

But at the laste thus he spak, and seyde: 1730
'My brother deer, I may do the namore.
What sholde I seyen? I hate, ywys, Cryseyde;
And, God woot, I wol hate hire evermore!
And that thow me bisoughtest don of yoore,
Havyng unto myn honour ne my reste   1735
Right no reward, I dide al that the leste.

'If I dide aught that myghte liken the,
It is me lief; and of this tresoun now,
God woot that it a sorwe is unto me!
And dredeles, for hertes ese of yow,   1740
Right fayn I wolde amende it, wiste I how.
And fro this world, almyghty God I preye
Delivere hire soon! I kan namore seye.'

Gret was the sorwe and pleynte of Troilus;
But forth hire cours Fortune ay gan to holde.   1745
Criseyde loveth the sone of Tideus,
And Troilus moot wepe in cares colde.
Swich is this world, whoso it kan byholde:
In ech estat is litel hertes reste.
God leve us for to take it for the beste!   1750

In many cruel bataille, out of drede,
Of Troilus, this ilke noble knyght,
As men may in thise olde bokes rede,
Was seen his knyghthod and his grete myght.
And dredeles, his ire, day and nyght,   1755

Ful cruwely the Grekis ay aboughte;
And alwey moost this Diomede he soughte.

And ofte tyme, I fynde that they mette
With blody strokes and with wordes grete,
Assayinge how hire speres weren whette;   1760
And, God it woot, with many a cruel hete
Gan Troilus upon his helm to bete!
But natheles, Fortune it naught ne wolde,
Of oothers hond that eyther deyen sholde.

And if I hadde ytaken for to write   1765
The armes of this ilke worthi man,
Than wolde ich of his batailles endite;
But for that I to writen first bigan
Of his love, I have seyd as I kan –
His worthi dedes, whoso list hem heere,   1770
Rede Dares, he kan telle hem alle ifeere –

Bysechyng every lady bright of hewe,
And every gentil womman, what she be,
That al be that Criseyde was untrewe,
That for that gilt she be nat wroth with me.   1775
Ye may hire giltes in other bokes se;
And gladlier I wol write, if yow leste,
Penelopeës trouthe and good Alceste.

N'y sey nat this aloonly for thise men,
But moost for wommen that bitraised be   1780
Thorugh false folk; God yeve hem sorwe, amen!
That with hire grete wit and subtilte
Bytraise yow! And this commeveth me
To speke, and in effect yow alle I preye,
Beth war of men, and herkneth what I seye!   1785

Go, litel book, go, litel myn tragedye,
Ther God thi makere yet, er that he dye,
So sende mygbt to make in som comedye!
But litel book, no makyng thow n'envie,
But subgit be to alle poesye;   1790

And kis the steppes, where as thow seest pace
Virgile, Ovide, Omer, Lucan, and Stace.

And for ther is so gret diversite
In Englissh and in writyng of oure tonge,
So prey I God that non myswrite the,   1795
Ne the mysmetre for defaute of tonge.
And red wherso thow be, or elles songe,
That thow be understonde, God I biseche!
But yet to purpos of my rather speche –

The wrath, as I bigan yow for to seye,   1800
Of Troilus the Grekis boughten deere.
For thousandes his hondes maden deye,
As he that was withouten any peere,
Save Ector, in his tyme, as I kan heere.
But weilawey, save only Goddes wille!   1805
Despitously hym slough the fierse Achille.

And whan that he was slayn in this manere,
His lighte goost ful blisfully is went
Up to the holughnesse of the eighte spere,
In convers letyng everich element;   1810
And ther he saugh, with ful avysement,
The erratik sterres, herkenyng armonye
With sownes ful of hevenyssh melodie.

And down from thennes faste he gan avyse
This litel spot of erthe, that with the se   1815
Embraced is, and fully gan despise
This wrecched world, and held al vanite
To respect of the pleyn felicite
That is in hevene above; and at the laste,
Ther he was slayn, his lokyng down he caste.   1820

And in hymself he lough right at the wo
Of hem that wepten for his deth so faste;
And dampned al oure werk that foloweth so
The blynde lust, the which that may nat laste,
And sholden al oure herte on heven caste.   1825

And forth he wente, shortly for to telle,
Ther as Mercurye sorted hym to dwelle.

Swich fyn hath, lo, this Troilus for love!
Swich fyn hath al his grete worthynesse!
Swich fyn hath his estat real above,   1830
Swich fyn his lust, swich fyn hath his noblesse!
Swych fyn hath false worldes brotelnesse!
And thus bigan his lovyng of Criseyde,
As I have told, and in this wise he deyde.

EPILOGUE

O yonge, fresshe folkes, he or she,   1835
In which that love up groweth with youre age,
Repeyreth hom fro worldly vanyte,
And of youre herte up casteth the visage
To thilke God that after his ymage
Yow made, and thynketh al nys but a faire   1840
This world, that passeth soone as floures faire.

And loveth hym, the which that right for love
Upon a crois, oure soules for to beye,
First starf, and roos, and sit in hevene above;
For he nyl falsen no wight, dar I seye,   1845
That wol his herte al holly on hym leye.
And syn he best to love is, and most meke,
What nedeth feynede loves for to seke?

Lo here, of payens corsed olde rites!
Lo here, what alle hire goddes may availle!   1850
Lo here, thise wrecched worldes appetites!
Lo here, the fyn and guerdoun for travaille
Of Jove, Appollo, of Mars, of swich rascaille!
Lo here, the forme of olde clerkis speche
In poetrie, if ye hire bokes seche!   1855

O moral Gower, this book I directe
To the and to the, philosophical Strode,
To vouchen sauf, ther nede is, to correcte,

Of youre benignites and zeles goode.
And to that sothefast Crist, that starf on rode,   1860
With al myn herte of mercy evere I preye,
And to the Lord right thus I speke and seye:

Thow oon, and two, and thre, eterne on lyve,
That regnest ay in thre, and two, and oon,
Uncircumscript, and al maist circumscrive,   1865
Us from visible and invisible foon
Defende, and to thy mercy, everichon,
So make us, Jesus, for thi mercy digne,
For love of mayde and moder thyn benigne.
    Amen.

COMMENTARY

Book I

1. *double sorwe:* in the first four lines the poet summarizes the whole course of the story (again I, 54). *Troilus:* a famous warrior and unhappy lover: about eighteen or nineteen years old. **2.** 'Who was the son of King Priam of Troy'. **5.** *fro ye:* 'from you'. Suggests presence of an audience. **6.** *Thesiphone:* four syllables, 'Tisiphone', one of the three Furies of classical mythology, though that they themselves suffer is not a classical notion. Cf. IV, 23. **7.** *vers, that wepen:* 'verses that weep', a curious conceit taken from *Il Filostrato* and *Boethius*. *write:* this suggests a poem written to be *read*, as well as heard (I, 5). Later Chaucer writes 'Thou, reader', V, 270 (not in present selection). **8.** *thow:* second person singular as in prayer. The difference between singular and plural forms is important. **13.** The 'woful wight' may be the poet and his 'dreary companion' Tisiphone; or the 'wight' may be the poem and the 'companion', the poet or his dreary appearance. That the 'action (i.e. the gesture of the teller) should suit the word' was a commonplace of rhetorical instruction. **15 ff.** The poet presents himself modestly, as rhetoricians advised, to obtain the sympathy of the audience or reader. **15.** *God of Love:* i.e. Cupid, often represented in the Middle Ages as a young, handsome and imperious king, as in Chaucer's *Prologue to the Legend of Good Women*. *God of Loves servantz serve:* this is a joking parody of the title of the Pope, who is described as 'the servant of the servants of God', and is also part of the poet's disclaimer of personal experience of love. **21.** *my thonk:* 'thanks due to me'. **27.** 'You have obtained love too easily if you do not realize how painful it can be.' **29-46.** A bidding prayer. **31.** *Love: hevene:* these terms are ambivalent, and might apply to either love or religion. **36.** *ben despeired:* 'are despairing'. **40.** *for:* 'by reason of'. **42.** *despeired out of:* 'in despair of'. *Despeir* and *grace* are religious terms, and ambivalent here: I, 41-2 are also applicable to Troilus's end. **44.** *God:* really God, not Cupid. **47 ff.** This can hardly be serious. **48.** *Loves servauntz:* a lover proved his love by 'serving' (on the analogy of serving a feudal superior) his

lady. 'To serve' and 'servant' became synonyms for 'to love' and
'lover'. **53.** *matere:* 'matter', almost a technical term; the sub-
stance of the story, Troilus's love and betrayal. **66.** *Calkas:*
'Calchas', priest and scientist, i.e. astrologer. **70.** *Daun Phebus or
Appollo Delphicus: daun* is *don,* from *dominus,* Latin 'master' or
'lord'. Phoebus Apollo was god of learning and light (hence of
the sun); his oracle was at Delphi. **71.** *calkulynge:* a play on
words. He made astrological calculation. **76.** *sort:* 'casting lots'.
77. *ye, wolde whoso nolde:* 'yes, whoever wanted or did not want
it'. Cf. *willy-nilly.* **88.** *casten:* the subject is to be understood as
'the townspeople'. **97.** Criseyde's isolation is emphasized. No
relative is mentioned. **98.** *dorste hir mone:* 'dared bemoan herself',
i.e. tell her sorrow. **104.** scan cré-á-túr-é. **106.** *alday herd at ere:*
'continually had in her ears'. **110.** *Ector:* 'Hector', eldest son of
Priam and chief Trojan warrior. **118.** Hector uses the polite
second person plural form. **119.** *yow good list:* 'it pleases you
well'. **120.** *don yow have:* 'cause you to have'. **126.** *and hom:* 'and
(went) home'. **132–3.** Boccaccio says quite clearly that she had no
children. Chaucer's comment is typical of the uncertainty and
insecurity with which he always associates Criseyde. There is
also a touch of flippancy here. **136.** *som day:* one day. *derre:*
dearer (comparative). **138–40.** 'Fortune raised them up and put
them down on her wheel, in her usual manner, all the time they
were angry.' The image is of Fortune's wheel, one of the dominant images of the poem. **142.** 'Does not fall to me to tell as (my)
purpose', i.e. 'it is not my intention to tell'. **144.** *yow to long to
dwelle:* 'too long for you to dwell', i.e. 'would keep you too long'.
Another direct address to the audience. **145–7.** Homer, the Greek
poet; Dares and Dictys were later Latin 'historians' of the Trojan
War. **153.** *heet Palladion:* 'called Palladium'–the sacred image of
Pallas Athene on which the safety of the city depended. It was
eventually stolen by Ulysses and Diomede according to Virgil,
but Benoît in the *Roman de Troie* says that the Trojans Antenor
(for whom, when he was captured, Criseyde was exchanged) and
Aeneas traitorously surrendered it. **156.** *Aperil:* the festival is a
pagan equivalent of Easter. **158.** *swote:* 'sweetly'; describes fresh
and growing things. (The parallel form *swete* describes persons
and what is 'sugary'.) **171.** *is now an A:* a complimentary reference to Queen Anne, married to Richard II in January 1382. But
of course our first letter has always been A, and there is an
equivocal note here. **172.** *makeles:* 'matchless', 'without an
equal'; perhaps also 'without a *make*' or mate, i.e. lover. **175.**
'Brightness' is the usual attribute of the medieval heroine, who
always had bright golden hair, etc. Criseyde's black dress was an
effective contrast. **180.** *neigh the dore:* a position of modesty. *ay*

under shames drede: 'always afraid of (incurring) shame'. **182.** *ful assured:* Criseyde is both very modest and very self-confident – she is presented with typical ambivalence. **196.** *the:* 'thee'. The singular form here expresses contempt. **197–203.** All these remarks will apply to Troilus's own love-affair. **198.** *lewede:* 'ignorant', hence 'foolish'. *observaunces:* 'rites', a semi-religious word. **202.** *veray:* 'true'. *nyce:* 'foolish'. **208.** *He kidde:* 'He (the God of Love) made known'. **210.** 'And still (nowadays) he can pluck as proud as a peacock (as Troilus was).' For the image, cf. V, 1546 (not in present selection). 'Proud as a peacock' is proverbial. **206–66.** All this passage is preparatory commentary on the glance that Troilus will cast on Criseyde, I, 273. **211–24.** What the rhetoricians call an *apostrophe.* The poet addresses somebody or something, and in so doing comments on the story, underlines a significant point, raises the feeling. Fundamentally serious, there is here perhaps a slight touch of exaggerated diction. There is also a contrast between the big solemn words, 211–14, on the one hand, and on the other the homeliness of the 'stair' image, and the elaborate but undignified simile of the horse, 'feeling his oats', brought to order with the carter's whip (I, 218–24). The whole passage is entirely original to Chaucer. **217.** Proverbial. **218.** *Bayard:* originally the name of a bay-coloured horse belonging to Charlemagne in the *chansons de gestes*; by the fourteenth century used with a touch of mockery for any horse. **221.** *praunce al byforn:* i.e. as the front horse in a tandem arrangement. **229.** *with a look:* i.e. the look Troilus will exchange with Criseyde, not yet described. **232–66.** Another address to the audience, and comment on the nature of love, original to Chaucer. Love is good and cannot be avoided. It depends on whom you love. The tone is varied, often light, not necessarily ironical, though there may be more to be said. The praise is traditional. **237.** That God, as Love, binds all things together is asserted by Boethius, in the passage rendered in Troilus's song, III, 1744 ff. (see note). Here the poet applies the words, perhaps ironically, to the more limited notion of love between the sexes. **238.** *fordon the lawe of kynde:* 'abolish the law of Nature'. In *The Parlement of Foules* Nature is 'the vicar of Almighty God' and impels creatures to love each other. **239.** *preved:* 'has proved (to be true), and still does so'. **241–2.** 'Men do not think that (there are some) people (who) have more intelligence than those who have been most enslaved by love'; i.e. even the wisest men fall in love. Solomon, Virgil, Aristotle were traditional examples, about whom comic stories were told. **243.** *strengest folk:* e.g. Samson, Hercules, and (in medieval story), Achilles, who all came to their deaths through love. **245.** Echoes the religious liturgy, the *Gloria Patri*, 'as it was in the beginning, is now, and ever shall be'. **257.** Proverbial. **260–6.** An empty stanza. **265.** *werk:* 'work' (but with an association of pain!). **267.** *pleyinge:* 'amusing (himself)'. **270.** *Wher so:* 'whether'. **272.** *percede:* it was believed up to Elizabethan times that sight was the product of rays streaming from the eye; cf. I, 305. **275.** *thrifty:* 'cautious'. **276.** *hastow:* Troilus uses the intimate second person singular in imaginary speech to Criseyde, as he never does in reality. **277.** *to devise:* 'to describe', i.e. to see. **281.** *nat with the leste:* i.e. of medium height. Cf. V, 806. **281 ff.** Criseyde's extreme femininity is emphasized. **285.** *pure wise:* 'very manner'. **294.** 'it seemed to him he had never seen'. **298.** *impressioun:* 'imprint'. An image of her was planted in the depths of his heart. *his:* Either 'of it' (i.e. her look); or 'his'. **300.** Proverbial. **306–8.** It was thought that the body was controlled by various 'spirits', highly refined substances or fluids passing through the arteries. The 'natural spirit' (which controlled emotions) originated in the liver, the 'animal spirit' in the brain, while the 'spirit of the heart' controlled pulse and breathing. The rays from Criseyde's eyes pierced through Troilus's own eye, went down to the heart, and so affected the spirit of the heart that his pulse and breathing stopped. **309.** *She, this . . .:* a familiar M.E. idiom, though grammatically here *she* should be *her*. *likynge:* 'pleasing'. **312.** *chere made:* 'revealed by his appearance'. **313.** *his manere,* etc.: 'in order to maintain his usual manner of behaviour'. **314.** *thing:* an old uninflected plural, 'things'. **321.** *Lest it were wist:* 'lest it should be known'. **330-50.** Troilus is being ironical, which, having regard to the true state of his feelings, is itself ironical. **330.** *lest:* the Kentish form of O.E. *lyst,* of which the East Midland form is *list* and the Western form *lust,* all meaning 'pleasure, desire', without the modern pejorative connotation. Chaucer varies the form for the sake of the rhyme. **333.** *tit:* contracted form of *tideth,* 'befalls'. **334.** A monetary image (sex and money are closely linked in most people's imaginations). **336.** *ordre:* derived from the notion of a religious order, i.e. a community obeying a particular rule. **337–8.** *observaunces:* cf. I, 160. 'Your rites are all uncertain except in a few trivial points.' **340.** *lay:* 'law'. **341.** *as mote I the:* 'so may I thrive', an empty exclamation for which no literal translation is possible. **351.** *say:* 'saw'. **353.** for the image cf. I, 210. **359.** *beddes feet:* 'foot of the bed'. Chairs were few even in palaces in the fourteenth century. Cf. Brewer, *Chaucer in His Time,* pp. 92 ff. 'Feet' is either an idiomatic plural or is an unusual form of the dative sing. **363.** *a-temple:* 'in the temple'. **365.** *mirour:* a mirror was an important instrument of perception to medieval minds, and the word was often used in the title of books. The mind was also thought of as a mirror. 'Mirror' was also used as an image of perfection. Cf. II, 266. **379–6.** ellipsis of parts of the verb 'to be'. **375–83.** He will keep his love private (rather than secret) unless he is successful; (*or*) unless he may gain anything by its being known (381). **379.** *loves craft:* skill in doing things that would please his lady. **383.** *desir in muwe:* 'desire in a cage'. His desire is thought of as a hawk cooped up in cage. **384.** *yblowe:* 'blown', i.e. scattered (as seed). The 'seed of love' is an image found in *Le Roman de la Rose*.

Book II

1 ff. Apart from a few specific suggestions from Dante and others, the first 264 lines or so of this book are original to Chaucer, while much that follows them is only lightly suggested by Boccaccio. **1–6.** The image of a poem as a boat was fairly common. **4.** 'That I can hardly steer it by my skill.' **7.** *kalendes:* first day of the month in the Roman calendar, hence, 'beginning'. **8.** *Cleo:* Clio, the classical muse of history. In this invocation the poet abandons the Fury of the first book. He pretends to think of his work here as an historical narrative, without *sentement* (personal feeling) (II, 13), and as translated from Latin, the language of learning (II, 14). He pretends merely to say what his source says, and once again proclaims his personal inexperience, with ironical, non-serious effect. **14–18.** References both to writing and a spoken address. **16.** *Of:* 'for'. **21.** Proverbial. **25.** *Us thinketh hem:* lit., 'it seems to us about them'. **26.** *spedde:* 'succeeded'. **27–42.** The many different fashions of love are emphasized. In lines 39–41 the poet (ironically?) implies that in his own day in England love was not secret, but wooing was carried on by open visiting and speech. **28.** Proverbial. **35.** 'I do not know; but it is no surprise to me.' **36–7.** Proverbial. *went:* 'wendeth'; *Halt:* 'holdeth'. **40.** 'in open behaviour or appearance'. **42.** Proverbial. **45–6.** 'For this may please you (one person) for *your* purpose, and you (another person) not at all: yet everything necessary is said sooner or later.' **48.** *bitit:* 'betideth', i.e. happens. **50.** May is 'mother' because 'she' begins the series of months of cheerful weather. **51.** *blew and white and rede:* conventional colours of flowers. **53.** *ful of bawme is fletyng every mede:* 'every meadow is swimming with sweet smells'. 'Wet' imagery suggests ease and warmth and fertility. **54–6.** Phoebus, the sun, entered the sign of the Zodiac called Taurus (the Bull) in Chaucer's time about 12 April, remaining there a month. On 3 May it was a little more than half-way through the sign. There is no astronomical reason for calling the Bull 'white'. It is a poetic flourish. This is a traditional passage of spring description. This date was one of the traditional unlucky days. Chaucer also uses it in *The Knight's Tale*, I, 1462–3, and *The Nun's Priest's Tale*, VII, 3190; it may have had some personal significance for him. **59.** *preche:* 'preach'. Pandarus's didacticism, contrasted with his personal failure, is mockingly hinted at. **61.** *So shop it:* 'it was so ordained'. **62.** Even Pandarus takes to his bed when miserable because of love. **64.** *Proigne:* Ovid tells the story of how Procne's husband Tereus raped her sister Philomela, then cut out her tongue. After the sisters had taken an equally terrible revenge on Tereus, Procne was changed to a swallow and Philomela to a nightingale. References to the story are very frequent: cf. *The Legend of Good Women*, 2228 ff. **71.** *gan to calle:* i.e. his servant. *dresse:* 'prepared'. **72–3.** 'Recalling to himself that his errand from Troilus, his great enterprise, had to be done.' **74.** *caste:* 'made an astrological calculation', i.e. about the future. *in good plit:* 'in favourable position'. It is now 4 May. **76.** Criseyde lives in a palace, at a higher social level than Boccaccio's heroine. **77.** *Janus:* Roman two-headed god of entrances. **81.** *sete:* 'seated'. **82.** *paved:* 'tiled'. **83–4.** This reading-party describes how much medieval poetry, including Chaucer's, must have been read. Cf. Brewer, *Chaucer in His Time*, 197 ff., and *Chaucer*, 51–2, 124–6. Cf. III, 613. **83.** *geste:* story. **84.** *siege of Thebes:* the story of the War of the Seven against Thebes was told in twelve books in the Latin *Thebais*, by Statius (first century A.D.), and in the twelfth century Anglo-Norman *Roman de Thèbes*, which Chaucer may also have had in mind. Cf. V, 937. **85.** *God yow see:* 'may God see (i.e. guard) you'. Pandarus addresses Criseyde with respect and distance as *Madame* and uses the polite second person plural (as does Criseyde to him). **87, 92.** The uncle-niece relationship is emphasized in the dialogue. **92.** *Ye, nece, yee:* 'yes, niece, you'. **95.** *preysen thus:* 'value so much'. **98.** *maistresse:* 'beloved' (the lady whom Pandarus is unsuccessfully in love with). Though polite, Criseyde is familiar enough. **101–2.** It was foretold at the birth of Oedipus that he would kill his father, King Laius. **103.** *lettres rede:* 'red letters' of a chapter heading in the manuscript book from which they were reading. **104.** *bisshop:* Chaucer, like the *Roman de Thèbes*, modernizes the title of the pagan priest. He was a soothsayer like Calchas. He foretold the result of the war and his own death, swallowed up by the earth. **110.** *barbe:* 'a piece of white plaited linen, passed over or under the chin, and reaching midway to the waist' (*O.E.D.*). Usually worn by nuns and widows. **112.** 'And let us pay some worship to May' (*or*)

'And let us do something appropriate to May'. **114.** 'Is that proper for a widow's life, Heaven help you?' **117.** *sate:* 'would suit.' **121.** *doon yow pleye:* 'to make you behave cheerfully'. **124.** Criseyde reveals her underlying insecurity. **132.** 'My wit is far too small to guess it'. **134.** *I youre borugh:* 'I your pledge', i.e. I give you my word. **151.** *unkouth:* 'unfamiliar'. **154.** i.e. protection for us and a scourge to the Greeks. **160–1.** Traditional knightly virtues. *gentilesse:* 'nobility'. *fredom:* 'generosity', *worthinesse:* (here specifically) 'bravery'. **164.** *gret deynte:* 'most estimable'. **178.** *of worthynesse welle:* 'the fountain (i.e. the very origin) of worthiness'. **181.** *pris:* 'praise'. **185 ff.** Troilus fulfils the traditional praise of the medieval knight, a lion in battle, a lamb in the hall. **189.** *me:* 'one'; lit., 'Of them that it would be most agreeable to one to be praised (by)', i.e. Of those one would most like to be praised by. **193 ff.** The emphasis on Troilus's valour is found in earlier writers, but not in *Il Filostrato.* **202.** *as that:* 'on that'. **205.** *Of gret estat:* 'of high rank'. *my lyve:* 'in my life'. **206.** *best felawshipe kan:* 'shows most friendship'. **207.** 'To such as seem to him able to do well.' **212.** *namelich:* 'especially'. **213–14.** 'I have (something) to do with you, to discuss what would be wise to do, before you go.' **217.** *hadde al that hem liste in honde:* 'dealt with everything they wanted to'. **218.** *tale:* 'talk'. **219.** 'about the management of her affairs'. **222.** *mischaunce:* i.e. to the devil. **232–4.** *Mynerve:* Minerva, classical goddess of wisdom. *Jupiter:* classical king of the gods, who controlled thunder; Jupiter was also a planet. *Venus:* classical goddess of love, also a planet. **236.** *Withouten paramours:* 'apart from (any) ladies I may be in love with'. **240 ff.** Criseyde's profession of indebtedness and affection, original with Chaucer, is not quite consistent with the isolation described when her father deserted her and she appealed to Hector. **244.** *as in my gylt:* 'through my fault'. **256 ff.** Pandarus is always interested in the artistry of narration. **260.** Proverbial, and also an axiom of the rhetoricians. **262.** *what:* 'why'. *peynte:* 'adorn (with rhetorical colours)'. **264.** *inwardly:* 'with concentration'. **266.** *mirour:* here an image of perfection. Cf. I, 365 n. **268.** *make a proces any whyle:* 'make a long story of it'. **271–3.** 'For unintelligent minds think that everything is deceit where they cannot plainly understand. Therefore I will try to adapt myself to her intelligence.' Pandarus has no high opinion of Criseyde's mind, and he is less frank to her than he appears. **274.** *bysi wyse:* 'attentive way'. **279.** *if ye / Be fortunat:* Pandarus is deliberately ambiguous, suggesting both 'Are you fortunate?' and 'How fortunate you are!' **280 ff.** The words *fortun(at), aventure, cas,* echo through these lines. **301.** Pandarus bullies a little here. **310.** *come of:* 'come on!' **314.** Criseyde's nervousness seems genuine. **315–85.** Most of Pandarus's speech is original to Chaucer. **318.** An interjection, creating slightly odd syntax, of a kind which survives in Dickens's Mrs Gamp. *Which:* 'who'. **319.** *the:* The second person singular emphasizes the personal feeling (and perhaps helped with the rhyme). Pandarus's normal accusative form to Criseyde is *yow,* as in 322. **323.** *sterve:* 'die'. Pandarus is pathetic in these lines on his own account, as well as Troilus's. **328.** *fisshed fayre:* 'fished well'. Images of fishing are not uncommon in love-poetry. **329.** 'How do you get better, if we get worse?' **330.** Troilus seems to be Pandarus's feudal lord, as well as bosom friend. **336.** 'Alas that God made you so beautiful!' **341.** *strecche:* i.e. be sufficient. **344.** *wo worth:* the repetition of these words is a rhetorical figure known as *anaphora.* Cf. V, 1828. There it seems to reflect genuine feeling: here it suggests Pandarus's deliberate working on Criseyde's feelings. **344–5.** It was believed that precious and semi-precious stones had magical and medicinal properties when worn, and many plants were similarly valued. **348.** *crop and roote:* common phrase signifying the whole. **349.** *routhe:* 'pity'. Chaucerian heroines are always requested to 'pity' rather than 'love' the hero. **352.** *thow:* with the singular form Pandarus shows passionate feeling, as in III, 356. **353.** *baude:* But a bawd or pimp is exactly what Pandarus is. **355.** *shame:* He is of course quite right. Knowing the end, the audience or reader is conscious of irony here. **361.** *feste:* 'feast', i.e. cheerful behaviour. **363.** *This:* 'This is', a frequent contraction. **366.** *doute of reson:* 'reasonable doubt'. **368.** *sen:* 'to see'. **370.** *fool of kynde:* 'natural fool'. **371.** *love of frendshipe:* 'friendly love', i.e. not 'of paramours'. Pandarus seems fond of using *of* + abstract noun as an adjective. Perhaps it suggests a deceitful tone here. **381.** *savacioun:* a clear, though trivial, example of anachronism. **384.** *daunger:* 'aloofness'. *Daunger* is the quality which keeps people off, reserve, haughtiness, a traditional, and obviously necessary, quality of the heroine, who would otherwise be cheap. *sucred:* 'sweetened', softened. **387.** Criseyde is also not entirely frank, though she is a child in cunning compared with Pandarus. **392.** *skilful guerdonynge:* 'reasonable reward'. **393.** Another kind of threat, though also a natural and traditional reflection. **396.** *the:* the singular form increases the feeling. **398.** as Pandarus says, proverbial. **400.** *fool:* court jester, who traditionally made satirical jokes at the expense of his superiors; but the remarks are natural, and also found in Ovid. **406.** 'Neice, I could wish you no greater sorrow'. **411.** *straunge:* 'strangers'. **413.** *Ret: redeth,* 'advises'. Criseyde is quite clear she should not love. **417.** *mannes creature:* 'creature of human kind'. **420.** *false world:* She feels

Pandarus has betrayed her, but the general notion is fundamental to the poem. **424.** *paynted proces:* 'specious argument'. Cf. II, 262, 292. The impression Criseyde has is exactly what Pandarus had tried to avoid. She is not so dim as he thinks. **425.** *Pallas:* one of the less usual names of Minerva. The Palladium (cf. I, 153 ff.) was an image of her. She was goddess of wisdom, and a virgin. Minerva became offended with the Trojans, and advised the Greeks to build the wooden horse by which they took Troy. Criseyde invokes Pallas again, V, 977, 999. **428–497.** Almost entirely original to Chaucer. **431.** *God toforn:* 'by God'. **435.** *Marte:* 'Mars', god of war. Pandarus, like Criseyde, invokes heathen gods. Local colour. **449–50.** Criseyde's timidity is insisted on by the poet. **452.** *sorwful ernest:* we may wonder about its sincerity. **460.** *no solas:* 'no comfort'; or 'no joke'. **461.** Criseyde is always anxious about what other people will think. Honour – and shame – which are the products of what other people think of one, are her chief concerns. Cf. I, 180, and II, 468, 762; III, 941 ff. **464.** 'Ah, Lord, what bad luck has befallen me.' **474.** *wis:* short for *iwis*, 'certainly'. Pandarus is lying. **475.** *peyne:* i.e. my best. **476.** 'I shall force my intention (*herte*) against my wish (*lust*).' **477.** 'except that I will not deceive him'. **485.** *proces:* 'matter'. **499 ff.** Criseyde shows her interest in her conquest. **500.** An anachronistic reference to the Christian God. **504.** 'for I shall the better provide (i.e. prepare) myself'. **506 ff.** Presumably the anecdote that Pandarus goes on here to tell 'by his truth' is untrue. **523 ff.** Modelled on religious language. **525.** *mea culpa:* Latin '(it is) my fault'. From the form of confession in the Latin service of the Mass. **526–8.** A Boethian echo, *Cons.* IV, pr. 6. **527–9.** 'controls the final end of every person by just foresight, graciously accept my humble confession'. **531.** *departe:* 'separate'. **538–9.** this proverbial illustration, also found in Ovid, is rather more in Pandarus's than Troilus's style. **545.** Pandarus reports his conversation in polite second-person plurals more consistently than is his normal usage to Troilus. **546.** *doth yow longe: either* 'does belong to you', *or*, 'causes you to yearn'. **548.** *or:* 'before'. **553.** *newe daunce:* 'latest dance'. **562.** *ner:* 'nearer'. **563.** an anachronistic oath. **565.** *engyn:* 'trick'. *loore:* 'advice'. **571.** *leche:* 'doctor'. Imagery of sickness, medicine, cure, doctor, etc. was commonly used for love. **576, 580, 581.** Pandarus protests a great deal. **583.** For the imagery, cf. II, 327 ff. **587–8.** Pandarus's expectations here run far beyond Criseyde's merely being kind to Troilus, as Criseyde laughingly, and not seriously upset, notes in the next line. **588.** *Ther:* an exclamatory intensive introducing a wish or imprecation. There is no modern equivalent. See Lang. **590.** *ye shenden every deel:*

'you spoil everything'. **594.** *my blood:* i.e. my blood-relation; 'cousin'. **615.** *cast up:* 'open'. **617–18.** *Dardanus:* one of the six gates of Troy. 'There is no other way from the gate of Dardanus where the chain is open.' Troy is envisaged like London and other medieval cities, where there were chains at the ends of streets to block them against horsemen, in case of riot or enemy attack. **621.** *happy day:* 'lucky day'. **622–3.** The note of destiny, ambivalently or ironically mentioned here, and awkwardly connected syntactically with the preceding lines, refers to Boethius, *Cons.,* V, pr. 6. **627.** *a pas:* 'at foot pace'. **628–30.** 'But such a chivalrous appearance, truly, without mistake, was not to be seen in Mars, who is god of battle, as was seen in Troilus'; i.e. he outdid even Mars in looking like a knight. This must be the general meaning, confused by the uncertainty between the transitive and intransitive senses of *syghte* and *To loke.* The literal sense, 'he did *not* look like Mars' – but was a man, seems impossible. Lines 628–37 are clumsy and repetitious. **634.** *that thing:* presumably meaning 'deeds of arms'. **635.** *hym dresse:* 'hold himself up'. **637.** 'It was a heavenly sight to see him.' **642.** *horn and nerf and rynde:* 'horn, sinew and hide' – general description of the materials of the shield. **651 ff.** *Who yaf me drynke:* 'Who has given me a love-potion?' Love was sometimes imaged as a drink, as in *Piers Plowman,* B-text, XVIII, 365. In the next five stanzas the poet dilates on the significance of Criseyde's remark and newly stirred feelings. II, 671–5 are particularly important and not apparently ironical or satirical. We have known from the beginning of the poem that Criseyde becomes Troilus's lover. The poet has here no difficulty in knowing what goes on in Criseyde's mind. **654.** *Which that:* 'who'. **656.** *for pure ashamed:* an idiomatic construction, 'for very shame'. **657.** *Gan in hire hed to pulle:* she had been looking out of her window. **671–2.** Proverbial. **677.** *myne:* 'penetrate'. **680–5.** *Venus:* the planet, astrological, i.e. for Chaucer the scientific truth underlying the poetic mythology. *hous* and *aspectes* are technical words. See Introd., p 35. **682.** *with aspectes payed:* i.e. shining in such a way as to seem pleased. **683.** *sely:* a word several times applied to Troilus in the poem. In Chaucer it has a range of meaning from 'innocent' to 'simple-minded' (foreshadowing the modern sense of 'silly'), and creates a sense of pathetic, defenceless goodness; but this sense is sometimes applied with a touch of mockery, as here. Translate 'simple'. **684.** *not al a foo:* Venus was not completely, only ultimately, hostile to Troilus. **687.** *Now lat us:* The poet associates himself with the audience. **691.** 'What position she would take up in the end.' **697.** 'So that she pleated many a fold very often', i.e. thought over and over again. **700.** The poet here attributes his knowledge of her thoughts to his source, Boccaccio's *Il Filostrato*, though he treats it with some freedom. **705–7.** Criseyde thinks it would benefit her reputation and her social estate, and give her a more cheerful life, to be nice to Troilus – and would also be good for him. **708–14.** It might also be dangerous to refuse him, she thinks, apparently forgetting his *gentilesse* and *worthynesse*, or not entirely believing them. **716–18.** A remark Chaucer found in *Le Roman de la Rose*, 5744–6. The literal sense is opposite to what is clearly meant. **720.** *ne aughte nat:* scan, *n'aughté nat*. **724.** *avantour:* 'one who boasts of his love affairs' – a cardinal sin in a lover. **728.** A metaphor from legal language, a clause being a binding stipulation. **729.** 'Now suppose a situation.' Perhaps *caas* has a legal flavour. Criseyde is arguing as Pandarus did, II, 367. **735.** *byleve:* 'go away'. **737.** *thriftieste:* 'most respectable'. **742.** *aventure:* 'fortune'.

745–6. scan *Al wolde I that noon wiste of this thought,*

I am oon the faireste, out of drede.

747. scan *goodlieste.* **750–1.** 'I am my own mistress, comfortably off. I thank God for it, as to my possessions'. **752.** *unteyde in lusty leese:* 'free in pleasant pasture'. She sees herself as a frisky young mare. **754.** checkmate is the term used to indicate prevention of the opponent's move (and thus victory) in chess. **759.** 'Why, good heavens, I am not a nun!' **784.** 'Our misfortune is this, to drink our own sorrow', i.e. to be left to endure our misery on our own – perhaps also here 'to face the consequences (e.g. an unwanted illegitimate baby) on our own.' Similar expressions were common. Cf. III, 1035. **787.** *lest:* 'desire', here corresponds with modern *lust*. As soon as the lover has slept with the girl he is satisfied and abandons her. **791.** Proverbial, presumably referring to over-sharpening a blade, which thus easily breaks. **792.** Criseyde's meditations on men's unfaithfulness have an obviously ironical effect here, since we know that it is she who will be unfaithful. **802–3.** 'For though there should be no cause, it seems to them that it is all for harm that people should please their friends.' **807–8.** Proverbial. **813 ff.** Criseyde's parlour, etc., were slightly above ground-level, probably built on deep cellars, so that she went down the steps at the back to the garden. Cf. Brewer, *Chaucer in His Time*, pp. 79 ff. The garden scene and Antigone's song are original to Chaucer. **814.** *neces thre:* These must be daughters of a married sister or brother of Criseyde, presumably dead, since her isolation has been insisted on. But to inquire too closely into such realistic detail, appropriate to a novel, is inappropriate here. Mention of the nieces here, with the other women, as in II, 81, provides an appropriate note of pleasant social domesticity, and yet suggests the grandness of Criseyde's establishment. The nieces are not important to the story, and are barely mentioned again. They are original to Chaucer. **816.** *Flexippe, Tharbe:* names invented by Chaucer presumably for local colour. *Antigone*, a Greek name, is also found in the story of Thebes. **826.** *it an heven:* 'it was heavenly'. **827.** Antigone's song establishes a warm, encouraging mood about love at this point of the story. It is an example of a *genre* of love-song in which a lady frankly expresses her own love and admiration for the beloved, and describes love as virtuous and mutual, without mention of 'art', 'craft', 'sovereignty' or 'secrecy', etc. **829-30.** 'I give all the desire of my heart as a payment to you, lord, for evermore, as best I can.' **843.** *of wit Apollo:* i.e. 'an Apollo as to his mind'. *stoon of sikernesse:* i.e. as steady as a rock. **849.** 'to bath in bliss' is a somewhat curious image, wet and warm, that Chaucer uses several times in the poem. **862.** *of kynde right:* 'in its proper nature'. **867-8.** Proverbial: cf. the modern proverb about glass houses. **882.** *let:* 'leads'. **890.** It was frequently stated in medieval literature (especially French) that a vulgar person could not know real love. **903.** *converte:* 'change' (her mind). **905.** *al this clepe I the sonne:* this phrase is perhaps the poet's joke against his own elaborate style. He makes the identical joke, if such it be, in *The Franklin's Tale*, V, 1017 ff. **918.** The nightingale was traditionally the bird of love. **925-31.** The dream symbolizes the traditional exchange of hearts between lovers, referred to in Antigone's song, II, 872-3. Lovers were often symbolized by birds, and an eagle symbolizes a royal and knightly lover, as in *The Parlement of Foules*. Troilus is himself compared to a sparrow-hawk seizing a lark, III, 1191. The dream is not in *Il Filostrato*. **926.** *whit as bon:* 'white as ivory'. Such a comparison was often made of the whiteness of the lady: why the eagle should be white is not clear – perhaps the whiteness signifies beauty and purity.

Book III

595. From here to III, 1190, is largely original to Chaucer. **601.** *stuwe:* 'a little room with a fireplace'. It is also a name for a brothel. No very dignified place for a prince of the blood royal to hide in. **602.** *bishet . . . in mewe:* 'cooped up'. **609.** 'there was no dainty to be fetched', i.e. none was lacking. **614.** *Wade:* an anachronistic mythological Germanic hero. No English story survives Cf. II, 83-4n. **615.** Proverbial. **617-23.** Suggested by Boethius.

Fortune controls or is the agent of Destiny (*wyrdes*) and works through the influence of the stars, mysteriously guiding our actions: as Criseyde's were guided. *wyrdes* is not a pagan word, but means the series of events in the world that add up to the 'way things are', which is destiny. In *The Legend of Good Women*, 2580, Chaucer writes of 'wyrdes' 'that we call Destiny'. Destiny includes adversity, but, as Boethius makes clear, *Cons.*, IV, p. 6, destiny is one aspect of God's Providence (*purveiaunce*). Fortune is thus a poetic word for worldly affairs, which are ultimately under the governance of God, but which are variable. Later, Chaucer says that Fortune has the 'permutation of things' committed to her by the providence (*purveiaunce*) and disposition of God (V, 1541–4, not in present selection). **623.** *bleve:* 'stay'. **624–6.** *bente moone:* 'crescent moon'. Saturn and Jove (Jupiter) are the planets joined with the moon in the sign of the Zodiac, Cancer (the Crab). This conjunction occurs only once in 600 years and in fact occurred in May 1385, which was about when Chaucer was finishing *Troilus and Criseyde.* The conjunction was thought to bring very heavy rain, which Pandarus had foreseen. **635.** Either Criseyde actually owned the house, or Pandarus is being very polite. **638–9.** 'Criseyde, who knew what was good as well as most people.' **640.** *ron:* 'rained'. **641.** *as good chepe:* 'as cheaply', i.e. as easily. **648.** *a-game:* 'in a joke'. **663 ff.** *closet:* It seems that Criseyde was to sleep in an inner room (*closet*), Pandarus's usual bedroom, off the small hall where they had eaten and had their party. The trestle tables were moved from this hall, a curtain (*travers*, III, 674) was drawn across the middle, and Criseyde's women slept in the inner section by the closet door, while Pandarus slept in the outer section. **671.** *The wyn anon!:* 'the wine now!' Before going to bed the well-to-do took a night-cap of wine (*the voidë*, III, 674), often accompanied with spices, cakes, raisins. **690–3.** The syntax is elliptical, half-quoting, half-reporting speech. 'There was to be no more skipping or tramping about, and if anyone stirred anywhere he was told to go to bed, curse him, and let those who were in bed sleep.' **695.** *The olde daunce:* a general French expression meaning 'the tricks of the game' but applied by Chaucer to love. **696.** *thyng:* an old uninflected plural, taking the plural adjective *alle*, but misunderstood as singular in the fourteenth century, hence the verb *was*. **702.** *word and ende:* 'from beginning to end'. A set phrase. **703.** *the:* 'thee'. Pandarus's intimate address in the second person singular contrasts with the polite and more distant second person plural he uses to Criseyde. He is brisk and down to earth. Troilus, with his invocations to Venus, is solemn. **705.** *thow me grace sende:* 'may you send me grace'; a subjunctive verb expressing a wish in prayer. **710.** *so thryve I:* subjunctive expressing wish in an intensifying phrase; 'so may I thrive', 'as I hope to prosper'. **711.** 'Or make a complete mess of it.' One of Pandarus's typically homely, semi-proverbial expressions. **713.** *wys:* 'surely'. **715-28.** Troilus's prayer, appropriately using the second person singular. He combines mythological and astrological attributes of the gods, thus giving both the local colour of an unenlightened pagan (the mythology) and touching on what were for the fourteenth century the underlying true scientific, i.e. astrological causes. The mythological stories were familiar: it is an irony obvious to the reader, unperceived by Troilus, that all these are stories of shame or disaster and atrocity caused by love. Mars, Jupiter, Apollo, the heroes, are the '*rascaille*' referred to in V, 1849-53. Chaucer clearly tremendously enjoyed reading Ovid, who tells these stories in the *Metamorphoses*, but he also shows a dry medieval contempt for the horrors which are the principal ingredients of classical mythology. Cf. Brewer, *Chaucer*, revised 2nd edition, 1961, p. 117. **716.** *aspectes badde of:* 'unfavourable influences from': *aspect* literally refers to position in the heaven; Troilus is thinking of his horoscope. **717.** *combust:* 'burnt up'. If a planet was too near the sun its good influence was *combust*, i.e. destroyed. **718.** *fader:* i.e. Jupiter, a benefic planet. **719.** *Of grace:* 'graciously'. **721.** *Adoun:* Adonis; Venus loved him: but he did not love her; he was killed by a boar when hunting. **722.** Jupiter (Jove), king of the gods, in order to carry off the beautiful Europa, assumed the form of a bull. After being raped she went mad and wandered through the world till death. **724.** the bloody cloak is a suitable attribute for Mars, god of war, who loved Venus, here called by her other name, Cipris. Venus's husband Vulcan caught Mars and Venus in a net and displayed them naked before the gods. **726.** Phoebus Apollo chased Daphne in an attempt to rape her. She escaped by being turned into a laurel. **729.** Mercury loved Herse, whose sister Aglauros was jealous of her. Mercury turned Aglauros to stone when she tried to hinder his love. Chaucer's memory of the details is vague. **731.** *Diane:* goddess of chastity. **733-4.** *fatal sustren:* 'sisters, the Fates': the three classical Fates, who spun and cut the threads of a man's life, i.e. decided his destiny, before even his first garment was made. Troilus believes his destiny has already been decided, but by a familiar human paradox also asks for help as if the outcome were still in doubt. Cf. V, 1-4 and note. The common modern meaning of *fatal* as 'ruinous' or 'disastrous' is not in Chaucer, nor recorded before the sixteenth century. **737.** *so that:* 'that'. **738.** *don:* 'put'. **739.** *the wite:* 'the blame'. **741-2.** The little room Troilus has waited in is connected with the room in which Criseyde is sleeping by a trap-door (and perhaps a passage and stairs as well). Pandarus pulls Troilus along by a fold (*lappe*) of his cloak, since it is dark and Troilus does not know the way. **748.** Pandarus, now in Criseyde's room, shuts the door which communicates with the hall where her women are sleeping. **754.** *ner:* 'nearer'. **757.** *benedicite:* 'bless

you!' an exclamation. Translate 'Good Heavens!' Scan *bendíste* (which is how it was sometimes written). It comes from the Canticle *Benedicite omnia*, sung by the Three Children in the fiery furnace. **764.** Proverbial. **781–4.** 'To Troilus, one of the worthiest knights of this world; and furthermore (you have) pledged your truth, that unless it were through his fault [*on hym along*, lit. 'because of him'] you would never betray him while you live.' **787.** *goter:* Even though Pandarus is lying, the implication is of a gutter, which, like a similar one in Chaucer's *Legend of Good Women*, 2705, needs a hole in a room's wall big enough for a man to squeeze through: perhaps it was a sort of drain, or even a latrine. **791.** *shal:* i.e. 'owe'. **796–7.** 'He says he has been told by a friend of his that you are said to love someone called Horaste.' Pandarus is lying again. The speech is not in Chaucer's sources; the name gives local colour. **800.** *colde:* 'grow cold'. **813–36.** Founded on Boethius, *Cons.*, II, pr. 4. The passage is formal, but the sentiments so natural and true that it does not make Criseyde less believable. That she speaks truth, but will prove it by her own falseness, is part of the irony of the poem. The instability of worldly joy is one chief theme of the poem. This passage is significantly placed before the description of the real though transient joy of the consummation of Troilus and Criseyde's love. Compare this passage with V, 1821 ff. **820.** *Brotel:* 'brittle'. **829.** *that:* is a pronoun, referring to the transitoriness of joy. **832.** 'And if he cares a farthing about losing his joy.' **834.** *diffyne:* 'conclude'. **844.** *Ye woot, ye:* 'You know, indeed'. **853.** Proverbial; delay brings danger. **855.** Proverbial. **860.** *benedicite:* cf. III, 757 n. *al among that fare:* i.e. 'while all that's going on'. **861.** Proverbial. The bird is flown; the opportunity lost. **872–5.** 'For if you make *me* an example of such love, *I* pray to God that I may never have joy if *I* would see him (i.e. allow him to be) sorrowful all night, for all the treasure in the town of Troy.' **885.** *blewe ryng:* ring with a blue gem-stone – the colour of constancy. **890.** *haselwodes shaken:* such references indicate derision and uselessness. Pandarus alone uses them; here and V, 505 (not in present selection) and 1174. **891–2.** Gem-stones were thought to have magical powers to confer benefits on the wearer, but none so strong as this! **900.** 'I would not value his sorrow at a farthing.' 901. *white:* 'fair'. 907. Pandarus cunningly plans ahead so that Troilus's ignorance of all this passion attributed to him may seem evidence of his depth of feeling. 919. *prime face: 'prima facie'*, 'at first sight'. Perhaps legal language. 922–4. 'It is not surprising, all things considered as they stood, and since she did all for good, if she did do him a favour then.' 925. *at reste:* i.e. in heaven. 931. *at dulcarnoun:* 'in two minds': *dulcarnoun* comes from an Arabic word meaning 'two-horned'. It was also used to describe the difficult 47th proposition of the first book of Euclid's geometry, which had a figure like two horns. 933. *flemyng of wrecches:* 'putting wretches to flight', the translation of a Latin term, *fuga miserorum*, which was used to describe another proposition of geometry. Pandarus likes to show his book-learning, but he is wrong in thinking that *dulcarnoun* (the 47th) is the same as *fuga miserorum*, which is Euclid's 5th proposition. Schoolboys had to learn these propositions. 934–5. 'It seems hard because wretches will not learn because of real idleness or other wilful faults.' Pandarus is self-condemned. His error symbolizes his speciousness and deceitfulness. 936. *This:* 'this is'. 937. *ye ben wis:* The low opinion Pandarus really had of Criseyde's mind is revealed earlier, II, 271. 938. *skilful:* 'reasonable'. 944–5. Criseyde's usual concern for honour, and her sense of helplessness, are conveyed here. 947. *Ther:* cf. II, 588. 'May that wise and noble heart of yours prosper!' 954. *sobrely:* 'humbly'. 964. The realistic and amusing cushion does not seem to be intended as a joke by Pandarus, though it must be so intended by the poet. 967 ff. The poet's ostentatious display of ignorance as to why Criseyde did not immediately dismiss Troilus draws attention to it. Her 'sighing sore' suggests her half-reluctant surrender. 979–80. 'And took a light and made a show of looking at an old romance.' 982. 'And stood clear in complete certainty', i.e. certainty that she had given Troilus no cause to be jealous. 1000. 'Have, and always shall, however it may hurt me.' 1009. *My goode myn:* lit. 'my good my own'; translate perhaps 'my own beloved and best'. *noot I:* 'I do not know'. 1029. 'And according to that, it ought to be called', i.e. love or (more likely) hate or anger. 1035. i.e. some jealousy does not express itself. For the idiom cf. II, 784. 1046–7. Three methods of proving her innocence are offered by Criseyde. *Ordal* was a test, such as holding a burning object, innocence being proved by rapidity of healing; by *oth*, was declaring one's innocence before God and calling down terrible penalties on oneself if the oath were false; by *sort* was drawing lots. Ordeal had been abolished in 1215, but 'purgation of oath' continued legally in Chaucer's time. The third method was popular rather than legal. **1056.** There is something absurdly but touchingly childish in Criseyde's hiding her head under the sheet. **1058.** The poet intervenes with a mock-anxious remark and typical comments on the alternations of worldly fortune, though he leaves out the usual completion of joy following sorrow, i.e. that sorrow follows joy. **1060–1.** Proverbial. **1067–71.** It seemed to him not like being beaten – far worse, he felt a deathly pain in his heart, to see his lady weep. **1088.** For spirits of the body see I, 306–8n; each spirit, of heart, liver, brain, contracted itself, so did not function, and Troilus fainted. **1108.** 'Than all the good encompassed by the sun', i.e. all the good in the world. **1125.** Criseyde uses the polite second person plural. **1135 ff.** The joke is here Pandarus's own. **1142.** *though:* it is impossible to see how *though* fits logically into the sentence structure. The underlying thought seems to be that though there was no need for Troilus to stay in bed with her, she nevertheless did not ask him to go. **1146–8.** Presumably these enigmatic remarks are meant to be taken as a joking sexual innuendo about Criseyde. Something less than oaths could have caused her to allow Troilus to stay with her – for all lovers wish only to be nice. **1154.** *bar hym on honde:* 'assured him'. **1161.** *al deere ynough a rysshe:* 'all not worth a rush'. **1165.** An anachronistically Christian reference. *bought:* 'redeemed'. **1191 ff.** Here the poet intervenes to comment overtly, to emphasize a new phase of the story, and also to cast responsibility on his source. **1192.** The fundamental and necessary sexual aggressiveness of the lover is here at last attributed to Troilus. **1194.** *sucre:* 'sugary'. *soot:* 'soot', i.e. bitter. **1199.** The poet again throws responsibility on his authorities, thus distancing the event at its most intimate moment. **1200.** The quivering of aspen leaves is a proverbial comparison. **1203.** The seven planets whose influence affects the earth are referred to. **1210–11.** In these two remarkable lines Criseyde expresses herself generously and with dramatic truth. *Ne hadde:* scan 'nad'. **1221.** 'to float in bliss' is characteristic of the 'wet' imagery of joy. **1224–5.** The poet again comments to his audience, this time with joking ambiguity about the 'need'. **1235.** *herde tale:* 'shepherd talk'. **1249.** *good thrift bad ful ofte:* i.e. 'wished many a blessing on'. **1254.** *O Love, O Charite:* charity can be Christian love but is obviously not so here. It is the same as Love, the offspring of Citherea, i.e. Venus, in the next line, thought of especially as the benevolent planet (III, 1257). The planet causes sexual love. The only other place where Chaucer links the words love and charity (in *Cons.*, III, pr. 11, 170–5) refers to natural physical desire 'coming not from the moving of the soul but from the intention of nature'. In other words, it is purely worldly and natural, though not evil. Cf. Brewer, *Chaucer*, 2nd edn, 1961, pp. 63–72. **1258.** *Imeneus:* 'Hymen', the classical god of marriage. Troilus, deceiving himself, thinks of his liaison as marriage. **1261.** Kindly love binds all things together, animate and inanimate; cf. III, 1744 ff. **1262.** *wol grace:* 'wishes for grace'. **1263.** *wol fle:* 'wishes to fly'. **1296.** *wommanliche wif:* 'pattern of womanliness': *wif* in the old sense of *woman: wommanliche* is always a word of high praise in Chaucer. **1299.** *breken youre defence:* 'do what you forbid'. **1301.** *lat sle me with the dede:* 'have me killed at the moment of the deed'. **1310 ff.** The poet comments in his own person. **1315–16.** Insecurity, between dread and certainty, accompanies even experience of the 'worthiness' of love. **1319–37.** The extravagance of language expressed by the poet, and his affectation of extreme envy, distances the events by a touch of absurdity that suggests, without expressing, a hint of criticism. The personal nature of his remarks here, his references to his source and to his own incompetence, his suggestion that the audience should 'increase' or 'diminish' his language, all lessen his own personal responsibility for the story and throw responsibility on the reader to make his own judgement. **1369.** *scripture:* i.e. an engraved posy. **1384.** *white:* 'silver'. *rede:* 'gold'. **1389.** *Mida:* Midas was granted his wish that everything he touched might turn to gold, and had his ears changed into the long ears of a donkey for his folly. **1391.** Crassus, a rich Roman consul, was killed in battle, 53 B.C. Molten gold was poured down his throat because he had been so avaricious in life. *affectis:* 'desires'. **1415.** *comune astrologer:* 'everyman's astrologer' – because he tells the time as it were from the stars. The learned phrase is in comic contrast with what it denotes. **1417.** *Lucyfer:* the morningstar, actually Venus, hence *hire* in III, 1418. **1420.** *Fortuna Major:* in origin the name of a pattern of six, here it refers to a group of six stars in the constellations Aquarius and Pegasus which were rising in the east at dawn about the time the poem was written. The name is also appropriate to the poem's concern with the ups and downs of Fortune. Troilus is symbolically on the upward turn of the wheel. *that:* we would expect *than*, 'then'; if the text is correct, the syntax of the sentence has become confused, though the sense is clear. **1422–70.** These speeches, whose blend of formality and passion reaches lyrical intensity, have no counterpart in *Il Filostrato*. They correspond to the traditional dawn-song, very widespread in the world's literature. That Criseyde begins testifies to her anxiety about her reputation, the loss of which would seem to her like eternal damnation (III, 1426). **1427 ff.** The second person singular is appropriate for passion, anger, and invocation of a mythological personification. **1428.** *Almena:* When Alcmena lay with Jove and begot Hercules, she miraculously extended the night to three times its usual length. **1434–5.** 'That whereas day would break us with labour you thus fly away and do not deign to rest us.' **1437–40.** 'You hasty night, may God, creator of nature, bind you so tight for ever to our hemisphere, because of your haste and unnatural vice, that you may nevermore revolve under the ground!' (i.e. to the other hemisphere). The exaggerated sentiment is perhaps slightly comic at Criseyde's expense. **1443–5.** *felte . . . teris:* 'felt – as it seemed to him then, because of his piteous distress – the bloody tears'. **1451.** Troilus is under no illusion that their love is not 'stolen and concealed'. **1453.** 'For every chink has one of your bright eyes', i.e. every chink into the dark room is bright with daylight. **1457.** *what:* 'how' ('why' in III, 1461). **1462.** Engravers of seals, who have very delicate work, need good light. **1464.** *Titan:* signifies the sun, often confused, as here, with the husband, Tithonus, of the Dawn (Aurora). **1469.** The ranting tone here again, as with parts of Criseyde's speech, is perhaps meant to be slightly comic to the audience, though Troilus himself is being portrayed as serious, sincere, and in real pain. **1470.** 'I pray God he may give you both sorrow.' *so:* an intensive, as in 'so help me', which modern English cannot translate. **1478.** *I not how:* 'I do not know how'. **1482.** *biteth:* 'cuts'. **1490.** *than thise worldes tweyne:* 'than two worlds such as this'. **1493 ff.** Criseyde's speech is sadly ironical to the reader, though meant sincerely by her. **1496.** *feere:* 'companion, mate'. **1501, 1503.** The solemnity of Criseyde's speech is enhanced by anachronistic but deeply felt Christian references to God. **1502.** *in the peyne:* 'under torture', which was applied to enemies and supposedly criminal witnesses in Chaucer's day. **1512.** *thyn:* the passion of this declaration is revealed by that rarest of grammatical uses between the lovers, the second personal singular, though even here not as a pronoun. **1514.** *er this:* she forgets, or did not love, her former husband. *mo:* 'more' in number. **1534.** *real:* 'royal'. **1546–7.** 'Desire all newly burned him, and lust (*or* longing *or* pleasure) began to grow more than before, and yet he took no heed'; i.e. he did not mind, or did not care, that far from being satisfied his desire was even greater than before. **1550.** *lust:* 'pleasure' or 'desire'. **1552.** *he so wel hire bisette: either* 'he (Love) placed her in such a favourable position'; *or* 'he (Troilus) so well occupied her'. **1555–89.** The visit of Pandarus is original to Chaucer. **1564–6.** Criseyde's angry answer, strictly inconsistent with her joy and satisfaction as just described, nevertheless recognizes Pandarus as the real deviser of the situation, and as a deceiver (*fox*). **1569–75.** Criseyde feels shame rather than guilt, and again covers her face; cf. III, 1056 and note. Pandarus's excited behaviour is itself almost sexual and betrays a freedom towards his niece not seen before. **1576.** The poet comments in his own person. **1577.** Not an anachronistic Christian reference, since it is spoken by the poet himself. The medieval freedom and casualness of reference to God is notable; this phrase was proverbial. It is theologically correct, Christ being God. *his deth:* 'his being put to death'. **1600.** *Flegetoun:* 'Phlegethon', one of the rivers of Hades, the classical hell. **1603.** 'It could not one whit suffice in (doing) that', i.e. it could not in the least repay you. **1606.** *inly:* 'extremely'. **1625–8.** An observation made by several medieval and later authors up to Tennyson, with his 'sorrow's crown'. **1625–38.** It is unusual for Pandarus to express something of the poem's theme of Fortune, and the transitoriness of worldly joy, but he does so with characteristic homely, realistic imagery and didacticism. **1642.** *heere:* 'her'. **1643.** *stere:* 'stir', i.e. discuss. **1650.** 'I never felt my love half as intensely as I do now.' **1661.** *ful to speke:* i.e. 'tired of speaking', For the idiom, cf. fed-up with'. **1663.** *bounte:* 'goodness'. **1667.** All events, whether agreeable (as here), or disagreeable, are 'under' Fortune. **1688.** *of for to seye:* 'for to speak of'. **1690.** The beauty of the relationship in which each obeys the other's desire, goes beyond the 'service' of a lover to his lady. This mutuality in true love is also represented in *The Franklin's Tale* and *The Wife of Bath's Tale.* **1691–2.** i.e. felicity, which wise and learned men (e.g. Boethius) commend so greatly, is an insufficient word in this case. The supreme joy the lovers feel is not denied or treated ironically. But it is, as the following stanzas show, transitory. **1703.** *Pirous:* 'Pyrois', one of the four horses of the chariot of the sun. **1705.** 'Have taken a short cut to spite me.' **1709.** 'But day needs must part them soon.' **1714 ff.** Fortune gives Troilus joy, and he leads a gay, expensive, fashionable life, in which his popularity does not spoil his faithfulness. The focus of the poem here, as ever, is on Troilus. Criseyde, however vivid a character, is an adjunct. **1721.** *as com hym wel of kynde:* 'as well became his nature'. **1730.** *Kynde:* 'Nature', the creative power that made the universe, and thus the creative aspect of God, cf. I, 238; also the universe as created by God, who is 'auctour of kynde', III, 1765. **1744–71.** Some manuscripts omit this song, and it may be one of several additions to the poem; cf. V, 1807–27 n. The song is based on *Cons.,* II, m. 8. Although formal, not dramatically realistic, the song conveys a noble image of the universe united by love, and expresses Troilus's deep desire to be part of it. The beauty of the song lies in the splendour of the ideas, the vigour and variety of diction, the power of the syntax that itself seems to enact the binding force of the divine love, and its expression of Troilus's own joy and aspiration. It is important to note that *Bynd* (1750) is a subjunctive, expressing Troilus's wish that his love *may* be part of the divine love, not an indicative signifying the fact. The poet himself expresses no opinion about this. But Troilus's own love is in fact true and stable (V, 1695–1701), like the love of God; to that extent his prayer is granted. That Criseyde is false is no reflection on the quality of Troilus's love, though he would have been happier if he had not sought a 'feynede love' as object (V, 1848). **1751.** *That that:* 'the fact that'; so III, 1758. **1752–4.** 'So varies its seasons harmoniously, that elements that are so discordant maintain a perpetually enduring bond between themselves.' **1766.** *vertu:* 'power'. **1772–1806.** The poet emphasizes the real goodness that love creates in Troilus. He avoided every vice. There is no irony here. Yet Troilus's liaison with Criseyde was irregular. Since it was not adulterous (neither being married) and bearing in mind Troilus's faithfulness, the poet ignores its immoral aspects. Nevertheless, the story shows that the irregularity of the love affair leaves it resting on the unstable foundation of Fortune. Had Criseyde been married she would hardly have been sent out of Troy. **1786.** *vertu:* 'goodness'. **1795.** *it:* i.e. in the service of love. This line naturally raises a question about Troilus in the reader's mind. **1796–9.** 'And beyond all this he could so express his feelings and dress himself so marvellously that every lover thought that whatever he said or did was well.' **1800–1.** This reference to the pride of royalty is hardly complimentary. **1805.** Four of the Seven Deadly Sins are here: the others are lechery, sloth, gluttony, included in the next line. **1806.** *gan to fle:* 'fled': *gan* here simply indicates the past tense. **1807.** *Dyone:* mother of Venus. **1809–10.** Helicon was erroneously thought in the Middle Ages to be a spring on Mount Parnassus, where the nine Muses dwelt. *listen for t'abide:* 'are pleased to dwell'. **1811–13.** 'That you have condescended to guide me so far I can say no more about other than, since you must depart, may you be praised for ever without end.' The Muses are 'departing' in that this book is coming to an end, and the presiding deities of the next books will be the Furies (IV, 22 ff.).

Book IV

7. 'Then she laughs and pulls a face at him.' **18.** *mynde:* 'memory'. **19–21.** The poet as usual leaves the 'truth' about Criseyde uncertain, and expresses an ambivalent sympathy.

22-4. *Herynes:* 'Erinyes', 'Furies'; cf. I, 6 n. **25.** *Quyryne:* Romulus, mythical founder of Rome, son of Mars. **26-8.** *ferthe book:* Chaucer here seems not to have expected to expand his poem into a fifth book.

Book V

1-2. *fatal destyne:* 'the inexorable course of events'; cf. III, 617 n., and III, 733 n. Boethius makes it clear that the course of events in the world, however mysterious or little to one's liking, is ultimately guided by God, here mythologically called Jove. **3.** *Parcas:* 'Parcae', the Fates, or 'fatal sisters', Lachesis (V, 7) Clotho, Atropos, who spin, measure and cut the thread of life. **4.** *don execucioun:* 'carry out'. **8-14.** A beautifully rhetorical way of describing the passage of the three years of the love affair. **10.** *Zepherus:* 'Zephyrus', the west wind. **12.** *Ecuba:* Hecuba, wife of Priam and mother of Troilus. **62-3.** The poet emphasizes Criseyde's sorrow at leaving Troilus here, and at V, 82, without irony. **71.** *Antenor:* the Trojan warrior for whom Criseyde was exchanged. **80.** 'And he rode nearer, to plead his cause.' **86.** *Diomede:* the Greek, son of Tideus, in charge of the exchange. **89-90.** The Creed was one of the first things a child learnt. Diomede was no beginner in these matters, and noted Troilus's distress. **95.** 'If I can help it, for I shall say something.' **98 ff.** Diomede's selfish egotism and his cool plan of seduction are made plain. **100.** *I am aboute nought:* i.e. I shall get nowhere. **101.** *make it tough:* 'press on boldly'. **106.** 'This Diomede, like one who knew what was good for him', i.e. being one who knew his own interests. **107.** *this:* i.e. his thoughts. **120.** 'it seems strange to you'. **122.** Either scan $Tr\acute{o} - \overset{\times}{i} - \acute{a}ns$, or as a 'headless' line with heavy stress on first syllable. Several scribes altered the line to improve the scansion. **124-6.** i.e. 'but God forbid you should not find a Greek among us as true and also as kind as any Trojan'. **130.** Diomede is a fast worker. **132.** 'Command me, however it may hurt me.' **137.** 'I do not know why, but without more delay.' **141.** Here *Troians* (like *Grekes*) is undoubtedly two syllables; cf. V, 122 n. **143.** *O:* 'one'. **151.** *this:* 'this is'. **155-61.** Troilus had genuinely been in this situation: as to Diomede's lie here, cf. V, 89-90, above. **156.** 'For as certainly as (I wish) God may gladden my heart.' **164-5.** The troubadour Jaufre Rudel was reputed to have fallen in love with the Countess of Tripoli on only hearing about her, and the notion is found elsewhere.

177. *as she that was:* 'since she was'. **180.** 'It seemed to her that her sorrowful heart would burst in two.' **189.** *As seyde she:* the placing of this phrase makes it a sceptical comment on Diomede's trustworthiness. **194.** scan *milde*. **204–5.** 'And there he gave free vent to his sorrows, which he had restrained, and cried out, "Death!"' **208.** Ceres, goddess of corn, hence food, and Bacchus, god of wine, were traditionally associated with Venus, goddess of love, here called by one of her alternative names, Cipride. **212.** Ixion was bound to a continually turning wheel in Hades. **784.** Criseyde had made use of the same proverb in her musings, II, 807–8. **790–1.** Diomede is as bookish, and as fond of a proverbial turn of phrase, as Pandarus. The reference is, however, vague, if not bogus, and no precise source is known. **796.** 'Thought in his heart, "Come what may".' **799 ff.** The following three portraits are to some extent garnered from Chaucer's sources, but they are also largely traditional portraits in a pattern descended from Latin and Greek literature, elaborated by rhetoricians and poets in the Middle Ages. **805.** Tydeus, Diomede's father, had been king of Calydon and Argos; cf. V, 932–5 and n. **806.** *mene:* 'moderate'. The usual heroine was tall, but Criseyde was traditionally not. **810.** A heroine's hair was always golden, as we are told Criseyde's was, IV, 736 (not in present selection). **813.** *browes joyneden:* joined eyebrows were a point of beauty to the Greeks, but not to medieval men. The philosopher and theologian Albertius Magnus considered joined eyebrows to be a sign of a treacherous nature. The medieval heroine's eyebrows were normally black, her eyes blue or grey. **820–6.** This stanza praises Criseyde's moral nature, her tender-heartedness, good education, etc.; her instability ('slydynge of corage', V, 825) is, however, an unusual quality among the traditional attributes of a heroine. A note of doubt is introduced only about her age. **821.** *ynorisshed:* 'brought up'. **825.** *slydynge of corage:* 'unstable of heart'. **831.** 'True as steel' was a traditional fixed phrase. **837.** *in durryng don:* 'in daring to do'; the phrase behind the modern false archaism *derring-do*. **859.** *demaunde:* 'question'. **860–1.** 'To ask her if the ways of the Greeks, and the things that they did, seemed strange to her.' **866.** *konnyng:* 'ability'. **868.** *semed:* 'seemed': the poet casts some doubt upon her apparent simplicity. **883 ff.** Diomede is not above a kind of bullying. **888.** *to mercy gon on-lyve:* lit. 'go alive to (or in) mercy', i.e. 'by way of mercy be allowed to escape alive'. **892–3.** *Manes:* Chaucer explains who he thinks them to be – it is not a classical notion. The Grecian vengeance on Troy will be so cruel that it will strike terror even into the gods of the Underworld. **897.**

ambages: Chaucer explains the meaning of this word in the next two lines because he took it direct from Boccaccio's Italian. The word was new, but the device is a very common part of Chaucer's own irony. **901.** *sen:* an infinitive, following *shal* in V, 900. **903.** 'Now pay attention, for that is what must be done.' **926–7.** *a litel wight* (bis): the repetition is comic and marks his insincerity. **931.** It is unimaginable that Troilus would have urged his suit by reference to his social status, as Diomede here does. **932.** Tydeus, father of Diomede, was one of the Seven against Thebes, whose war was the subject of the book Criseyde and her ladies were reading (II, 84). He was killed at Thebes. Why Diomede would have been king of his father's kingdom if his father had *lived* is not clear, but Chaucer is translating Boccaccio here. **938.** 'To the harm of Polynices and many a man.' Polynices was the chief of the Seven. **940.** cf. V, 155–61. **955.** *strangely:* 'distantly'. **958.** *doth it care:* 'cause it sorrow'. **971.** *Orkades and Inde:* 'the Orkneys and India' – limits of the known world. **976.** *The whos:* 'whose'. **977.** *Pallas:* Pallas Athene, patron saint of the city: cf. I, 153, and II, 425. **982.** *scornen:* i.e. mock by making offers of love. **984–5.** i.e. 'I would rather, if I might do it, lament and sorrow until my death'. **986.** *after:* 'in the future' – somewhat inconsistent with the previous lines. **992.** *say:* 'saw'. **1015.** *al was wel:* i.e. he was sure of success. **1016–22.** A passage that is decorative and also tells the date. Venus as an evening star following the sun (Phebus) was visible just above (and so she indicated) where the sun had set. Cynthia, the moon-goddess, reached over her chariot-horses in urging them on to leave the Zodiacal sign of the Lion (Leo). In IV, 1590–6 (not in present selection) Criseyde had promised to return before the Moon passed out of Leo, so she has been with the Greeks nearly ten days – her time is almost up. The stars in the Zodiac (the *candels* of *Signifer*) are bright. **1025.** *His grete estat:* 'his high rank', rather than his riches. **1030.** *gostly:* 'spiritually', i.e. 'truthfully'. **1032.** 'And, to be brief, lest you interrupt my tale.' From here to l. 1053 we are made especially aware of the poet addressing us, and his care to hold a possibly restive audience. **1038–9.** Diomede, according to earlier accounts, won the horse and gave it to Criseyde, who gave it back to him. **1041.** *Troilus:* 'Troilus's', gen. sing. **1048.** *kepen:* 'look after'. **1050.** *I not:* 'I do not know'. As so often, the poet disclaims knowledge about Criseyde. But, considering the series of examples of devotion to Diomede he has just given us, this disclaimer has an ironical, sceptical tone. **1062.** *my belle shal be ronge:* a semi-proverbial expression suggesting malicious talk about a genuinely bad reputation. **1086–1100.** In these lines we are again made more aware of the poet as commentator. Attention is directed towards Criseyde's ultimate unfaithfulness, of which our knowledge serves as background to the account of Troilus's expectations when the story returns to the tenth day. The poet's expression of sorrow, V, 1093–9, may be taken at its face value, though some may detect irony, emphasizing guilt while pretending to seek excuse. **1107.** *laurer-crowned:* a non-realistic attribute of the sun-god. **1110.** *Nysus doughter:* Scylla, who betrayed her father for love of Minos and was turned into a lark. **1140.** *holden up the yate:* the gate was a portcullis. **1141.** *as naught ne were:* 'as if for nothing'. **1149.** *kan hire good:* 'knows what is good for her'. **1161.** *where arte?:* i.e. 'where do you think you are?' **1174.** *joly Robin* is not Robin Hood but the shepherd Robin, who was the subject (with the shepherdess Marion) of many artificial pastoral French songs and of a famous comedy by Adan de la Halle in the thirteenth century. 'The hazelwood, where jolly Robin played' is therefore 'never-never land'. **1176.** Proverbial. **1641.** *as faste:* 'very soon'. **1652.** *Deiphebe:* Deiphebus, a brother of Troilus. **1653.** *Lollius:* Chaucer's pretended source. **1658.** *werk:* 'embroidery'. **1664.** 'And she in return laid her faith as a pledge', i.e. 'and she in return pledged her faith'. **1666.** 'His lady was no longer to be trusted.' **1672.** *after deth:* 'for death'. **1677.** *feeste:* 'enjoyment'. **1679.** *in trouthe to me stonde:* 'stay faithful to me'. **1709–15.** Troilus refers to a dream he had dreamt of a boar embracing Criseyde, which Pandarus had pooh-poohed. Cassandra his sister had explained the boar meant Diomede, V, 1233 ff. (not in present selection). **1731.** 'My dear brother, I can do no more for you.' **1732.** Pandarus says he hates Criseyde; Troilus has said he cannot stop loving her, 1696–8. **1736.** *reward:* 'regard'. **1742.** *almyghty God:* a more than usually anachronistic invocation. **1765.** Once more the poet's comment in his own person distances the action of the story; here begins a more complete withdrawal. From here onwards almost all is independent of Boccaccio's *Filostrato.* **1771.** *Dares:* one of the Latin historians of the Trojan War. **1778.** Penelope was the wife of Odysseus (Ulysses) and remained faithful to him during his twenty years' absence. Alcestis, wife of King Admetus, volunteered to die in her husband's place. They were types of faithful wives in classical literature. The story of Alcestis is briefly told, V, 1527–33 (not in present selection). **1783.** Address to the ladies in the audience. **1786.** *tragedye:* In his translation of the *Consolation of Philosophy* Chaucer defines tragedy as a poem 'of a prosperity for a time, that endeth in wretchedness', II, pr. 2, 70–80. **1788.** *comedye:* a poem with a happy ending. **1789–90.** 'But, little book, do not strive with other writing, but be under all poetry.' **1791.** *steppes:*

'foot-prints'. Imitated from the end of the *Thebaid*. **1792**. Virgil
wrote the *Aeneid*; Ovid *Metamorphoses, Heroides* and others;
Homer the *Iliad* and *Odyssey* (in Greek and known only by
reputation to the Middle Ages); Lucan *Pharsalia*; Statius the
Thebaid. **1793–8**. A passage all editors and students may take to
heart. **1797**. *songe:* The expression is presumably conventional.
1799. *rather:* 'earlier'. **1805**. 'But alas, except that it was God's
will.' **1807–27**. These stanzas are based on three from Boccaccio's
Teseida (source of Chaucer's *The Knight's Tale*), where they refer
to the death of Arcita, and may be a later addition of Chaucer's.
1809. *eighte spere:* 'eighth sphere'; probably the sphere of the
fixed stars, numbered outward from the earth. **1810**. 'Leaving
behind every element.' **1812**. *erratik sterres:* 'the wandering
stars', i.e. the (seven) planets. **1812–13**. *herkenyng armonye:* presumably it is Troilus who is listening to the harmony of the
spheres, with its sounds full of heavenly melody. **1823–5**. The
short-sighted pursuit of transient earthly instead of eternal
heavenly pleasure is condemned. **1827**. It was one of the duties of
the god Mercury to escort the souls of the dead to their proper
place. Chaucer does not tell us where Troilus was finally placed.
1828–34. *Swich fyn:* the end referred to is probably the end of
his love affair, showing how little his merit counted for in
worldly life and success. For this stanza Chaucer goes back to *Il
Filostrato*, where the same rhetorical figure of repetition (*anaphora*) is used. **1830**. *estat real:* 'royal rank'. **1832**. *brotelnesse:*
'brittleness', i.e. insecurity. **1835 ff**. The story has now been
finally left behind, and the poet addresses his audience direct.
This ending has been much discussed. It is less moralistic than
sometimes thought – more a reflection on the world's mutability
and transience under Fortune than a condemnation of its morals.
1844. *starf:* 'died'. **1849–55**. This stanza is a comment on paganism in general as the extreme example of doomed and futile
worldliness, of which the story of the unfortunate Troilus is one
particular instance. The distaste for the hopelessness of paganism
is found elsewhere in Chaucer, e.g. *The Legends of Good Women*,
and at the end of other medieval works, e.g. by Boccaccio, cf.
III, 715 n. **1849–55**. 'See, in this example, what the cursed
ancient rites of pagans come to! See how much all their gods
can help! See these miserable worldly desires! See the end and
reward for labour that are given by Jove, Apollo, Mars and such
scoundrels! See what is the spirit (*or* meaning) of what ancient
writers say in poetry, if you look at their books!' **1854**. *forme:*
either 'essence', as in scholastic philosophy and Chaucer's *The
Legends of Good Women*, 1582–3; or 'shape', hence 'meaning'.
1856. *O moral Gower:* 'moral' because of his long poems, one in

Latin, one in French, on the sorry state of human life and of England. John Gower (c. 1330–1408), a Kentish landowner, lived in London, was a friend of Chaucer, and was known to Richard II and the court. In 1390 he completed his long English poem *Confessio Amantis*, in the earlier editions of which he praises Chaucer, though the reference was later cut out. The dedication to Gower and Strode suggests a poem meant to be read. **1857.** *philosophical Strode:* philosophy included both theology and science. A Ralph Strode was fellow of Merton College, Oxford, before 1360 and author of learned works. He was a friend of Wycliffe but opposed his views, especially his determinism. The Merton Strode may well also have been the lawyer of the same name who was busy in London from 1373 to 1387 and who is mentioned with Chaucer in a legal document in 1382. **1858.** The modest request for correction is not unusual, especially in Boccaccio's works. **1863.** The Trinity, Father, Son and Holy Ghost. **1863–9.** The conclusion of a long poem with a prayer or reference to God was very common. Chaucer in this stanza of great dignity translates from Dante's *Il Paradiso*, XIV, 28–30, where Dante is among the doctors of philosophy and theology.

GLOSSARY

The aim of the Glossary is to help with the understanding of the text of this edition. It is not a general analysis of the language. In intention all words and forms that may give difficulty by unfamiliarity of appearance or meaning are included. Some common variations are only noted where there seems likelihood of confusion. Thus the variations between *c* and *k*; *-e-* and *-i-* and *-y-*; *-u-* and *-w-*; *-an-* and *-aun-*; single and double vowels and consonants; are usually disregarded. The presence or absence of final *-e*, etymological or scribal, in various forms of the same word, is usually only generally noted, though the reader should notice that its presence may indicate a change of case or number, etc. If a word that seems to offer difficulty does not appear in the Glossary where the reader first looks for it, he should consult these variations or revise his notion of the alphabet. Words identical or almost identical (e.g. lawe = law) with their modern forms and meanings are not included. Occasionally words entered in the Glossary with only their former meaning may also have their modern meanings in some contexts. The context is the guide. The reader may also sometimes prefer a synonym to the word actually given in the Glossary, e.g. *siker* (sure) could equally well be translated (certain). But for many words some alternatives have been offered, either to fit different contexts or to suggest possible nuances.

The principal grammatical labels used are old-fashioned but still the most useful; *adj* (adjective), *adv* (adverb), *conj* (conjunction), *demon* (demonstrative), *excl* (exclamation), *n* (noun), *v* (verb), *acc* (accusative), *gen* (genitive), *dat* (dative), *pt* (preterite, i.e. past tense), *subj* (subjunctive mood), *pp* (past participle), *part* (present participle), *s* (singular), *pl* (plural), etc. Where no indication of the tense of a verb is given the present is to be understood; where no indication of mood, the indicative. Numbers in the Glossary refer to the grammatical person.

A

a *indefinite article* a

a *prep* on

abaysed *pp* startled; **abayst** abashed, cast down

abedde *adv* in bed

abet *n* abetting

abide *v* wait

aboughte *pp* paid for

aboute(n) *adv, prep* about, around

above *adj, adv, prep* above, on high, excessively, more than

abreyde *v* start (from sleep), wake up, come to

accident *n* occurrence

accusour *n* betrayer

acorse *v* curse

acoye *v* quiet, tame

adawe *v* awake, come to

aday *adv* by day

afer *adv* afar

a-fere *adv* on fire

affectis *n pl* desires

aftir *adj, adv, prep* after-(wards), later, in the future; according to, in accordance with, for

a-game *adv* playfully

agaste *v* frighten

agayn(e)s, aye(y)ns *see* ageyn

age *n* age, old age; **ages** *pl* periods of time

ageyn, ayeyn *adv, prep* against, in return, again

agilten *v* do wrong, offend

ago(n) *pp* gone

agrief *adv* amiss, unkindly

agroos *3 s pt* was frightened

ake *v* ache

al, alle *adj, pron* all, every, quite; **alle thyng** every thing; all, everything; **alle and some** one and all; **al**

and som the sum total; **aller, alder** *gen pl* of all

al *adv* all, quite, entirely

al *conj* (*followed by inverted word-order*) although, even if

alday *adv* continually, constantly

alderbest *adj* best of all

alderwisest *adj* wisest of all

aldirmost *adv* most of all

aleye *n* alley, garden path

alighte *v* alight; **alighte s** *pt*

alliaunce, *n* alliance

along (on) *adj* on account of

aloonly *adv* solely

al-outrely *adv* completely, absolutely

als *adv* also

also, al so *adv* also; **also . . . as** as . . . as; **as** *expletive particle*

alwey *adv* always

ambages *n pl* circumlocutions, ambiguities

amenden *v* correct, reform, remedy, make amends

among *adv, prep* round about, all the while, among, during

amonges *prep* amongst

and *conj* if, and

answerynge *part* suitable

apeired *pp* injured

apere *v* appear

apese *v* appease, pacify, quiet

apoynte *v* set a time, say definitely; **a. hire** *refl* decide, determine

appaire *1 pl* suffer harm, deteriorate

approche(n) *v* approach

arace *v* root out; **arace** *3 s subj*

arayed *pp* dressed; arranged

arede *v* explain, foretell, guess, conjecture

argumenten *3 pl* argue; **argumented** *3 s pt*

aright *adv* rightly, truly, well

armes *n pl* weapons

armonye *n* harmony, music

array *n* dress

art *n* skill, craft, craftsmanship; principles governing an activity which involves knowledge or skill

arwe *n* arrow

aryse, arise *v* arise

as *conj* as, since; **as ferforth as** as far as, the same as if; **swich . . . as** such . . . as

as *adv* (*and adverbial uses*), as, so, very, to the greatest possible extent; **as faste** very soon, very quickly

as +*prep:* **as for** for; **as in my gylt** through fault of mine; **as to** according to

as +*adv* **as paramours** passionately, in the manner of a lover; **as tho** at that time; **as yit** yet

as +*infin* **as to speke of** speaking of

as *prep* like, as

as *expletive particle, introducing* (a) *an imperative,* (b) *a hortatory subjunctive of wish, imprecation, etc* (a) **as beth nat wroth** be not angry; (b) **as wolde God** would God

asay *v* try; **asaieth** *3 s*; **assayinge** *part*; **assaied** *pp* experienced

ascaunces *conj* as if to say

ascry *n* outcry, shout

ashamed *pp* put to shame, disgraced; **for pure ashamed** for very shame

asken *v* ask; **asketh** *3 s* demands

asonder *adv* apart, asunder

asp *n* aspen tree; **aspes** *gen s*

aspectes *n* relative position of heavenly bodies, aspects

aspie(n) *v* catch sight of; see, notice; observe; **aspied** *pp* seen, discovered

assege *n* siege, besieging force

assegeden *3 pl pt* besieged

assent *n* consent, opinion; **of thyn assent** complying with thee; **by oon assent** with one accord

asshen *n pl* ashes

assure *v* assure; acquire confidence; **assured** *pp* assured, confident, self-possessed

astoned *pp* astonished, bewildered, stunned

asure *n* blue

aswowne *adv* in a swoon, unconscious

at *prep* at, in

athynken *v* (*impersonal*) cause regret

atire, *n* dress

atwixen *prep* between

a-two *adv* in two

atwynne *adv* apart

auctorite *n* authority

auctour *n* author, creator

aught *adv* in any way

aungelik *adj* angelic

availle *v* help, advance (a cause); *3 pl* be worth, do any good

avale *v* descend

avantour *n* boaster

avaunce *v* advance, cause to prosper, benefit

avaunt *n* boast

aventure *n* chance, fortune, fate, (one's) lot; adventure, experience avowe *v* avow, assert

avyse, avise *v* consider, take counsel, reflect on (*often refl*), contemplate; **was avysed** had considered; **sodeynly avysed** by a sudden resolution; **avise** *2 pl* observe, stare at

avysement *n* consideration, reflection, contemplation

awhaped *pp* disconcerted, bewildered

axe(n) *v* axe at ask of; **axeth** requires

ayens *see* ageyn

B

bad *see* bidde

baiten *v* feed

balaunce *n* balance; **in balaunce** in danger

bane *n* bane, death

bar *see* bere

barbe *n* barb (a pleated covering for the throat, or chin, and the chest, worn by widows and nuns)

bare *adj* bare; mere

baroun *n* baron

bataille *n* battle; **god . . . of bataylle** god of war

baudc *n* bawd, pimp

bawme *n* balm, fragrance

be- *see* bi-

bede *v* offer; **boden** *pp* bidden, commanded

beele *adj* fair

been *n pl* bees

beere *see* beren

ben, bee(n) *v* be; **arte** *2 s* (*interr*); **ar, are, be(n), been** *pl*; **be** *2 pl subj*; **beth, beeth** *pl imp*

benched *pp* provided with benches

bende *v* bend, turn; **benten** *3 pl pt* bent; **bente** *pp* crescent

benignyten *n* benignity, graciousness, kindness; **benignites** *pl*

berd *n* beard; **in the berd** resolutely, face to face

bere *n* bear

bere, beere *v* bear, carry; **bar** *3 s pt*; **bar . . . on honde** accuse, assert, assure

bet *adj* better

bete *v* beat

beth *see* ben

beye *v* buy; **boughten** *3 pl pt*; **ybought, bought** *pp*

bi- *see* by-

bidde *v* request, beseech, beg, pray; **biddeth** *3 s*; **bid** *s imp*; **biddeth** *imp pl* pray; **I bidde wisshe** I intend to wish; **bad** *3 s pt* besought, commanded, told; wished

bide *s imp* wait

bigon, by- *pp as adj*; **wel bygon** fortunate; **wo-bigon** miserable

bigyle *v* cheat, deceive

bigynne, by- *v* begin; **bigan** *1 & 3 s pt*; **bigonne** *pl pt*; **bigonne** *pp*

biheste *n* promise

bihight *pp* promised

biholde *v* look, look at; **byheld** *s pt*; **byhelde** *3 s pt, subj*

bihovely *adj* profitable

bileve *see* bleven

biloved *pp* beloved

bilynne *v* cease

bipath *n* short-cut

biraft(e) *see* bireve

bireve *v* take away, remove, deprive (of)

biseche *v* beseech; **bisoughtest** *2 s pt*

biseke *v* beseech

bisette *3 s pt* set, placed; **byset** *pp*

bishet *pp* shut up

biside, bisyde *adv, prep* besides, also, aside, away; beside, without; **ther b.** nearby

bisily *adv* busily, without delay

bisoghte *see* **biseche**

bistowe *v* bestow; **bistowed** *pp* placed

bisy, besy, bysi *adj* busy; anxious; **in a bysi wyse** attentively

bisynesse *n* activity, endeavour

bitake *v* commit, commend

bithought *pp* thought of

bitraised *pp* betrayed; **bytraise** *3 pl*

bittre *adj* bitter

bitwene, by- *adv, prep* in between; between

bitwixe(n), bitwix *prep* between

bityde(n) *v* happen, take place; **bitit** *3 s*; **bitidde** *s pt*

blak *adj* black; **blake** *pl*

blent *3 s* blinds

bleve(n), bileve *v* remain; depart

bleynte *s pt* turned away

blisful, blys- *adj* happy, fortunate

blody, bloody *adj* bloody

blosmy *adj* covered with blossoms

blyve *adj* quickly; **as b., also b.** immediately, as soon as possible

boghte *see* **byen**

Bole *n* Bull (the sign Taurus)

bon *n* bone; **fel and bones** skin and bones

bond *n* something that binds; binding force; **bittre bondes** *pl* mental anguish

boor *n* boar

boot *n* boat

boot(e), bote *n* remedy

bore *n* hole

borneth *3 s* makes bright, *lit* burnishes

botme *n* bottom

brast(e) *see* **breste**

bred *n* bread

brede *n* space, breadth

brede *v* grow

breke(n) *v* break, cut short, interrupt; **broken** *pp*

brenne(n) *v* burn, be burnt

brest *n* breast

breste *v* burst, break; **breste** *3 pl pt*; **brast** *3 s pt, ind & subj*

briddes *n gen s* bird's

bright *n* brightness

broche *n* brooch

brode *adv* plainly

brotel *adj* brittle, fragile, insecure

brotelnesse *n* fragility, insecurity

broun *adj* brown, dark

brydel *n* bridle

brynge(n) *v* bring; **brynge** *3 s subj*; **broughte** *3 s pt*

burthe *n* birth

but *adv, conj* only, unless, but; **but if** unless

by- *see* **bi-**

by *adv, prep* nearby, by, concerning; **faste by** near

bycometh *3 s*; **wher bycometh it** what becomes of it

bye(n), beye v buy; **boughten** pl pt; **ybought** pp

byfalle(n) v happen

byfor(e), byforn, biforn adv & prep before, previously, in front of; **here-biforn** before now

byhynde(n) prep behind

byjaped pp ridiculed; fooled

byleve see **bleven**

bylyve adv quickly, soon

bytrent 3 s encircles

C

cacche v seize; **kaughte** pp

calkulyng n reckoning, divination

calle n caul, hairnet, close-fitting cap; **maken an howve above a c.** engage in double dealing

can see **conne**

candele n candle

care n worry, sorrow

cas n something that occurs or happens; an event, occurrence, experience; situation, circumstances; example, supposition; **upon cas** by chance

cast n throwing

caste(n) v throw, cast, lit & fig (a stone, the eyes, etc.); turned, calculated (astrol); determined, resolved; **cast** pl imp lay aside, put away; **cast** pp; **caste up** raise, open

cause n cause, plea; **by the c.** because; **in c. of** responsible for, to blame

cedre n cedar

cerclen v encircle

certes adv certainly

certeyn, -ein, -ayn adj, adv certain(ly)

cesse v cease; **cesse** 3 s subj if it cease; **cessed** s pt

chace v chase, **c. at** speak roughly to

chambre n room, bedroom

char n chariot

charge n burden, matter, concern

char-hors n pl chariot-horses

charitable adj kind, loving

chaunce n unexpected event, accident

chaunge n change

cheere, chiere, chere n face, manner; look, change of countenance; gladness, merriment, mirth; **make(n) c.** be pleasant or agreeable

chek mat n checkmate

chep(e), cheep n cheapness, bargain; **as good chep** as cheaply, as easily

cherice(n) v cherish

chese v choose

cheterynge n chattering

chiere see **cheere**

chivalrous adj brave

chymeneye n fireplace

circumscrive v encompass

cite n a walled town, city

clause n clause, sentence, a few words; stipulation

cleer(e), clere adj, adv clear, bright, shining

clene, cleene adj clean; honourable

clene adv clean, completely

clepe(n) v call, name, cry out; **clepe** 1 s; **clepid** pp; **clepe ayein** recall

clere v clear

clerk n a member of the clergy or one preparing for the

clerk—*cont.*
priesthood, one who can read and write, a learned person, scholar
clippe *1 s* embrace
clomben *pp* climbed
closet *n* small room, bedroom
coghe *v* cough
colde *v* grow cold
coler *n* collar
collateral *adj* incidental, of secondary importance
combust *pp* burnt up
comedye *n* poem or tale with happy ending
come(n) *v* come; **com(e) of** come on, hurry up; **com** *3 s pt* came **come(n)** *pp*
comfort *see* **confort**
commeveth *3 s* moves
commune, comune *adj* common, common to all, general, familiar
compaignye, companye *n* company; companionship
complet *adv* completely
comprende *v* contain
condicioun, -ion *n* state, status
conforte(n) *v* comfort; assuage
conne, konne *v* be able; **can, kan** *1 & 3 s*; **koude** *pl pt*; **koude his good** knew what was best for him
connyng(e) *see* **konnynge**
constreinte *n* distress
constreyne *v* compel, force; **constreyneth** *3 s* restrains
contenaunce, coun-, -ance *n* behaviour, demeanour, bearing; **fond his c.** assumed an attitude or appearance
contree *n* land, country

contrepeise *v* balance, counterbalance
convers *n* **in convers** on the other side, behind
converte *v* change the opinion; change one's mind
cope *n* cape
corage *n* heart, spirit
correccioun *n* correction
cors *n* body, corpse
corsen *v* curse; **corsed** *pp*
cote-armure *n* coat-armour (tunic with heraldic devices worn over armour)
cours *n* movement, passage; course of the sun
coye *v* quiet, pacify
craft *n* skill, art
crecche *v* snatch, grab
crepe *v* creep; **cropen** *pp*
crie(n) *v* cry, cry out, proclaim
crop *n* top
cropen *see* **crepe**
croys *n* cross
cure *n* care, charge; duty; **besy c.** diligence, zeal
curteis, -eys *adj* courteous
curteisye *n* courtesy

D

dan *see* **daun**
dar *s & pl pr* dare; **dorste** *cond* would dare
dart *n* arrow
daun, dan *n* master, lord (title of respect)
daunce *n* dance; **the olde d.** the tricks of the game, the ways of love-making
daunger *n* power to hinder the lover; distant manner, haughtiness
dauntest *2 s* dost subdue, control; **daunteth** *3 s*
dawyng *n* dawn

de- *see* **di-**
debat *n* strife
debonaire *adj & n* gracious (person)
declare *v* explain
dede *n* deed
deed, ded, dede *adj* dead
deele(n), dele *v* have to do with
deeth, deth *n* death
deface *v* spoil
defame *v* slander; **defamen** *3 pl*
defaute *n* lack
defence *n* prohibition
defende *v* defend, forbid
degre *n* rank
deignous *adj* haughty, disdainful
delit *n* delight, pleasure
delite *v* delight, take pleasure (often reflexive)
demaunde *n* question
deme(n) *v* judge, decide; suppose, consider
departe(n) *v* separate; go away, depart
depe *adv* deeply
depper *adv compar of* **deep**; deeper
dere, deere *adv* dearly
derk *adj* dark
derre *adj, adv* more dear, more dearly
des- *see* **dis-**
desteyned *pp* stained, blemished
destourbed *pp* upset, altered
devoir *n* duty
devyn *n* priest (of Apollo), soothsayer
devyne *v* suspect, guess
devyse(n) *v* decide, determine; suggest, recommend; express; arrange

dewete *n* duty
deye(n) *see* **dye(n)**
deyn *v* deign, condescend
deynte *n* pleasure, delight; a delicacy; something estimable
diffyne(n) *v* conclude, state in conclusion
dighte *v* appoint, ordain; **the first in armes dyght** the first one armed
digne *adj* worthy
dignitee *n* worthiness
directe *I s* address, dedicate
dirke *see* **derk**
dis- *see* **des-**
disavaunce *v* injure, repel
disaventure *n* misfortune
disblameth *imp s* excuse
discrecioun *n* discretion; judgement
disese *n* distress
disese(n) *v* cause distress
disesperaunce *n* despair
disfigure *v* destroy (one's) attractiveness
dispeyred *pp* in despair
dispit *n* contempt, scorn, indignation, anger; **have in d.** bear a grudge against
dispitous(e) *adj* spiteful, malicious
disporte(n) *v* amuse, entertain, divert
disseveraunce *n* parting, separation
dissimulen *v* dissemble
distreyne *v* oppress; **destrayned** *pl pt* oppressed, occupied
disturne *v* turn aside
dom *see* **doom**
don *see* **do(on)**
donne *adj* dun, dull brown
doom *n* judgement

do(on), do(ne) *v* perform, put, do; **do wey** remove

dorste *see* **dar**

doun *adv* down; **up and doun** up and down, back and forth, over and over

doutaunce *n* doubt; *pl* uncertainties

doute *n* fear; doubt

douteles *adv* without doubt

dradde *see* **drede**

drawe(n) *v* draw, pull

drecchyng *n* delay

drede *n* fear, anxiety, doubt, uncertainty; **out of drede** without doubt; **withoute(n) drede** without doubt

drede *v* fear; **dredde, dradde** *1 & 3 s pt* feared, dreaded; was afraid; **drad, ydred** *pp*

dredeles *adv* without doubt

dredful, drede- *adj* fearful, timid

drem, dreem *n* dream

dremen *v* dream

drenche(n) *v* drown

dresse *v* prepare, array (*often refl*) hold oneself erect

dreye *see* **drye(n)**

drope *n* drop

dronke(n) *pp* drunk

drye(n) *v* suffer, endure

dryve(n) *v* drive; **drof** *3 s pt*

dulcarnoun *n* at d. completely perplexed

durre *v* dare

durryng *n* daring

dwelle *v* remain

dye(n), deye(n) *v* die; **deyde** *3 s pt*

E

ech *adj*, *pron* each, every, everyone

eche *v* increase, add; **eched** *pp*

echon, -oon *pron* each one

eek, ek, eke *adv* also

eet *see* **ete(n)**

effect *n* result, consequence, intent; matter of consequence

eft *adv* again

eighe *see* **eye**

elde *n* age, old age

element *n* element (fire, air, earth, water); **elementz** *pl*

elles, -is *adv* otherwise, else

em *n* uncle; **emes** *gen s*

embrace, en- *v* embrace; **embraced** *pp*

emforth *prep* to the extent of

emprise *n* undertaking

enchesoun *n* reason, cause

enclyne *v* bow; be disposed

encres *n* increase

encresse *v* increase

endite(n) *v* compose (*a letter, poem, etc.*); tell, express

endure(n) *v* continue; endure, stand

engyn *n* skill, subtlety

enquere(n) *v* inquire

ensample *n* example

enseled *pp* sealed up, preserved

enspire *s imp* inspire

entecched *pp* imbued with, endowed

entencioun *n* intention, purpose, will, understanding

entende *v* intend, plan, incline (to)

entent(e) *n* intention, intent, endeavour, diligence

ententif *adj* eager, desirous

entrechaungeden *pl pt* exchanged

entune *v* sing

envye *n* ill-will, envy

envie *s imp* vie with, strive with, challenge

er *adv, conj, prep* before

ere *n* ear; **erys** *pl*

ernest *n* seriousness

erratik *adj* wandering; **e. sterres** planets

erre *v* do wrong; **erre(n)** *3 pl* are wrong, mistaken

erst *adv* before, formerly

eschue(n) *v* avoid; refrain from; **eschuwe** *2 pl*

ese, eyse *n* ease; **do(on) his (my) herte an e.** relieve one's mind, gratify

ese(n) *v* ease, give comfort to; **esed** comforted, relieved

esily, esilich *adv* easily

est *adj* east

estat *n* condition, state, position; economic or social position, status

estatly, estatlich *adj* dignified

esy *adj* easy; gentle

ete(n) *v* eat

ethe *adj* easy

even *n* evening

even(e) *adj adv* even; equally

ever(e) *adv* for ever, always

ever(e)mo *adv* evermore, continually

everich *adj pron* every, each (one)

everichon *pron* every one, each one

executrice *n* controller *or* agent

experience *n* first-hand knowledge, experience; proof

eye, eighe *n* eye

eyle, aile *v* ail, trouble, afflict; **what eyleth, aileth** what ails

eyr *n* air

eyse *see* **ese**

F

face *see* **prime**

fader *n* father

fair *adj* fair, beautiful; *n* a fine thing to do

fair(e) *adv* fairly, well

faire *n* fair, market

falle(n) *v* fall, descend; happen; **fallen forth** engage in; **fil** *s pt* fell, happened

fals *adj* false

false(n) *v* prove false, betray, deceive; **falsed** *s pt, pp*

fantasye *n* imaginary experience, illusion, delusion

fare *n* behaviour, conduct, activity, business, fuss; **frendes fare** friendly behaviour

fare-carten cart for produce

fare(n) *v* travel; go; experience; get on, proceed

faste *adv* firmly, closely, tightly; eagerly; steadily; **as f.** very quickly, as quickly as possible

fatal *adj* to do with the Fates; predestined

faukoun *n* falcon

favour *n* favour; favourable feeling, partiality

fayn *adj, adv* fain, glad(ly), willingly

fecche(n) *v* fetch, bring

fecches *n pl* vetches, beans

feeblesse *n* feebleness

feffe *v* grant, bestow upon

feith *n* faith; honour, truthfulness

feithfully *adv* piously, devoutly; faithfully

fel *n* skin

felaweshipe *n* fellowship, company; companionship

feldefare *n* fieldfare

fele(n) *v* feel; find out; understand

feloun *adj* angry, sullen

fer, ferre *adj, adv* far, distant

ferde, fered *n* fear: **for f.** for fear

fere *n* fear

fere, feere *n* companion; **feres** *pl*

ferforth *adv* far; **as f. as** as far as, to the extent that; as long as; **so f.** to such an extent

ferfulleste *adj* most fearful, timid

fern *adj* former; **ferne yere** last year

ferther *adv* farther

fery *adj* fiery

feste, feeste *n* religious festival; rejoicing, joy; **maketh (made) feste** welcomes, welcomed; **make hym ... moore feste** show more pleasure in seeing

fette *v* fetch, bring (to be sought); **fette** *s & pl pt*

feyne *v* concoct, invent; deceive; **feyned hym** *s pt* pretended; **feyned** *pl pt, adj* false

fiers(e) *adj* proud, noble

figure *n* shape, form; image

fil *see* **fallen**

fir *n* fire

firy *adj* fiery

fixe *pp* fixed

fle(e) *v* flee; **fleest** *2 s*; **fled** *pp*

fle(en) *v* fly; **fleigh** *3 s pt*

flemen *v* banish

flemyng *n* banishment

flesshly *adj* fleshy

flete *v* float, bathe, swim;

flete *3 pl* bathe; **fletynge** *part*

flour *n* flower

folde *v* fold, clasp

fonde *v* test; strive, endeavour

fo(o) *n* foe; **foon** *pl*

for *conj, prep* because; for

forbeede *v* forbid; **forbet** *3 s*; **forbede** *3 s subj*

forby *adv* by, past

fordo(on) *v* destroy, ruin; abolish

forgo(n) *v* go without; **forgoth** *3 s* gives up; **forgon** *pp* lost

forme, fourme *n* shape, form, pattern; beauty

fors *n* (the usual spelling of **force** in the sense of 'importance', 'something that matters'); **no fors** no matter; **what f. were it** what would it matter

forshapen *pp* transformed

forth *adv* forth, forward, on; further, in addition

forther *adv* further

forther over *adv* moreover; **forther over this** furthermore

forthy *adv* therefore

fortunat *adj* fortunate, favoured by fortune

for-why *conj* because; therefore; for what reason

foryete(n) *v* forget

foryeve *v* forgive

foul *adj* unclean, defiled; miserable, wretched, poor

fredom *n* liberality, nobility; freedom

fre(e) *adj* generous, noble; unbound, at liberty

frend *n* friend; **frendes** *gen as adj* friendly

frendlich *adj* friendly; **frendly** pleasant

frendshipe *n* friendship

fremde *adj* strange

frenetik *adj* frantic

fressh *adj* fresh; active, vigorous

fro *prep, adv* from

frote *v* rub

fruyt *n* fruit

ful *adj* full; satiated, surfeited; **atte fulle** full on

ful *adv* full, entirely, very

fulfille *v* fulfil

fyn *n* end, aim

fynde(n) *v* find; **fond, fownde** *2 s pt*; **fond his contenaunce** assumed an appearance; **founde(n)** *pp*

fynder *n* discoverer, inventor

fyne *v* finish; cease, stop

G

game *n* amusement; **a-game** in jest

gan *see* **gynne**

gape *v* gape; **gape after** *3 pl* wish, long for

gat *see* **geten**

gaude *n* trick

gaure(n) *v* gape, stare

gayneth *3 s impers* avails, profits; **gayned** *s pt*

geant *n* giant

general *adj* general

gentil *adj* well-born, noble

gentilesse *n* gentility, nobility

gentilly *adv* courteously

gere *n* equipment

gesse *v* suppose, imagine, think

gest *n* stranger

geste *n* story

gete(n), gette *v* get, obtain; **gat** *3 s pt* got

gilt *n* offence, fault; **in my g.** through fault of mine

giltif *adj* guilty

gise *n* manner, ways, custom

glade *v* gladden, cheer up; **gladed(e), gladded** *s pt*

gladly *adv* willingly, readily

gladnesse *n* cheerfulness, happiness

gledes *n pl* embers

go(n), goon *v* go; **yede** *3 s pt* went

good *adv*; **whil yow good list** as long as you please

good *n* property, goods, wealth; **koude his good** knew what was good for him

goodly *adj* pleasing; kind; beautiful

goodly *adv* graciously, patiently

goodlyhede *n* goodliness; **goodlihed(e)** goodness; comeliness

gost *n* soul, spirit

gostly *adv* spiritually; **gostly for to speke** to tell the truth

goter *n* gutter, drain

governaunce *n* management, direction, control

grace *n* favour, a favour; **of grace** through kindness, graciously

grame *n* anger; suffering

graunt mercy *excl* many thanks

grave(n) *v* dig; engrave, scratch; carve

gree *n* favour, goodwill; **in g.** favourably, graciously

greet *adj* great; **the grete** *n* the chief part, gist

grene *adj* green

gres *n* grass

grete *v* greet

gretter *adj compar* greater

greve *n* thicket, grove

greve *v* annoy, cause discomfort; *refl* feel annoyed; **greveth** does harm

greyn *n* grain; very small amount

grone *v* groan

ground *n* ground; foundation

groyn *n* grumbling, scolding

grucche *v* grumble, complain

gruwel *n* gruel

guerdoun *n* reward

guerdonynge *n* reward

gyde *n* guide

gyde(n) *v* guide, conduct

gyle *n* deceit

gynne *v* begin; **gynne** *1 s*; **gynneth** *3 s*; **gan** *3 s pt*; *as auxiliary v* did

gynnyng(e) *n* beginning

gyse *n* manner, method, way; custom

H

habit *n* dress

habundaunce *n* abundance

halvendel *n* half

han *see* **have**

hap *n* chance, fortune

happe(n) *v* happen

hardely *adv* assuredly, certainly

hardynesse *n* boldness, courage

harm *n* harm, hurt, injury; pity, a pity

haselwode *excl* implying scepticism; **haselwodes shaken** for heaven's sake!

haten *v* hate

hatte *pp* called

have, han *v* have; **hastow** hast thou; **han** *pl pr* have

hawe *n* haw (fruit of the hawthorn), something of little value

he *3 pers pron* he; **his, hise** *gen*; **him** *acc & dat*; **he ... he, he ... hym** *as indef pron* this one ... that one; **hym** *refl* himself

hed(e) *n* heed

hed(e), heved *n* head

heet *pp* called

hegge *n* hedge

heigh, hye *adj, adv* high; proudly

hele *n* health, well-being, prosperity

helen *v* cure

helm *n* helmet

helmed *pp* wearing a helmet

helply *adj* helpful

hem *see* **they**

hemself *pron* themselves

hemysperie *n* hemisphere

henne(s) *adv* hence

hennesforth *adv* henceforth

hente *v* seize, catch, get; **hent** *3 s* catches

hepe *n* heap, crowd, large number; **to-hepe** together

her *see* **they**

herafter *adv* hereafter

here *see* **she**

herebefore, -forn *adv* herebefore

here(n) *v* hear; **hereth** *3 s*

heres *n pl* hair

herie *v* praise; **herye** *1 s*; **heryed, yheried** *pp*

herken *v* listen (to)

herte *n* heart; sweetheart; **hertes, herte** *gen s* heart's

hertely *adv* genuinely, earnestly, heartily

heste *n* behest, bidding, command; **hestes** *pl* commands

hete *n* heat

heve *imp s* raise

heven *n* heaven; **hevene(s)** *gen s* heaven's; **hevene blisse** heavenly bliss

hevenyssh *adj* heavenly

hevynesse *n* sorrow

hewe *n* colour; **hewis** *pl* colours, pigments

hierde, herde *n* shepherd; **hierdes** *pl* guardians

highte *n* height

hight(e) *pp* called; promised

hir *see* **they**

hire *n* payment, wages; **quite youre hire** repay you

hire *see* **she, they**

hir(e)self, hir(e)selve(n) *pron* herself

hit, it, *pron* it

hit *see* **hyde**

holde(n) *v* keep, hold, maintain; consider; continue; **held** *s pt*; **holde(n), yholde** *pp* beholden; **to holde in honde** encourage with false hopes, deceive

holpen *pp* helped

holwnesse *n* hollowness; inner side

hond *n* hand; **bar . . . on honde** accuse, assert, assure

hondred *n* hundred

honeste *n* good repute

honge(n) *v* hang

honour *n* honour, reputation, good name

honoure(n) *v* honour, worship

hool *adj* whole, entire; **al hool of** recovered from

hool *adv* wholly; **al hool** completely

hoolly *adv* wholly

hoot *adj* hot (*in lit and fig senses*)

hoote *adv* hotly, fervently; intensely

hors *n* horse; **hors** *pl*

hound *n* dog

hous *n* house; **outer hous** portion of the great hall separated by a traverse; **hous of hevene** division of the sky

hove *v* hover

how *adv* however

howve *n* hood; **maken an howve above a calle** engage in double dealing

hust *imper s* hush; **hust** *pp* hushed, silent

humble *adj* modest

hye *n* haste, speed; **in hye** quickly, soon

hye *v* hurry; **hiest** *2 s* hastenest; **hyed** *pp*

hye *see* **heigh**

hymself, hymselve(n) *pron* himself; **himself, himselve** itself; (*as pers pron*) he himself

I

I *1 pers pron*; **ich** (*Midl and Southern occ before vowels*); **my** *gen*; **myn** *see separate entry*; **me** *dat, acc*

ijaped *pp* made sport

ilke *adj* same

illusion *n* illusion, delusion

ilost *pp* lost

ilyved *pp* lived

imedled *pp* mingled

impossible *n* impossibility

impresse(n) *v* impress

impressioun *n* imprint; *pl* thoughts, emotions

in *adv*, *prep* in, within, inside

in- *see* **im-**

infortune *n* ill fortune, misfortune

injure *n* injury

in-knette *s pt* contracted

inly *adv* extremely

inne *adv* in, within

into *prep* into, to, unto; on, upon

inwardly *adv* intently, with concentration

inwith *prep* within

ire *n* anger

ise *see* **ysee**

isought *pp* sought

issue *n* outlet

isworn *pp* sworn

itake *pp* caught

iwis *see* **ywis**

iwryen *pp* covered, hidden; *see* **wrye**

J

jalous *adj* jealous

jalousie *n* jealousy

jangle *v* talk loudly or much; **jangle** *3 pl*

jape *n* joke, trick

jape(n) *v* joke, jest; trick, mock; **ijaped** *pp* made sport (of)

japer *n* trickster

joly *adj* jolly

joyned *3 s pt* joined; **joyneden** *pl pt*; *pp* in conjunction

juggen *v* judge; **juggeth** *pl imp*

jupartie *n* jeopardy, risk

juste(n) *v* joust; **jousteth** *3 s*

K

kalendes *n pl* the first day of the Roman month; a beginning

kan, kanst *see* **conne**

kaught(e) *see* **cacche**

kene *adj* sharp

kep(e) *n* heed, care; **took . . . kep** paid . . . attention

kepen *v* take care of, look after, guard

kerve *v* cut

kid(de) *see* **kithe**

kithe *v* make known; **kidde** *s pt*; **kith(e)** *s imp*

knotte *n* knot

knowe *n dat s* knee; **knowes** *pl*

knowe(n) *v* know

knytte *v* knit (*lit & fig*); **knetteth** *3 s*; **yknet** knit

konne(n) *see* **conne**

konnyng(e), con- *n* ability; skill, knowledge; **of my connynge** by my ability

konnyng(e) *adj* capable; clever, wise

konnyngeste *adj superl* cleverest

koude, koud *see* **conne**

kyn *n* kindred, family descent

kynde *n* nature

kynrede *n* kindred, family

L

ladde *see* **leden**

laft(e) *see* **leven**

lakke(n) *v* disparage

lappe *n* flap, fold

large *adj* broad, large; full-cut, flowing; **of tonge l.** free with his tongue

lasse *adj*, *adv*, *n* less

last *adj*, *adv*, *n* last; **atte laste** at last, finally; **to the laste** in the end

laste *v* last, continue; **laste** *s pt*

lat, laten *see* leten

late *adv* late(ly)

laude *n* praise

laughe(n) *v* laugh; lough *s pt*; loughe *pl pt*

laurer-crowned *pp* laurel-crowned

lay *n* law, doctrine, religion

leche *n* physician

lede(n) *v* take, carry; lead; ladde *s & pl pt*

leef *n* leaf

leese *n* pasture

leet *see* leten

leful *see* leveful

leggen *see* leye

leigh *see* lye

lene *adj* lean

lenger *adj, adv* longer

lengest *adj superl, adv* longest

Leoun *see* lyoun

lepe *v* leap, spring

lere *v* teach, learn; leere *pl imp* teach

lerne *v* learn; teach

lese(n) *v* lose; lorn *pp* lost; ilost *pp*

lest *n dial var* (*Kentish*) *of* lust pleasure, desire, happiness

lest *3 s impers* (*Kentish form*) it pleases. *See* list

leste *adj superl* least

lesyng *n* losing

lete(n), late(n) *v* let, let go; late *1 & 3 s* let; lette, lete, leet, let *1 & 3 s pt* let; pretended; considered; lat *s imp* let

lette *n* hindrance; delay

lette(n) *v* hinder, prevent; lette *s imp* hinder; let *pp* hindered

lettre *n* letter (of alphabet)

leve *see* lief

leve *n* leave, permission; bisyde his (hire) l. without his (her) permission

leve *v* believe

leve *3 s subj* grant: God leve may God grant; leve *s imp* grant

leveful, leful *adj* lawful, permissible

leve(n) *v* leave (allow to remain)

lever(e) *adj* more agreeable; rather; me were levere one would rather

levest *superl adj* most dear; me were l. one would prefer

lew(e)d *adj* ignorant; foolish

leye, legge(n) *v* lay; cause to lie, lodge; bet; adoun leyde soothed

leyser *n* leisure

lief *adj* dear, agreeable; leve *wk decl* dear; it is me lief I am glad; *see* levere

lif *n* life; lyve *dat* on, in (his, my) life; my lif in my life

lige *adj* liege

ligge(n) *v* lie; liggen *2 & 3 pl*; liggeth *imp pl*; *for other forms see* lye

lighte *v* lighten, alleviate; unburden

lighte *v* illuminate, brighten

like(n) *v* please, be pleasing to; to be liked; liketh *3 s impers*; likynge *part* pleasing

likker(e) *adj* more like

likly *adj* likely

likyng *n* pleasure, inclination

lisse *v* alleviate; lissed, ylissed *pp* eased, relieved

list *n* pleasure; desire

list *3 s impers* it pleases; listen *3 pl* are pleased

lite *adj* little; **a l.** *as adv*
litel *adj* little
lofte *n dat*: **on-lofte, o-lofte, alofte** aloft, above
loke(n) *v* look; **loked** *pp* looked
lokyng *n* look, glance, gaze
lond *n* land
longe *adj, adv* long, a long while
longe(n) *v* long, yearn
longe(n) *v* belongs to; **longeth** *3 s*
loore *n* advice; learning
looth, loth *adj* displeasing, hateful; reluctant; *as adv* unwillingly
lordshipe *n* sovereignty
lorn *see* **lesen**
los *n* loss
loude *adv* loud(ly), aloud
lough *see* **lowe**
loute *v* bow
lowely *adv* humbly
lufsom *adj* lovesome
lust *n* pleasure, joy, happiness, desire, wish, will, lust
lust *3 s* (it) pleases, is pleasing (to); **luste** *3 s pt* it pleased
lusty *adj* pleasant
lye *v* lie, recline, remain; **lay** *1 & 3 s pt* lay, lodged; **layen** *pl pt* lay; *see* **liggen**
lye(n) *v* lie, misrepresent
lyk *adj, adv* alike
lym *n* limb, organ, part of the body; **lymes, lymmes** *pl*
lyme *v* smear with bird lime (so as to catch)
lyne *n* line; fishing line
lyoun *n* lion: **Leoun** Lion (*sign of the Zodiac*)
lyve *see* **lif**
lyvynge *n* living, way of life

M

madde *v* rage
makeles *adj* matchless
make(n) *v* make, compose (verse, etc.); **maad** *pp*
makere *n* maker, poet
makyng *n* composing, writing
maladye *n* illness
male *n* wallet, (travelling) bag
malencolie *n* melancholy
man *indef pron* one; **men** *pl* people, they
manere *n* manner, proper behaviour, way; **maner(e)** (*with ellipsis of* **of**) kind of
manhod *n* manliness
mannyssh *adj* masculine
mansuete *adj* gentle, meek
many *adj, pron*; **many oon** many a one
mateer(e) *n* matter, subject-matter
maugre *prep* in spite of
mede *n* meadow
medle *v* mix; **medled, imedled** mingled
meene *n* instrument, means
meeste *adj* highest in rank; **at the m.** at the most
melodye *n* music
melte *v* melt; **molte** *pp*
memorie *n* memory; remembrance
men *indef pron* one
mene *adj* average
mene(n) *v* say; **meneth** *3 s* intends, means; **mente** *3 s pt* thought
meschaunce *n* bad luck, misfortune, harm; **to m.** to the devil
meschief *n* misfortune, trouble, unfortunate condition

mete(n) v dream; **meete** *1 s*;
mette *s pt*

meve v move

mevynge n moving, movement

meyne n household

mischaunce *see*
meschaunce

misericorde n mercy

mo(o) *adj, pron* more; others

moche(l) *see* **muche(l)**

moeved *see* meve

moevyng *see* mevynge

mokre v hoard

mone n moan, lament

mone n moon

mone v *refl* bemoan, reveal
one's sorrow

moost(e) *superl adv & adj*
most, greatest

moot, mot *1 s* may, must;
moot, mot *3 s*; **moste** *3 s*
pt

moote n particle

more, moore *comp adv &*
adj more, greater, larger,
further

more, moore *pron* more;
namore no more

morwe n morning, morrow

most, moste(n) *see* moot

motre v mutter

mowe n grimace

mowen v be able

moyst(e) *adj* moist

muable *adj* changeable

muche, moche *adj* much,
great

muche(l), moche(l) *adv*
much, greatly

muwe, mewe n coop, pen;
in muwe secretly

muwet *adj* mute

myght n power, ability

myn *poss pron* mine; **my good**

m., O goodly m. *as n* my
own

myne v penetrate, undermine

mysbyleved *pp* misbelieving

mysconstruwe v misconstrue

mysse v fail

mysseyest *2 s* speakest falsely,
dost slander

myte n small copper coin,
farthing, anything worthless

N

nadde *s pt* ne + hadde had
not

nam *1 s pt* ne + am am not

namelich *adv* especially

narwe *adv* closely

nas *s pt* ne + was was not

nat *adv* not

natheles(s) *adv* none the less,
nevertheless

naught *adv* not

nay *adv* no

ne *adv* not; *often combined with*
following word. See **nam,**
nas, nyl, *etc*

ne *conj* nor

nece n niece

nede v be necessary; **nedeth**
3 s impers is necessary; **what**
nedeth what is the need of

nedeles *adv* unnecessarily

nedes *adv* necessarily

neer *adv* near

neer, ner(e) *adv* nearer

neigh, nygh, ny(e) *adj* near,
close-by; *quasi prep* near (to)

neigh *adv* near; **wel n.** wellnigh, almost

nekke n neck

nere *s pt, subj* ne + were
were I (it) not, would not be

nerf n sinew

new(e) *adv* newly, lately, anew

noblesse *n* nobleness

no fors no matter; *see* **fors**

noght, nought *adv* not, not at all

nolde *s & pl pt* **ne + wolde** would not; **noldestow**

nome, ynome *pp* taken

noon *n* noon

noon, none *adj, pron* none, no (*esp. before vowel*)

noot, not *1 & 3* **ne + wot** know(s) not

norissed *pp* brought up; **ynorissed**

not *see* **noot**

nother, nouther *conj, pron* neither; **nother . . . nor, n. . . . ne** neither . . . nor

nothyng, no thyng *adv* not at all, in no wise

noumbre *v* count; **noumbred** *pp* numbered

nouncerteyn *n* uncertainty

novelrie *n* novelty

noyse *n* noise; clamour, rumour

nyce *adj* foolish

nycely *adv* stupidly

nycete *n* foolishness

n'y *1 pers pron* **net y** nor I

ny(e) *see* **neigh**

nyghte *v* grow dark

nyl, nil *1 & 3 s* **ne + wyl** will not

nys *3 s* **ne + ys** is not

nyste *s pt* **ne + wyste** knew not

O

o, oo *adj* one

obeisaunce, *n* obedience

oblige *v* pledge (myself); **obliged** *pp* be under obligation

observaunce *n* customary rite or practice; attention, conventional act of respect

occupie *v* occupy

of *prep* of; by; in, in respect to

of *adv* off

offende(n) *v* offend

office *n* duty, task

ofte *adj* many, many a

ofte *adv* often; **ful o. a day** many times a day

ofter *adv* more often

o-lofte *see* **lofte**

on *prep* on, in

ones *adv* once, at one time

on-lofte *see* **lofte**

on lyve *adv* alive

oon, on *adj, pron* one, a

oost *n* host, army

ooth *n* oath

oother, other *adv* otherwise

oppresse *v* suppress, overcome; **oppressed** *pp* weighed down

or *conj* ere, before

ordal *n* ordeal

ordinaunce *n* arrangement, plan

ordre *n* order, disposition of things; religious or other constituted body

other(e) *indef pron pl* others

oure, oures *see* **we**

out of *prep* without

out-brynge *v* bring out, speak, say something

outher, other *conj* or

outrely *adv* utterly

over *prep* over

overal *adv* everywhere

overraughte *3 s pt* reached over, encouraged

oversprede *v* overspread, cover; **oversprat** *3 s* overspreads; **overspradde** *3 s pt*

overthwart *adv* opposite
owher(e) *adv* anywhere

P

pace, passe(n) *v* go, proceed, move on; pass for, be accepted as; *trans. uses:* **paste** *pl pt*; **passynge** *part* surpassing
paleys *n* palace
paramours *n pl* lady-loves
paramours *adv* in the manner of a lover
parde *excl* par Dieu, by God, assuredly; **pardieux**
paregal *adj* equal
parfit *adj* perfect
part *n* portion; **every p.** everywhere
parte(n) *v* divide, share; **parte** *1 s* depart
party(e) *n* part, portion
pas *n* footpace, walk; **a pas** slowly
passe(n) *see* **pace**
passioun *n* suffering
paumes *n pl* palms (of the hand)
payens *n pl gen* pagans'
paynted *adj* highly coloured, specious
pecok *n* peacock
penaunce *n* penance, distress, suffering
pencel *n* token, streamer
peple *n* people
peraunter *adv* perhaps
perce(n) *v* pierce
peyne *n* pain, suffering, grief; **doon my (doost thy) p.** make an effort
peyne *v* inflict pain (upon); *refl* put (oneself) to trouble, endeavour

peynte *v* paint, colour; adorn with (rhetorical) colours; **paynted** *pp as adj* as highly coloured, specious
piete *n* pity; **with p.** dutifully
pitee, pyte *n* pity
pitous, pietous *adj* pitiful, sad; pitying, tenderhearted
pitously *adv* piteously, pitifully
place *n* place, dwelling-place
platly *adv* flatly, plainly, bluntly
plesaunce *n* pleasure
pley *n* pastime, entertainment
pleye(n) *v* play, be merry or sociable, joke; *refl* amuse oneself; **pleye** *2 s* act; **pleyde** *s pt*; **pleyde** *pl pt*
pleyinge *adj* playful
pleyn *adj* full, perfect
pleyne *v* complain, lament
pleynly[1] *adv* frankly, openly, clearly. (*Sometimes merging into* **pleynly**[2])
pleynly[2] *adv* fully, completely
pleynte *n* plaint, lament
plighte *1 s* plight, pledge; **yplight** *pp*
plit(e), plyt *n* plight; situation
plite *v* fold; **plited** *pp* folded; turned back and forth
poure *v* pore, look closely, stare; **poured** *pp* gazed
pous *n* pulse
poynt *n* point, detail, essential matter, sharp end, particle
pray(e), prey(e) *n* victim
prees, press *n* crowd
prenten *v* print, impress
prest *adj* ready; resourceful
preve *v* prove
preye(n), prayen *v* pray beseech

preyse *v* praise, commend; **preysen** *2 pl* value; **preysed** *pp*

prime *adj* first; **at p. face** on first appearance

pris *n* worth, esteem, renown, value

prive *adj* private, secret

prively *adv* privately, secretly

proces *n* course of events, matter, affair; subject, story, account, discourse; **paynted p.** highly-coloured story; **in p.** in due course

profre *v* offer; **profrestow** *2 s* dost thou offer

prow *n* advantage

prowesse *n* bravery

prye *v* look closely

pryketh *3 s* drives on

pryme *n* prime (*canonical hour*); the period from about 6 a.m. to 9 a.m., especially the latter; beginning: **of lusty Veer the pryme** the beginning of the pleasant spring-time

pulle *v* pull, draw; pluck

punyce *v* punish; **punysshed** *pp* made to suffer

purchace *v* purchase, acquire

pure *adj* very

pure *adv* very; **for pure ashamed** for very shame

purpos *n* purpose, intention; question, subject, matter; **took p.** reached a decision

purveiaunce *n* providence, foreknowledge

purveye *v* provide, prepare; **purveye** *s imp* provide

putte, put *v* put; **put** *pp*

pyne *n* pain, grief

pyte *see* **pitee**

Q

quake *v* quake, tremble; **quook** *3 s pt*

quemen *3 pl* please

quenche(n) *v* quench, put an end to

quod *s pt* quoth, said

quook *see* **quake**

quyk(e) *adj* quick; alive

quyken *v* quicken; become alive

quysshen *n* cushion

quyt *pp* paid, satisfied, requited, paid back

R

rakel, rakle *adj* hasty

rakle *v* act rashly

rascaille *n* rabble

rathe *adv* early, soon

rather *comp adj & adv* earlier, former; sooner

raughte *see* **reche**

ravysshen *v* carry off by force

ravysshyng *n* carrying off

rayled *pp* enclosed

real *adj* royal

recche, rekke *v pers & impers* care, have concern for

reche *v* reach, hand; **raughte** *3 s pt* started, proceeded

recorde *v* call to mind; **r. on** *s imp* think about, reflect on

recovere(n) *v* gain, obtain; **recovered** *pp* benefited

rede(n) *v* think, guess; counsel, advise; **ret** *3 s* advises; **rede(n)** *pl*

redere *n* reader

redresse *v* set right, correct

reed, red(e) *n* counsel, advice

reed(e) *adj* red

refere *v* return, revert

reherce(n) v rehearse, repeat, say

releve v relieve

relyk n sacred image

rende v tear; rente of tore away; yrent pp

rente n income; to r. as payment due

repaire v return; repeyreth imp pl

repentaunce n repentance; regret

repressioun n restraint, control

repreve n reproof

requere v request 1 s; requere 2 pl

rescowe v rescue

resoun n reason

respect n respect; to r. of in comparison with

respit n delay

reste n rest, repose

reste v rest

retourne v return; retourne 1 s subj; retornyng part turning over (in the mind); retourned pp

reven v take away, deprive; reft 3 s pt

reverence n respect

revoken v restore to consciousness, bring to

reward n regard

rewen v feel sorry, repent; rewe 3 s subj

reyn n rain

reyne n rein

reyne v rain; ron 3 s pt rained

right adv very

right n right, privilege

roche n rock

rode n rood, cross

rollen v turn over (in the mind)

romen v roam; romyng part

ron see reyne

route n company

route v roar

routhe n pity

routheles adj without pity

rowe adv angrily

rynde n hide (?)

rynge v ring; ronge pp

ryse v. rise; rist 3 s refl; ro(o)s 3 s pt

rysshe n rush

S

sad adj sober

salue, saluwe v greet, salute

samyt n samite, a costly silk

saugh see seen

savacioun n salvation, safety

save prep, conj save, except

save(n) v save, keep, preserve

savour n smell, odour; taste, pleasure

sawe n saying; sawes pl expressions

say see seen

sayn see seyen

scapen v escape

scarmuch n skirmish

scarsly adv scarcely

scathe n harm

science n learning, knowledge

scorne(n) v mock; scorned 3 s pt derided, mocked

scripture n posy, inscription in a ring

seche, seke(n) v seek; seche 1 s; sekestow seekest thou; isought pp

secree adj secret

see(n), se(n) v see, behold; se 1 s; seest 2 s; seth 3 s; se(e), seen pl; se pr, subj;

seen(n)—*cont.*
> **God yow see** may God watch over you; **saigh, saugh, say, sey** *1 & 3 s pt*; **sey, syen** *3 pl pt*; **sayn, seye** *pp*

selde *adv* seldom
selve *adj* same
sely *adj* blissful; simple; hapless
selynesse *n* happiness
seme *v* seem
sende(n) *v* send
sentement *n* feelings
sentence *n* opinion, thought, meaning
serve(n) *v* serve (*often implying* love)
sette(n) *v* set, place; value, care; **sette** *2 pl* value; **I sette the worste** I suppose the worst possibility; **sette a caas** suppose an imaginary case
seur *adv* surely
seurte *n* pledge; security, confidence
sey, sey(n) *see* **seen**
seye(n), seyn(e), sayn(e), say *v* say; **seistow** sayest thou; **seye** *3 pl subj*; **as who seyth** as one may say
shadwe *n* shadow
shadwe *v* shadow
shal *1 s* owe, owe to; *1 & 3 s future auxiliary* shall, must; **sholde, sholden** *pl pt*
shame *n* shame; reproach, insult
shap *n* shape
shape(n) *v* shape, arrange, see to it; **shoop, shop** *1 & 3 s pt* determined; **shape(n), yshapen** *pp* shaped, formed, decreed

shawe *n* grove, thicket
she *pron*; **hir, hyr, hire, her** *acc gen dat*
sheene *adj* bright, beautiful
sheld *n* shield
shende *v* put to shame, harm; **shenden** *pl* spoil; **shente** *1 & 3 s pt* injured; **shent** *pp* spoiled
shere *v* shear, cut; **shorn** *pp* clipped
sherte *n* shirt
shette(n) *v* shut; **shetten** *pl pt* shut up
shewe(n) *v* show
shof *3 s pt* pushed; **shove** *pp*
shorte *v* shorten
shot *n* arrow; **shotes** *pl*
shour *n* shower; **shoures** *pl* combats, battles
shrewednesse *n* evil, wickedness
shryve *1 s* shrive; **shryven** *pp* disclosed
shulder *n* shoulder
sik, syk, sek *adj* sick, ill; **sike, seeke** *pl*
sike *v* sigh; **sighte** *3 s pt*
siker *adj* sure
siker *adv* surely; confidently
sikerly *adv* surely
sikernesse *n* certainty, safety, security
singynges *n pl* singing songs
sith *conj, prep* since
sithen *conj* since
sithen *adv* afterwards, then
sitte(n) *v* sit; **sitte** *2 s subj* mayst sit; **it sate her (me)** it were fitting, would suit; **sete(n)** *pl pt*
skile *n* reason; **skiles** *pl*
skilful *adj* reasonable
slake *v* lessen; *3 s subj* wane

slee(n) v slay; **sle** 3 s subj; **slawe** pp slain

sleighly see **slyly**

sleight(e) n cunning, trickery, craftiness; skill, ingenuity

slepe(n) v sleep; **slep** 1 & 3 s pt; **slepte(n)** pl pt

slomberynge n slumbering

slouthe n sloth, laxness in one's duty

slydynge adj unstable

slyly, sleigh- adv craftily; secretly; cautiously

slyvere n sliver, portion

smale adj small, slender

smal adv little

smert adj; **smerte** pl sharp, bitter, painful

smert(e) n pain

smerte v smart, feel pain, suffer; **smerte** 3 s subj impers it may pain; **smerte** 3 s pt felt pain

smyte(n) v strike; **smot** 3 s pt struck

snowisshe adj snowlike

so adv so; as intensive introducing imp & subj (command, wish, etc.); **so, so that** as intensive (= how) introducing excl

so conj so, that, provided; **so that** provided

sobre adj grave; quiet, discreet

sobrelich(e), sobrely adv gravely; quietly, seriously; humbly, modestly

socouren v help

sodeyn adj sudden; impetuous

sodeynly, sodeynliche adv suddenly

softe adv softly, gently, timidly

sojourne v tarry, delay; **sojorneth** 3 s remains

solas n entertainment; comfort

som adj, pron some

somdel adv somewhat

somer n summer; **someris** gen

somtyme adv for a time, at some time

sonded pp covered with sand

sone adv soon

song n singing; song

sonne n sun; **sonnes** gen

sonner adv sooner

soor(e) adj sore

soore, sore adv sorely; bitterly; violently

soot n soot

sooth(e), soth(e) n truth, what is correct or accurate

sooth, soth adj, adv true, correct; truly

soothly, sothly adv truly

soper n supper

sort n divination, lot

sorted 3 s pt allotted

sorwe n sorrow

sorweful adj sad

sorwe(n) v sorrow, grieve; **sorweth** 3 s; **sorwynge** part

sory adj mournful, sad; sorry; unfortunate

sothfast adj true

soun n sound

sowen v sow; **sowe(n)** pp

sownde adv in good health

sownen v conduce to; **sowneth** 3 s

space n space of time

span-newe adj brand-new

spare v refrain; **spared** pp restrained

special adj special; **in s** especially

spede v succeed; *3 s subj* may (God) assist

speed n success; help

speke(n) v speak; **speke, spake** *pl pt*

spere n sphere

spille v spill, drop

spirit n soul, spirit

sporneth on it *3 s* kicks it; comes across it

sprede v spread; expand

spyen v keep watch, spy, look (*for something*)

spynne v spin; **sponne** *pl pt*

squier n squire

staat n condition, state

stal *3 s pt* stole; crept away

stalke v steal up quietly

stant *see* **stonden**

starf *see* **sterven**

steppes n foot-prints

stere n rudder; helmsman

stere v steer, guide, govern; **steere** *1 s*

stere v stir; urge; **stirynge** *part*

sterne *adj* stern; **sterne wynd** rough wind

sterneliche *adv* hard

sterre n star

sterte v spring, leap, make a quick, sudden movement; go (quickly)

sterve(n) v die; **starf** *3 s pt* perished

steven(e) n voice, sound; report

steyre, staire n stairs

stiken v stick, penetrate; **stiketh** *3 s* sticks; **stak** *3 s pt* fixed

stille *adv* quietly, motionless

stonde(n) v stand; **stant** *3 s*

stoon n stone; **stoon of sikernesse** rock of security

storie n story; history

stounde n space of time, time, hour, a while

straunge *adj* foreign, strange; surprising; *as n* strangers

straungely *adv* coldly, distantly

strecche v stretch, extend

streight, streght *adj*, *adv* straight

stremes *n pl* rays

strengest *adj*, *adv* strongest

streyne v clasp tightly; afflict

strif n strife

stryve v strive; **strof** *3 s pt* strove

stuwe n a small heated room; **stuwe door** door to such a room

stynte v stop, stay, leave off; **stynten** *1 pl*; **stynte** *3 s pt*; **stente** (*in rhyme*) *3 s & pl pt*; **stynt** *pp*

subgit *adj* subject

subgit n subject

subtil *adj* subtle; **s. stremes** penetrating rays; **s. art** cunning art

subtilte n cunning

sucre *adj* sugary, sweet

sucre n sugar

sucred *pp* sugared

suffisaunce n sufficiency; fullness of heart's desire

suffise v suffice

suffre(n) v allow, suffer; **suffrest** *2 s*; **suffren** *pl*; **suffre** *2 pl subj*

supprised *pp* seized, overtaken

surmounteth *3 s* surpasses, overcomes

surquidrie n pride, arrogance

suster n sister; **sustren** *pl*

suwe v follow

swalwe *n* swallow

swere *v* swear; **swerith** *3 s*; **swor** *1 & 3 s pt*; **isworn** *pp*

swete *adj* sweet (*used of people*, charming, beloved, *etc.*)

swete *n* sweetheart

swetnesse *n* sweetness

swich *adj, pron* such

swollen *pp* **s. herte** heart swollen with rage

swough *n* swoon

swote *adj* sweet, fresh, fragrant (*used of growing things*)

swowneth *s imp* faint

sye *v* sink down, fall

syn *conj* since

synge(n) *v* sing; **song** *3 s pt*; **songe, y-songe** *pp*

synke *v* sink, cause to sink

sythe *n pl* times

T

take(n) *v* take, consider; **tak** *s imp*; **taketh** *pl imp*; **take(n), ytake(n)** *pp* undertaken; **itake** caught

tale *n* narrative, story, account; talk

tarie *v* delay; **tarie** *1 s*; **tarieth** *3 s*

taryinge *n* delay

tecches *n pl* faults

techen *v* teach

telle(n) *v* tell

tene *n* sorrow, grief

terme *n* period of time

testif *adj* impetuous

text *n* text, a writing

thank, thonk *n* thanks, good will

thanke(n), thonke(n), thank *v* thank; **thank(e), thonke** *1 s*; **thanked, ythanked, thonked** *pp*

than(ne) *adv* then

that *demons pron* that, the

that *rel pron* that, which; that which, what

that *conj* that; so that; as that; as; as well as; as if

the *see* **thow**

the *v* thrive, prosper; **so (as) moot I thee(n)** as may I thrive

the *def article* the

theigh *conj* although, though

thennes *adv* thence

ther(e) *adv* there; *rel adv, conj* where; *redundant, introducing a wish, imprecation, etc.*

ther-ayeins *adv* there against

theras *conj* whereas; where

thewes *n pl* qualities (mental and moral)

they *pers pron*; **hir, hire, her** *gen* their; **hem** them

thider *adv* thither

thikke *adj, adv* thick, close together

thilke *adj* the same, that same; **thilke, thilk** (*before vowel*) *pl* those

thing *n* thing; **thing, thynges** *pl*

thirled *pp* pierced

this *demon adj & pron*; **this** *pl*; **thise** *pl* these, those; **thise, these** (in generalizing sense); **thise bokes** those books (that will be written)

this *contr of* **this is**

tho *demon adj & pron* those

tho *adv* then

thogh *conj* though, although

thoght *n* anxiety

thonder *n* thunder

thonk, thonken *see* **thank, thanken**

thorugh-darted *pp* pierced through

thorugh-shoten *pp* shot through

thow *2 pers pron* thou; **the(e)** *acc, dat*; **thyn** *gen* thine

thralle(n) *v* enslave

threed *n* thread

threste *3 s pt* thrust

thrie *adv* three times

thrift *n* prosperity, success; **by my t.** *a mild oath*; **good thrift** good fortune (to)

thriftieste *adj as n* most respectable

thrifty *adj* prudent

throwe *n* little while, moment

throwes *n pl* throes, pangs

thyn *see* **thow**

thynke *v* seem; **thynketh** *3 s impers* it seems; **thoughte, thoghte** *3 s impers pt* it seemed

thynke(n) *v* think, imagine, conceive, call to mind, remember, consider, believe, intend; **thynkest** *2 s*; **thynketh** *3 s & pl*

thyself, thyselven *refl pron*; *as intensive*; *as pers pron* thou thyself.

tid *see* **tit**

til *prep* to

til *conj* until

tit *3 s impers* (it) happens, befalls: **tid** *pp* befallen

to *prep* to; of; **to respect of** in comparison with

to *adv* too

tobreste *v* burst or break in two

todasshed *pp* battered

toforn *prep* before; **God toforn** by God

to-hepe *adv* together

tohewen *pp* cut

to-morwe *adv* tomorrow

tonge *n* tongue

torende *3 pl subj* may tear to pieces

torne, turne *v* turn, return; **turnest** *2 s*; **torneth** *3 s*

tough, towgh *adj* hard, difficult; **make it t.** press on boldly; **made it t.** behaved haughtily

toun *n* town

trappe *n* trap

trappe-dore *n* trap door

traunce *v* tramp *or* run about

travaille *n* labour; trouble

travers *n* curtain screening off part of a room, traverse

trays *n pl* traces

trede *v* tread; **tret** *3 s*

tre(e) *n* wood

treson, -oun *n* treason

tresor, -our *n* treasure

trespace *v* commit an offence against

trete *v* treat (*a person*)

trewe *n* truce

trewe *adj* true

trist *n* trust

triste *v* trust

trouthe *n* truth, faith, troth, pledge; integrity, faithfulness

trowe(n) *v* believe; **trowed** *pp*

tweye *adj* two

tweyne *adj* two

twiste *n* branch

twiste *v* twist, wring; **twiste** *3 s subj pt*

twyne *3 s subj* twist, spin

twynne *v* separate, be parted; depart; **twynne** *3 pl pt*

U

unavysed *pp* unaware

uncircumscript *pp* uncircumscribed

under *adv, prep* beneath
undertake *v* guarantee
unhappes *n pl* misfortunes
unkouth *adj* unusual, marvellous
unkynde *adj* unnatural; cruel, faithless
unkonnyng *adj* stupid
unliklynesse *n* unattractiveness
unloven *v* cease to love
unmyghty *adj* unable
unnethe *adv* scarcely
unnethes *adv* scarcely
unpynne *v* unbolt
unsely *adj* unhappy
unsittynge *adj* not fitting
unstable *adj* unstable, unreliable
unswelle *v* become less swollen (with emotion)
until *prep* unto; unto, to
unto *prep* unto, to
untrewe *adj* untrue, false; *adv* falsely, inaccurately
untriste *adj* distrustful
unwar *adj* unaware
unwist *adj* unaware
up *adv, prep* up; upon
up-born *pp* respected
upon *prep* upon, on
usage *n* practice, habit
use(n) *v* use, practise

V

vanyte *n* futility, worthlessness
variaunce *n* changeability
Veer *prop n* Spring
vengeaunce *n* revenge
verray *adj* true
verre *n* glass
vers *n* verse, line; **vers** *pl*
vertu *n* power, virtue, goodness

vertulees *adj* without efficacy
veyn *adj* worthless
viage *n* trip, journey, expedition, undertaking
vice *n* vice; wrong
vileynye, vilanye *n* rudeness of speech or manner, characteristic of a villein; shame, wrong; reproach
voidë *n* wine, with cakes, etc. taken before retiring
voide *adj* devoid
vouchen sauf *v* condescend, deign; **vouchesauf** *2 subj pl* graciously permit
voiden *v* depart; **voided** *pp* gone away

W

wade *v* go; enter
wake(n) *v* be awake, stay awake; **wook, wok** *3 s pt* awoke
walke *v* walk; **welk** *1 s pt*
walwe *v* wallow; **walweth** *3 s* tosses
war *adj* aware; **be war** take warning, beware; **beth wel war** be very careful
war(e) *v* (*refl*) beware
warne *v* warn; **warned** *pp* informed
wawe *n* wave
waxen *v* grow, become; **wax** *3 s pt*
waymentynge *n* lamentation
wayten *v* watch, watch for
we *1 pl pers pron*; **oure(s)** *gen*
wede *n* cloak, garment
weder *n* weather
weel *adj, adv* well
weet *adj* wet
weet *see* **wite(n)**
weldy *adj* vigorous

wele *n* well-being, welfare, prosperity; happiness, good fortune

welle *n* spring, source

wel-willy *adj* beneficent

wende(n) *v* go, go away, leave; **wendeth, went** *3 s* goes; **wende** *2 pl subj*; **wente** *3 s pt* went; went on; **wente(n)** *pl pt*

wene(n) *v* think, suppose; **weneth** *3 s*; **wende** *1 & 3 s pt*; **wend, ywent** *pp* supposed

wente *n* turn; twisting and turning; passage

wepe(n) *v* weep; **wepeth** *3 s*; **wepen** *3 pl*; **weep, wepte** *3 s pt*; **wepten** *pl pt*

were *v* wear; **werest** *2 s*

werk *n* work, busy-ness, activity; embroidery

werke(n) *v* act, work

werre *n* war; **of w.** in war

wers(e) *adj, adv* worse

wery *adj* weary

westren *v* move westward

wete *v* wet

wexen *v* grow, become; **wex** *3 s pt*

wey *n* way; **other weyes** otherwise; **do wey** not at all!

weylaway *excl* alas; **so w.** alas

weyven *v* cast aside

whan *conj* when

what *rel pron* what; who

what *interrog pron & adj* what

what *indef pron* whatever; **what so** whatever

what *conj* however, as much as; **what . . . what** both . . . and

what *interrog adv* why; how

what *interj* what!

wheither *indef pron* whichever; **the w.** which (of two)

wheither *interrog adv* (*introducing a direct question involving alternatives*) whether

whennes *adv* whence

wher *conj* whether; **wher so** whether

wher *interrog adv* (*introducing a direct question involving alternatives*) whether

wher as *adv, conj* where

wherby *conj* whereby; **w. that** by which

wherof *conj* of what

whette *pp, pt* whet, sharpened

which(e) *rel pron & adj* which, who, whom; **which that** who, what; **which, whiche** *pl*

which *interrog pron & adj* which, what; *in exclamations* **which a** what a; **whiche** *pl* what

whielen *v* wheel, turn round

whil *conj* while

while *n* time, while; **in the meene whiles** meanwhile

whiles *conj* while, whilst

whit(e) *adj* white; fair

wif *n* woman, wife

wight *n* creature, being, person, fellow; **a little w.** a little bit

wikke *adj* wicked, evil; *as n* bad

wilfully *adv* voluntarily; intentionally

wille *v* wish

wir *n* wire

wisly *adv* certainly, surely

wit *n* mind; understanding, intelligence, wisdom, judgement, opinion

wite *n* blame

wite *v* blame

wite(n) *v* know; **wot, woot** *1 & 3 s*; **wost** *2 s*; **wiste** *1 & 3 s pt*; **wystestow** if thou didst know; **wiste(n)** *pl pt*

withal, with alle *adv* also, in addition

witholde *v* w. of restrain from

withoute *adv* outside

withoute(n) *prep* without, apart from

withstonde *v* oppose, withstand; **withstonde** *pp* withstood

wityng, wyttynge *n* knowledge

wo *adj* unhappy

wodebynde *n* woodbine

wol(e) *1 s* will, want, wish; **wol(e)** *3 s*; **wol(e)** *pl*; **wolde** *1 s pt* intended; *3 s pt* wished; *3 pl pt* intended; **wolde God** would God, God wishes; **wolde whoso nolde** willy-nilly

wommanhede *n* womanliness

wommanliche *adj* womanly; **w. wif** pattern of womanhood

wonder *adj* wonderful, strange

wonder *adv* wonderfully

wonderly, -lych *adv* wonderfully

wondre(n) *v* wonder, show amazement; **wondre** *1 s* wonder; **wondreth** *3 s*; **wondred** *3 s & pl pt*; **wondreden** *3 pl pt*; **wondred** *pp*

wone *n* custom

wone *v* dwell; **woned** *3 s pt*; **woned** *pp*

woned, wont *adj* wont, accustomed

wood *adj* mad

woodnesse *n* madness

word *n properly* ord: **word and ende** from beginning to end

word *n* word, expression

worshipe *v* honour, reverence

worshyp(e) *n* honour

worthen *v* be, dwell; **wo (wel) worth(e)** woe (well) be it (to)

worthily *adv* worthily, deservedly

worthy *adj* worthy, excellent, brave

wostow *see* **witen**

wot, woot *see* **witen**

wowe *v* woo

wrath(e) *n* anger

wrecche *n* exile, wretch, wretched person

wrecche *adj* wretched

wrecchednesse *n* wretchedness, misery, meanness

wreche *n* vengeance; **wrecche** affliction, misfortune

wreigh *see* **wrye**

wreke(n) *v* avenge; **wroken** *pp* revenged

wreththe *see* **wrathe**

write *v* write; **wroot** *1 & 3 s pt*

writhe(n) *v* turn; **writh** *3 s* twists, winds

wroken *see* **wreken**

wrooth *adj* wroth, angry

wrye *v* cover; cover up, conceal; **wrien** *3 pl*; **wreigh** *3 s pt* covered; **wry** *s imp* wrap; **wrie, iwryen** *pp* covered, hidden

wrye(n) *v* turn, change course

wrynge *v* wring; **wrong** *3 s
pt* wrung
wyd(e) *adj* wide, broad, exten-
sive
wyde *adv* widely
wydwe *n* widow
wyke *n* week
wyle *n* trick; trickery, subtlety
wyn *n* wine
wynde *v* pass around, en-
twine, embrace; revolve,
turn over; bend; *2 s subj*
may pass, go; **wynt** *3 s*
turns
wynke *v* close the eyes; **loke
or w.** look or not look
wynne(n) *v* win; **wynnen
from** get away from; **wan**
s & pl pt; **wonne(n)** *pp*
wynter *n* winter, year;
wynter *pl*
wyrdes *n* events
wys(e) *adj* wise, prudent; *as
n* wise one
wys *adv* certainly, surely; **also
wys (as), as wys (as)** as
surely as
wyse *n* way, manner; **in w. of**
after the fashion of
wystestow *see* **wite(n)**
wyt *see* **wit**
wyte *see* **wite**
wyvere *n* viper, snake

Y

y *1 pers pron* I
yate *n* gate
yblowe *pp* spread abroad
ybought *pp* bought
ydel *adj* idle; **on y.** in vain
ydrawe *pp* drawn
ydred *pp* dreaded
ye *2 pl pers pron* ye; **youre,**
gen; **youres; yow, you** *dat*

acc; **fro ye** (*unstressed*) from
you
ye, yee *adv* yes
yë *n* eye; **yen** *pl*
yede(n) *see* **gon**
yeer(e) *n* year; **yeer** *pl*
yelde(n) *v* pay, surrender,
give up; **yelt** *3 s* yields;
yeldeth *pl imp* yield, give
in; **yold** *pp* given up
yerd *n* yard, garden
yerde *n* rod, stick
yeve(n), yive *v* give; **yaf**
1 2 & 3 s pt; **yave** *3 s subj
pt*; **yaf, yave** *pl pt*; **yif,
yef, yeve** *s imp*
yfeere *adv* together
yif *see* **yeven**
yis *adv* yes
yit *adv* yet
yive *see* **yeven**
yknet *pp* knit together
ylost *pp* lost
ymagynen *v* imagine
ymet *pp* met
ynogh, ynough, ynow(e) *adj,
pron* enough, plenty
ynogh, ynough, ynow *adv*
enough
ynome, nome *pp* taken
ynorissed *pp* brought up
yold *pp* given up
yong *adj* young
yore *adv* formerly, in the past,
before
your(e)self, your(e)selven
pron (*refl & intensive*) yourself; *as pers pron* you yourself
yrent *pp* torn
yronne *pp* run; completed
yse(e) *v* see, behold; gaze;
yseyn, yseye *pp* seen
ysene *adj* visible
yserved *pp* served

yshapen *pp* shaped, formed, decreed
ysonge *pp* sung
ysounded *pp* sunk, penetrated
yt *see* **hit**
ytake *pp* taken; **ytaken** undertaken
ythe *v* thrive
ythonked *pp* thanked
ythrowe *pp* thrown

ytressed *pp* braided
yvel *adj*, *n* evil, ill
ywar *adj* watchful, on guard
ywis *adv* certainly, surely

Z

zeles *n pl* zeal (*of more than one person*)